COLLECTED WHEEL PUBLICATIONS

VOLUME 1

NUMBERS 1 – 15

BPE

BPS Pariyatti Editions

BPS Pariyatti Editions
An imprint of Pariyatti Publishing
www.pariyatti.org

Although this is an American edition, we have left any British spelling of words unchanged.

Note that WH 09 "Karma and Rebirth" by Nyanatiloka Mahathera is omitted from Volume 1 and has been republished as Wheel 394/96.

First BPS Pariyatti Edition, 2018
ISBN: 978-1-68172-124-8 (Print)
ISBN: 978-1-68172-125-5 (PDF)
ISBN: 978-1-68172-126-2 (ePub)
ISBN: 978-1-68172-127-9 (Mobi)
LCCN: 2018940050

Contents

WH 01 The Seven Factors of Enlightenment
Piyadassi Thera 1

WH 02 Vedānta and Buddhism
Helmuth von Glasenapp 27

WH 03 Buddhism and Science
K. N. Jayatilleke, Robert F. Spencer, Wu Shu 41

WH 04 The Greatest Adventure
David Maurice 69

WH 05 The Buddha
Piyadassi Thera 101

WH 06 The Four Sublime States
Nyanaponika Thera 151

WH 07 The Practice of Loving-Kindness (*Mettā*)
Ñāṇamoli Thera 169

WH 08 Kālāma Sutta
Soma Thera 193

WH 10 Sakka's Quest
Sister Vajirā 205

WH 11 Anattā and Nibbāna
Nyanaponika Thera 235

WH 12 & 13 The Case for Rebirth
Francis Story, The Anāgārika Sugatānanda 259

WH 14 Everyman's Ethics
Nārada Thera 317

WH 15 Dependent Origination
Piyadassi Thera 343

Key to Abbreviations

A	Aṅguttara Nikāya	Paṭis	Paṭisambhidamagga
Ap	Apadāna	Peṭ	Peṭakopadesa
Bv	Buddhavaṃsa	S	Saṃyutta Nikāya
Cp	Cariyāpiṭaka	Sn	Suttanipāta
D	Dīgha Nikāya	Th	Theragātha
Dhp	Dhammapada	Thī	Therigātha
Dhs	Dhammasaṅgaṇī	Ud	Udāna
It	Itivuttaka	Vibh	Vibhaṅga
Ja	Jātaka verses and commentary	Vin	Vinaya-piṭaka
Khp	Khuddakapāṭha	Vism	Visuddhimagga
M	Majjhima Nikāya	Vism-mhṭ	Visuddhimagga Sub-commentary
Mil	Milindapañha	Vv	Vimānavatthu
Nett	Nettipakaraṇa	Nidd	Niddesa

The above is the abbreviation scheme of the Pali Text Society (PTS) as given in the *Dictionary of Pali* by Margaret Cone.

The commentaries, *aṭṭhakathā*, are abbreviated by using a hyphen and an "a" ("-a") following the abbreviation of the text, e.g., *Dīgha Nikāya Aṭṭhakathā* = D-a. Likewise the sub-commentaries are abbreviated by a "ṭ" ("-ṭ") following the abbreviation of the text.

The sutta reference abbreviation system for the four Nikāyas, as is used in Bhikkhu Bodhi's translations is:

AN	Aṅguttara Nikāya	DN	Dīgha Nikāya
MN	Majjhima Nikāya	Sn	Saṃyutta Nikāya
J	Jātaka story	Mv	Mahāvagga (Vinaya Piṭaka)
Cv	Cullavagga (Vinaya Piṭaka)	SVibh	Suttavibhaṅga (Vinaya Piṭaka)

The Seven Factors of Enlightenment

Satta Bojjhaṅga

by

Piyadassi Thera

WHEEL PUBLICATION NO. 01

Introduction

The Tipiṭaka, the Buddhist canon, is replete with references to the factors of enlightenment—*bojjhaṅga*—expounded by the Enlightened One on different occasions. In the Book of the Kindred Sayings, V (*Saṃyutta Nikāya, Mahā Vagga*) we find a special section under the title *Bojjhaṅga Saṃyutta* wherein the Buddha discourses on the *bojjhaṅgas* in diverse ways. In this section are three discourses or sermons that have been recited by Buddhists since the time of the Buddha as a protection (*paritta* or *pirit*) against pain, disease and adversity.

The term *bojjhaṅga* is composed of *bodhi* + *aṅga*. *Bodhi* denotes enlightenment; to be exact, insight concerned with the realization of the four Noble Truths, namely, the Noble Truth of Suffering, the Noble Truth of the Origin of Suffering, the Noble Truth of the Cessation of Suffering and the Noble Truth of the Path leading to the Cessation of Suffering. *Aṅga* means factors or limbs. *Bodhi* + *aṅga* (*bojjhaṅga*), therefore, means the factors of enlightenment, or the factors for insight, wisdom.

> "*Bojjhaṅgas*! *bojjhaṅgas*! they are called, Venerable Sir. Now, in what respect are they called *bojjhaṅgas*?" queried a monk of the Buddha. The succinct reply of the Master was "They conduce to enlightenment, monk, that is why they are so called." *(Bodhāya saṃvaṭṭanīti kho bhikkhu tasmā bojjhaṅgā ti vuccanti.)*[1]

> Further says the Buddha:

> "Just as, monks, in a peaked house all rafters whatsoever go together to the peak, slope to the peak, join in the peak, and of them all the peak is reckoned chief, even so, monks, the monk who cultivates and makes much of the seven factors of wisdom, slopes to Nibbāna, inclines to Nibbāna, tends to Nibbāna."[2]

---

1. S V 72 (P.T.S.).
2. *The Kindred Sayings*, S V, p. 63.

The seven factors are:
1. Mindfulness (*sati*),
2. Keen investigation of the dhamma (*dhammavicaya*),[3]
3. Energy (*viriya*),
4. Rapture or happiness (*pīti*),
5. Calm (*passaddhi*),
6. Concentration (*samādhi*),
7. Equanimity (*upekkhā*).

One of the three discourses on the bojjhaṅgas mentioned above begins:

Thus I heard. At one time the Buddha was living at Rājagaha, at Veḷuvana bamboo grove, in the squirrels' feeding-ground. At that time the venerable Mahā Kassapa, who was living in Pipphalī Cave, was sick, stricken with a severe illness.

Then the Buddha rising from his solitude at eventide visited the venerable Mahā Kassapa, took his seat, and spoke to the venerable Mahā Kassapa in this wise:

> "Well, Kassapa. how is it with you? Are you bearing up, are you enduring? Do your pains lessen or increase? Are there signs of your pains lessening and not increasing?"
>
> "No, Lord. I am not bearing up, I am not enduring. The pain is very great. There is a sign not of the pains lessening, but of their increasing."
>
> "Kassapa, these seven factors of enlightenment are well expounded by me, cultivated and much developed by me, and when cultivated and much developed they conduce to full realization, perfect wisdom, to Nibbāna. What are the seven?
>
> 1. "Mindfulness. This, Kassapa, is well expounded by me, cultivated and much developed by me, and when cultivated and much developed, it conduces to full realization, perfect wisdom, to Nibbāna.

---

3. *Dhamma* is a multi-significant term. Here it means mind and matter (*nāma-rūpa*); *dhammavicaya* is the investigation or analysis of this conflux of mind and body, and all component and conditioned things.

2. Investigation of the dhamma...
3. Energy...
4. Rapture...
5. Calm...
6. Concentration...
7. Equanimity, Kassapa, is well expounded by me..."

"These seven factors of enlightenment, verily, Kassapa, are well expounded by me, cultivated and much developed by me, and when cultivated and much developed they conduce to full realization, perfect wisdom, to Nibbāna."

"Verily, Blessed One, they are factors of enlightenment! Verily, Welcome One, they are factors of enlightenment!" uttered Mahā Kassapa.

Thus spoke the Buddha, and the venerable Mahā Kassapa rejoicing welcomed the utterances of the Worthy One. And the venerable Mahā Kassapa rose from that illness. There and then that ailment of the venerable Mahā Kassapa vanished.[4]

Another discourse (*Mahā Cunda Bojjhaṅga Sutta*) of the three mentioned above reveals that at one time the Buddha himself was ill, and the venerable Mahā Cunda recited the *bojjhaṅgas*, factors of enlightenment, and that the Buddha's grievous illness vanished.[5]

Man's mind tremendously and profoundly influences and affects the body. If allowed to function viciously and entertain unwholesome and harmful thoughts, mind can cause disaster, even kill a being; but mind also can cure a sick body. When concentrated on right thoughts with right understanding, the effects mind can produce are immense.

"Mind not only makes sick, it also cures. An optimistic patient has more chance of getting well than a patient who is worried and unhappy. The recorded instances of faith healing include cases in which even organic diseases were cured almost instantaneously."[6]

Buddhism (*Buddha-dhamma*) is the teaching of enlightenment. One who is keen on attaining enlightenment should first know clearly the impediments that block the path to enlightenment.

---

4. S V 79.
5. S V 81.
6. Aldous Huxley, *Ends and Means* (London, 1946), p, 259.

Life, according to the right understanding of a Buddha, is suffering, and that suffering is based on ignorance or *avijjā*. Ignorance is the experiencing of that which is unworthy of experiencing, namely evil. Further it is the non-perception of the conglomerate nature of the aggregates; non-perception of sense-organ and object in their respective and objective natures; non-perception of the emptiness or the relativity of the elements; non-perception of the dominant nature of the sense-controlling faculties; non-perception of the thusness—the infallibility—of the four Truths. And the five hindrances (*pañca nīvaraṇāni*) are the nutriment of (or condition for) this ignorance. They are called hindrances because they completely close in, cut off, and obstruct. They hinder the understanding of the way to release from suffering. These five hindrances are: sensuality (*kāmacchanda*); ill will (*vyāpāda*); obduracy of mind and mental factors (*thīnamiddha*); restlessness and flurry (*uddhaccakukkucca*); and doubt (*vicikicchā*).

And what is the nutriment of these hindrances? The three evil modes of life (*tini duccaritāni*)—bodily, vocal and mental wrongdoing. This threefold nutriment is in turn nourished by non-restraint of the senses (*indriya asaṃvaro*), which is explained by the commentator as the admittance of lust and hate into the six sense organs of eye, ear, nose, tongue, body, and mind.

The nutriment of non-restraint is shown to be lack of mindfulness and of complete awareness (*asati asampajañña*). In the context of nutriment, the reason for non-restraint is the drifting away of the object (*dhamma*)—the lapsing from the mind of the knowledge of the *lakkhaṇas* or characteristics of existence (impermanence, suffering, and voidness of self), and forgetfulness of the true nature of things. It is when one does not bear in mind the transience and the other characteristics of things, and one allows oneself all kinds of liberties in speech and deed, and gives rein to full thought imagery of an unskilful kind. Lack of complete awareness is lack of these four: complete awareness of purpose (*sāttha sampajañña*); of suitability (*sappāya sampajañña*); of resort (*gocara sampajañña*); and of non-delusion (*asammoha sampajañña*). When one does a thing without a right purpose, when one looks at things or does actions which do not help the growth of the good, when one does things inimical to improvement, when one forgets the Dhamma which is the true resort of one who strives, when one deludedly lays hold of things, believing them to be pleasant, beautiful, permanent and substantial, when one behaves thus, then too non-restraint is nourished.

And below this lack of mindfulness and complete awareness lies unsystematic reflection (*ayoniso manasikāra*). The books say unsystematic reflection is reflection that is off the right course; that is, taking the impermanent as permanent, the painful as pleasure, the soulless as a soul, the bad as good. The constant rolling-on that is *saṃsāra* is rooted in unsystematic thinking. When unsystematic thinking increases, it fulfils two things: ignorance and lust for becoming. Ignorance being present, the origination of the entire mass of suffering comes to be. Thus a person who is a shallow thinker, like a ship drifting at the wind's will, like a herd of cattle swept into the whirlpools of a river, like an ox yoked to a wheel-contraption, goes on revolving in the cycle of existence, *saṃsāra*.

And it is said that imperfect confidence (*assaddhiyaṃ*) in the Buddha, the Dhamma and the Sangha is the condition which develops unsystematic reflection, and imperfect confidence is due to non-hearing of the True Law, the Dhamma (*asaddhamma savanaṃ*).

Finally, one does not hear the Dhamma through lack of contact with the wise, through not consorting with the good (*asappurisa saṃseva*). Thus want of good friendship, *kalyāṇa mittatā*, appears to be the basic reason for the ills of the world. And conversely, the basis and nutriment of all good is shown to be good friendship that furnishes one with the food of the sublime Dhamma which in turn produces confidence in the Triple Gem, *Tri Ratana*, the Buddha, Dhamma and the Sangha. When one has confidence in the Triple Gem there come into existence profound or systematic thinking, mindfulness, and complete awareness, restraint of the senses, the three good modes of life, the four arousings of mindfulness, the seven factors of enlightenment and deliverance through wisdom, one after another in due order.[7]

---

7. *Sammohavinodanī.*

I

Let us now deal with the enlightenment factors one by one. The first is *sati*, mindfulness, It is the instrument most efficacious in self-mastery, and whosoever practises it has found the path to deliverance. It is fourfold: mindfulness consisting in contemplation of the body (*kāyānupassanā*); feeling (*vedanānupassanā*); mind (*cittānupassanā*); and mental objects or mind contents (*dhammānupassanā*).[8]

The man lacking in this all-important quality of mindfulness cannot achieve anything worthwhile. The Buddha's final admonition to his disciples on his death bed was this: "Transient are all component things. Work out your deliverance with heedfulness!" (*vaya-dhammā saṅkhārā, appamādena sampādetha*).[9] And the last words of the venerable Sāriputta, the foremost disciple of the Buddha who predeceased the Master, were these: "Strive on with heedfulness! This is my advice to you!" (*sampādetha appamādena, esā me ānusāsanā*). In both these injunctions the most significant and pregnant word is *appamāda*, which literally means incessant heedfulness. Man cannot be heedful unless he is fully aware of his actions, whether they are mental, verbal or physical, at every moment of his waking life. Only when a man is fully awake to and mindful of his activities can he distinguish good from bad and right from wrong. It is in the light of mindfulness he will see the beauty or the ugliness of his deeds.

The word *appamāda* throughout the *Tipiṭaka* is used to denote *sati*, mindfulness; *pamāda* is defined as absence of mindfulness. Says the Buddha in the *Aṅguttara Nikāya*:

> "Monks, I know not of any other single thing of such power to cause the arising of good thoughts if not yet arisen, or to cause the waning of evil thoughts if already arisen, as heedfulness. In him who is heedful, good thoughts not yet arisen do arise, and evil thoughts, if arisen, do wane."

---

8. Satipaṭṭhāna Sutta, MN 10 or DN 2. See *The Wheel No. 19: The Foundations of Mindfulness*.

9. Mahāparinibbāna Sutta, DN 16.

Constant mindfulness and vigilance are necessary to avoid ill and perform good. The man with presence of mind who surrounds himself with watchfulness of mind (*satimā*), the man of courage and earnestness, gets ahead of the lethargic, the heedless (*pamatto*), as a racehorse outstrips a decrepit hack.[10] The importance of *sati*, mindfulness, in all our dealings is clearly indicated by the following striking words of the Buddha: "Mindfulness, disciples, I declare is essential in all things everywhere. It is as salt is to the curry."[11]

The Buddha's life is one integral picture of mindfulness He is the *Sadā sato*, the ever mindful, the ever vigilant. He is the very embodiment of mindfulness. There was never an occasion when the Buddha manifested signs of sluggish inactivity or thoughtlessness.

Right mindfulness or complete awareness, in a way, is superior to knowledge, because in the absence of mindfulness it is just impossible for a man to make the best of his learning. Intelligence devoid of mindfulness tends to lead a man astray and entice him from the path of rectitude and duty. Even people who are well informed and intelligent fail to see a thing in its proper perspective when they lack this all-important quality of mindfulness. Men of good standing who have acted or spoken thoughtlessly and without due consideration to the consequences, are often subjected to severe and justifiable criticism.

Mindfulness is the chief characteristic of all wholesome actions tending to one's own and others' profit (*Appamādo mahato atthāya saṃvattati*[12]) "mindfulness is conducive to great profit," that is, to highest mental development, and it is through such attainment that deliverance from the sufferings of *saṃsāra* is possible.

> "The man who delights in mindfulness and regards heedlessness with dread is not liable to fall away. He is in the vicinity of Nibbāna."[13]

---

10. Dhp 29.
11. MN, Satipaṭṭhāna Commentary.
12. SN, Sagāthaka Vagga.
13. Dhp 31.

II

The second enlightenment factor is *dhammavicaya*, keen investigation of the Dhamma. It is the sharp analytical knowledge of understanding the true nature of all constituent things, animate or inanimate, human or divine. It is seeing things as they really are; seeing things in their proper perspective. It is the analysis of all component things into their fundamental elements, right down to their ultimates. Through keen investigation one understands that all compounded things pass through the inconceivably rapid moments of *uppāda*, *ṭhiti* and *bhaṅga*; or of arising, reaching a peak, and ceasing, just as a river in flood sweeps to a climax and fades away. The whole universe is constantly changing, not remaining the same for two consecutive moments. All things in fact are subjected to causes, conditions, and effects (*hetu*, *paccaya* and *phala*). Systematic reflection (*yoniso manasikāra*) comes naturally through right mindfulness, and it urges one to discriminate, to reason and investigate. Shallow thinking, unsystematic reflection (*ayoniso manasikāra*), makes men muddle-headed, and then they fail to investigate the nature of things. Such people cannot see cause and effect, seed and fruit, the rise and fall of compounded things. Says the Buddha: "This doctrine is for the wise and not for the unwise."[14]

Buddhism is free from compulsion and coercion, and does not demand of the follower blind faith. At the very outset the sceptic will be pleased to hear of its call for investigation. Buddhism, from beginning to end, is open to all those who have eyes to see and minds to understand. The Buddha never endeavoured to wring out of his followers blind and submissive faith in him and his teaching. He tutors his disciples in the ways of discrimination and intelligent inquiry. To the inquiring Kālāmas the Buddha answered: "Right is it to doubt, right is it to question what is doubtful and what is not clear. In a doubtful matter, wavering does arise."

14. AN 8:30.

We find this dialogue between the Master and his disciples:

"If, now, knowing this and perceiving this, would you say: 'We honour our Master and through respect for him we respect what he teaches'?"

"Nay, Lord."

"That which you affirm, disciples, is it not only that which you yourselves have recognized, seen and grasped?"

"Yes, Lord."[15]

And in conformity with this thoroughly correct attitude of true inquiry, the philosophers of later times observed: "As the wise test the purity of gold by burning, cutting and examining it by means of a piece of touchstone, so should you accept my words after examining them and not merely out of regard and reverence for me."[16] Thus blind belief is condemned in the analytic teaching (*vibhajjavāda*) of the Buddha. The truth of the Dhamma can be grasped only through calm concentrative thought and insight (*samatha* and *vipassanā*) and never through blind faith. One who goes in quest of truth is not satisfied with surface knowledge. He wants to delve deep and see what is beneath. That is the sort of search encouraged in Buddhism. That type of search yields right understanding.

We read in the texts the following story: "On one occasion Upāli, a fervent follower of Nigaṇṭha Nātaputta, the Jain, visited the Buddha, thoughtfully listened to the Dhamma, gained *saddhā* (confidence based on knowledge) and forthwith manifested his readiness to become a follower of the Master. Nevertheless, the Master said: 'Of a truth, Upāli, make thorough investigation,' and thus discouraged him." This clearly shows that the Buddha was not keen on converting people to his way of thinking, and to his fold. He did not interfere with another man's freedom of thought; for freedom of thought is the birthright of every individual. It is wrong to force someone out of the way of life which accords with his outlook and character, spiritual inclinations and tendencies; compulsion in every form is bad. It is coercion of the blackest kind to make a man gulp down beliefs for which he has no relish. Such forced feeding cannot be good for anybody, anywhere.

15. MN 38.

16. *Jñānasārasamuccaya* p. 31 (ascribed to Āryadeva).

He that cultivates *dhammavicaya*, investigation of the Dhamma, focuses his mind on the five aggregates of grasping, the *pañcupadānakkhandhā*, and endeavours to realize the rise and fall or the arising and passing away (*udaya-vaya*) of this conglomeration of bare forces (*suddha-saṅkhāra-puñja*), this conflux of mind and matter (*nāma-rūpa-santati*). It is only when he fully realizes the evanescent nature of his own mind and body that he experiences happiness, joyous anticipation. Therefore, it is said:

> *Yato yato sammāsati—khandhānaṃ udayabbayaṃ*
> *Labhati pīti pāmojjaṃ—amataṃ tam vijānataṃ*[17]

> Whenever he reflects on the rise and fall of the aggregates, he experiences unalloyed joy and happiness. To the discerning one that (reflection) is deathless Nibbāna.

What is impermanent and not lasting he sees as sorrow-fraught. What is impermanent and sorrow-fraught, he understands as void of a permanent and everlasting soul, self, or ego entity. It is this grasping, this realization of the three characteristics or laws—transiency *anicca*, sorrow *dukkha*, and no-self (soullessness) *anattā*—which is known to Buddhists as *vipassanā-ñāṇa* or penetrative insight, and which, like the razor-edged sword, entirely eradicates all the latent tendencies (*anusaya*). With it, all the varied ramifications of sorrow's cause are finally destroyed. A man who ascends to this summit of vision is an arahat, a perfect one, whose clarity of vision, whose depth of insight, penetrates into the deepest recesses of life and cognizes the true nature that underlies all appearance. No more can he be swept off his feet by the glamour of things ephemeral. No more can he be confused by fearful and terrible appearances. No more is it possible for him to have a clouded view of phenomena; for he has transcended all capacity for error through the perfect immunity which penetrative insight alone can give.

17. Dhp 374.

III

The third enlightenment factor is *viriya*, energy. It is a mental property (*cetasika*) and the sixth limb of the Noble Eightfold Path, there called *sammā vāyāma*, Right Effort.

The life of the Buddha clearly reveals that he was never subjected to moral or spiritual fatigue. From the hour of his enlightenment to the end of his life, he strove tirelessly to elevate mankind, regardless of the bodily fatigue involved, and oblivious to the many obstacles and handicaps that hampered his way. He never relaxed in his exertion for the common weal. Though physically he was not always fit, mentally he was ever vigilant and energetic. Of him it is said:

> Ah, wonderful is the Conqueror,
> Who e'er untiring strives
> For the blessing of all beings,
> For the comfort of all lives.

Buddhism is for the sincerely zealous, strong and firm in purpose, and not for the indolent (*āraddhaviriyassāyaṃ dhammo, nāyaṃ dhammo kusītassa*).[18] The Buddha has not proclaimed himself a saviour willing and able to take upon himself the evil of mankind. On the contrary, he declares that each person has to bear the burden of his own ill deeds. In the words of the Buddha, each individual has himself to put forth the necessary effort, and work out his own deliverance with diligence The Buddha is only a path-revealer and not a saviour who endeavours to save 'souls' by means of a revealed religion. The idea that another raises a man from lower to higher levels of life, and ultimately rescues him, tends to make a man indolent and weak, supine and foolish. Others may lend us a helping hand indirectly, but deliverance from suffering must be wrought out and fashioned by each one for himself upon the anvil of his own actions. "Be ye islands unto yourselves, be ye your own refuge."[19] Thus did the Master exhort his followers to acquire self-reliance.

---

18. AN 8:30.
19. Mahāparinibbāna Sutta, DN 16.

A follower of the Buddha should not under any circumstances relinquish hope and effort; for the Buddha was one who never gave up courage and effort even as a Bodhisatta. As an aspirant for Buddhahood, he had as his motto the following inspiring words: *mā nivatta, abhikkama*, "Falter not, advance". The man who is mindful (*satimā*) and cultivates keen investigation should next put forth the necessary effort to fight his way out.

The function of *viriya* or energy is fourfold. It is defined as: 1. the effort to eradicate evils that have arisen in the mind; 2. the effort to prevent the arising of unarisen evil; 3. the effort to develop unarisen good; and 4. the effort to promote the further growth of good already arisen.[20]

"Just," says the *Vitakkasaṇṭhāna Sutta* of the *Majjhima Nikāya* (No. 20), "as a competent carpenter or a carpenter's apprentice with a slender pin will knock out, remove and dispose of a thicker one, so also, when through dwelling on some idea that has come to him, evil, unsalutary considerations connected with desire, hate and delusion arise in the monk, then he should engender in his mind an idea other than that former idea and connected with salutary things; whereupon the evil unsalutary considerations will disappear, and with their disappearing his mind will become settled, subdued, unified, concentrated."[21]

Thus the path of purification is impossible for an indolent person. The aspirant for enlightenment (*bodhi*) should possess unflinching energy coupled with fixed determination. Enlightenment and deliverance lie absolutely and entirely in his own hands. "Man must himself by his own resolute efforts rise and make his way to the portals of liberty, and it is always, at every moment, in his power so to do. Those portals are not locked; the key is not in possession of someone else from whom it must be obtained by prayer and entreaty. They are free of all bolts and bars, save those the man himself has made."

By precept and example, the Buddha was an exponent of the strenuous life. Hear these words of the Buddha: "The idler who does not strive, who, though young and strong, is full of sloth,

---

20. AN 4:13.

21. Adapted from Sīlācāra, *Discourses of Gotama the Buddha*. A translation of this discourse has been published in *The Wheel No. 21*.

who is weak in resolution and thought, that lazy and idle man will not find the way to wisdom, the way to enlightenment."[22]

Following in the footsteps of the Buddha the disciple thinks: "Though only my skin, sinews and bones remain, and my blood and flesh dry up and wither away, yet never will I give up my quest and swerve from the path of rectitude and enlightenment."

IV

The fourth enlightenment factor is *pīti*, rapture or happiness. This, too, is a mental property (*cetasika*) and is a quality which suffuses both the body and mind. The man lacking in this quality cannot proceed along the path to enlightenment. There will arise in him sullen indifference to the dhamma, an aversion to the practise of meditation, and morbid manifestations. It is, therefore, very necessary that a man striving to attain enlightenment and final deliverance from the fetters of *saṃsāra* should endeavour to cultivate the all-important factor of happiness. No one can bestow on another the gift of happiness; each one has to build it up by effort, reflection and concentrated activity. As happiness is a thing of the mind it should be sought not in external and material things, though they may in a small way be instrumental.

Contentment is a characteristic of the really happy individual The ordinary worldling seems to think that it is difficult to cultivate and develop contentment; but by dint of courage, determination, systematic attention and thought about the things that one meets with in everyday life, by controlling one's evil inclinations, and by curbing the impulses, the sudden tendencies to act without reflection, one can keep the mind from being soiled, and experience happiness through contentment.

In man's mind arise conflicts of diverse kinds, and if these conflicts are to be controlled, while still not eliminated, man must give less rein to inclinations and longings; in other words, he must cultivate contentment. Hard it is to give up what lures and holds us in thrall; and hard it is to exorcise the evil spirits that haunt the human heart in the shape of ugly and unwholesome thoughts. These evils are the manifestations of lust, hate and

22. Dhp 280.

delusion (*lobha*, *dosa* and *moha*). Until one attains to the very crest of purity and peace by constant training of the mind one cannot defeat these hosts completely. The mere abandoning of outward things, fasting, bathing in rivers and at hot springs, and so forth, do not tend to purify a man; these things do not make a man happy, holy and harmless. Hence the need to develop the Buddha's path of purification: morality, meditation and insight (*sīla*, *samādhi* and *paññā*).

When discussing happiness in the context of *sambojjhaṅgas*, we must bear in mind the vast difference between pleasure and happiness. Pleasure—pleasant feeling—is something very momentary and fleeting. Is it wrong to say that pleasant feelings are the prelude to pain? What people hug in great glee in this moment turns to be a source of pain in the next. "The desired is no more there when the outstretched hand would grasp it, or being there and grasped, it vanishes like a flake of snow."
In the words of Robert Burns:

Pleasures are like poppies spread.
You seize the flower, its bloom is shed;
Or, like the snowfall in the river,
A moment white, then melts for ever.

Seeing a form, hearing a sound, perceiving an odour, tasting a flavour, feeling some tangible thing, cognizing an idea, people are moved, and from those sense objects and mental objects they experience a certain degree of pleasure, but it is all a passing show of phenomena. Unlike the animal whose sole purpose is to derive a feeling of pleasure from any source, at any cost, man should endeavour to gain real *pīti* or happiness. Real happiness or rapture comes not through grasping or clinging to things animate or inanimate, but by giving up (*nekkhamma*). It is the detached attitude toward the world that brings about true happiness. The *Satipaṭṭhāna Sutta*, the Discourse on the Foundations of Mindfulness, speaks of pleasant worldly feeling (*sāmisa sukha*) and pleasant unworldly feeling (*nirāmisa sukha*). *Nirāmisa sukha* is far superior to *sāmisa sukha*.

Once the Buddha did not receive even a single morsel of food when he went on his alms round, and an intruder (i.e. *Māra*) remarked that the Master was apparently afflicted with hunger.

Thereupon the Supreme Buddha breathed forth the following verse:[23]

> Ah, happily do we dwell—we who have no impediments!
> Feeders on joy shall we be—even as the radiant devas![24]

Unalloyed joy comes to a man who ponders thus: "Others may harm, but I will become harmless; others may slay living beings, but I will become a non-slayer; others may live unchaste, but I will live pure; others may utter falsehood, I however will speak the truth; others may slander, talk harshly, indulge in gossip, but I will talk only words that promote concord, harmless words agreeable to the ear, full of love, heart-pleasing, courteous, worthy of being borne in mind, timely, fit and to the point. Others may be covetous, I will not covet. Energetic, steeped in modesty of heart, unswerving as regards truth and rectitude, peaceful, honest, contented, generous and truthful in all things will I be." Thus conducive to full realization, perfect wisdom, to Nibbāna is this fourth enlightenment factor *pīti*, happiness.

V

Passaddhi, calm or tranquillity, is the fifth factor of enlightenment. *Passaddhi* is twofold. *Kāya passaddhi* is calm of body. *Kāya* here means all the mental properties rather than the physical body; in other words, calm of the aggregates of feeling (*vedanākkhandha*), perception (*saññākkhandha*) and volitional activities or conformations (*saṅkhārakkhandha*). *Cittapassaddhi* is the calm of the mind; that is, the aggregate of consciousness (*viññāṇakkhandha*).

Passaddhi is compared to the happy experience of a weary walker who sits down under a tree in the shade, or the cooling of a hot place by rain. Hard it is to tranquillize the mind; it trembles and it is unsteady, difficult to guard and hold back; it quivers like a fish taken from its watery home and thrown on the dry ground. It wanders at will.[25] Such is the nature of this ultra-subtle mind. It is systematic reflection (*yonisomanasikāra*) that helps the aspirant for

23. Dhp, 200.
24. Devas are deities.
25. Dhp 33–34.

enlightenment to quieten the fickle mind. Unless a man cultivates tranquillity of mind, concentration cannot be successfully developed. A tranquillized mind keeps away all superficialities and futilities. Many a man today thinks that freedom and unrestraint are synonyms, and that the taming of the self is a hindrance to self development. In the teaching of the Buddha, however, it is quite different. The self must be subdued and tamed on right lines if it is to become truly well. The Tathāgata the Tamed, teaches the Dhamma for the purpose of taming the human heart (*danto so Bhagavā damatāya dhammaṃ deseti*)[26].

It is only when the mind is tranquillized and is kept to the right road of orderly progress, that it becomes useful for the individual possessor of it and for society. A disorderly mind is a liability both to the owner of it and to others. All the havoc wrought in the world is wrought by men who have not learned the way of mental calm, balance and poise. Calmness is not weakness. The calm attitude at all times shows a man of culture. It is not too hard a task for a man to be calm when all things around him are favourable. But to be composed in mind in the midst of unfavourable circumstances is hard indeed, and it is this difficult quality that is worth achieving; for by such control one builds up strength of character. The most deceptive thing in the world is to imagine that they alone who are noisy are strong, or that they alone who are fussily busy possess power.

The man who cultivates calm of the mind does not get upset, confused or excited when confronted with the eight vicissitudes of the world (*aṭṭha-lokadhamma*). He endeavours to see the rise and fall of all things conditioned; how things come into being and pass away. Free from anxiety and restlessness he will see the fragility of the fragile.

A story in our books tells us how when a mother was asked why she did not lament and feel pain over the death of her beloved son, said: "Uninvited he came, uninvited he passed away, as he came so he went, what use is there in lamenting, weeping and wailing?"[27] Such is the advantage of a tranquillized mind. It is unshaken by loss and gain, blame and praise, and undisturbed

26. DN 25.
27. Uraga Jātaka, J 354.

by adversity. This frame of mind is brought about by viewing the sentient world in its proper perspective Thus calm, *passaddhi,* leads man to enlightenment and deliverance from suffering.

VI

The sixth enlightenment factor is *samādhi,* concentration. It is only the tranquillized mind that can easily concentrate on a subject of meditation. The calm, concentrated mind sees things as they really are (*samāhito yathābhutaṃ pajānāti*). The unified mind brings the five hindrances (*pañca nīvaraṇāni*) under subjugation.

Concentration is the intensified steadiness of the mind comparable to an unflickering flame of a lamp in a windless place. It is concentration that fixes the mind aright and causes it to be unmoved and undisturbed. Correct practise of *samādhi* maintains the mind and the mental properties in a state of balance like a steady hand holding a pair of scales.

Right concentration dispels passions that disturb the mind, and brings purity and placidity of mind. The concentrated mind is not distracted by sense objects; concentration of the highest type cannot be disturbed under the most adverse conditions.

One who is intent on *samādhi* should develop a love of virtue, *sīla*, for it is virtue that nourishes mental life, and makes it coherent and calm, equable and full of rich content. The unrestrained mind dissipates itself in frivolous activity.

Many are the impediments that confront a yogi, an aspirant for enlightenment, but there are five particular hindrances that hinder concentrative thought, *samādhi*, and obstruct the way to deliverance. In the teaching of the Buddha they are known as *pañca nīvaraṇa*, the five hindrances. The Pali term *nīvaraṇa* denotes that which hinders or obstructs mental development (*bhāvanā*). They are called hindrances because they completely close in, cut off and obstruct. They close the doors to deliverance. The five hindrances are:

1. *kāmacchanda*—sensual desires,
2. *vyāpāda*—ill will,
3. *thīnamiddha*—obduracy of mind and mental factors,
4. *uddhaccakukkucca*—restlessness and worry,
5. *vicikicchā*—doubt.

Kāmacchanda or sensual desires or intense thirst for either possessions or the satisfaction of base desires is the thirst that binds man to *saṃsāra*, repeated wandering, and closes the door to final deliverance. What is this sensuality? Where does this craving (*taṇhā*) arise and take root? According to the Discourse on the Foundations of Mindfulness (*Satipaṭṭhāna Sutta*) "where there is the delightful and the pleasurable, there this craving arises and takes root." Forms, sounds, smell, taste, bodily contacts and ideas are delightful and pleasurable; there this craving arises and takes root. Craving when obstructed by some cause is transformed to frustration and wrath. As the Dhammapada says:

Taṇhāya jāyati soko—taṇhāya jāyati bhayaṃ
Taṇhāya vippamuttassa—natthi soko kuto bhayaṃ[28]

From craving arises grief, from craving arises fear;
To one who is free from craving, there is no grief, no fear.

The next hindrance is *vyāpāda*—ill will, hatred or aversion. Man naturally revolts against the unpleasant and the disagreeable, and also is depressed by them. To be separated from the loved is painful, and equally painful is the union with the loathed. Even a disagreeable dish, an unpleasant drink, an unlovely demeanour, or a hundred other trifles, may cause indignation. It is wrong thinking, unsystematic reflection, that brings about hatred. Hatred on the other hand breeds hatred and clouds the vision; it distorts the entire mind and its properties, and thus hinders awakening to truth, blocks the way to freedom. This lust and hatred based on ignorance, the crowning corruption of all our madness (*avijjāparamaṃ malaṃ*), are indeed the root causes of strife and dissension between man and man, nation and nation.

The third hindrance consists of a pair of evils; *thīna* and *middha*. *Thīna* is lassitude or morbid state of the mind, and *middha* is a morbid state of the mental properties. *Thīnamiddha*, as some are inclined to think, is certainly not sluggishness of the body; for even the arahats, the perfect ones, who are free from this pair of evils, also experience bodily fatigue. *Thīnamiddha* retards mental development; under its influence mind is inert like butter too stiff to spread or like molasses sticking to a spoon.

28. Dhp 216.

Laxity is a dangerous enemy of mental development. Laxity leads to greater laxity until finally there arises a state of callous indifference. This flabbiness of character is a fatal block to righteousness and freedom. It is through *viriya* or mental effort that one overcomes this pair of evils.

The fourth hindrance also comprises twin drawbacks: *uddhacca* and *kukkucca*, restlessness and brooding, or flurry and worry. As a rule anyone who commits evil is mentally excited and restless; the guilty and the impatient suffer from this hindrance. The minds of men who are restless and unstable are like flustered bees in a shaken hive. This mental agitation impedes meditation and blocks the upward path. Equally baneful is mental worry. Often people repent over the evil actions they have committed. This is not praised by the Buddha; for it is useless to cry over spilt milk. Instead of brooding over such shortcomings one should endeavour not to repeat such unwholesome deeds. There are others who worry over the good deeds omitted and duties left undone. This, too, serves no purpose. It is as futile as to ask the farther bank of a river to come over that we may get to the other side. Instead of uselessly worrying over what good one has failed to do, one should endeavour to perform wholesome deeds. This mental unsteadiness (*kukkucca*) also hinders mental progress.

The fifth and last hindrance is *vicikicchā*, doubt. The Pali term *vi* + *cikicchā* literally means medicine-less. One who suffers from perplexity is really suffering from a dire disease, and until and unless one sheds one's doubts, one will continue to suffer from it. So long as man is subject to this mental itching, so long will he continue to take a cynical view of things which is most detrimental to mental development. The commentators explain this hindrance as the inability to decide anything definitely; it also comprises doubt with regard to the possibility of attaining the *jhānas*, concentrative thought.

In this connection, one may add that even non-Buddhists and yogis who are not concerned with the Buddha, Dhamma and the Sangha at all can inhibit doubt (*vicikicchā nīvaraṇa*) and gain the *jhānas*. The yogi who attains the *jhānas* inhibits all five hindrances by five *jhānaṅgas*, characteristics or factors of *jhāna*. *Kāmacchanda* is inhibited by *ekaggatā* (one-pointedness or unification of the mind); *vyāpāda* by *pīti* (joy); *thīnamiddha* by *vitakka* (applied thought); *uddhaccakukkucca* by *sukha* (happiness); and *vicikicchā* by *vicāra* (sustained thought). The attainment of *jhānas*, however, is not the end aimed at. *Jhānas* should be made to lead to *vipassanā*, intuitional insight. It is through insight that the yogi eradicates the latent corruptions (*anusaya kilesa*), and attains perfect purity.

So long as impurities or taints (*kilesas*) exist latent in man's mind, so long will the arising of *papa* (evil) in him continue. The practiser of *jhāna* whose purpose is to attain *vipassanā* commits no ill action because the hindrances are inhibited, but he has the latent impurities in his make-up, and therefore he is not yet in a state of absolute security. But the arahat, the perfect one, wipes out all the latent impurities with their rootlets and brings this repetitive wandering, *saṃsāra*, to a standstill. He is one whose *saṃsāra* is indubitably ended; for by him the noble life has been perfected and the task done. For him there is no more rebirth.[29]

A sincere student, who is bent on deep study, cuts himself off from sense attractions, and retiring to a congenial atmosphere, holds fast to his studies, and thus steering through all disturbing factors, attains success in his examinations. In the same way, seated in a cloister-cell or some other suitable place "far from the madding crowd's ignoble strife," the yogi, the meditator, fixes his mind on a subject of meditation (*kammaṭṭhāna*), and by struggle and unceasing effort inhibits the five hindrances; and washing out the impurities of his mind-flux, gradually reaches the first, the second, the third, and the fourth *jhāna*. Then by the power of *samādhi*, concentrative thought, thus won, he turns his mind to the understanding of reality in the highest sense. It is at this stage that the yogi cultivates *vipassanā*, intuitional insight. It is through *vipassanā* that one understands the real nature of all component and conditioned things.

Vipassanā aids one to see things as they truly are. One sees truth face to face and comprehends that all tones are just variations struck on the one chord that runs through all life—the chord which is made up of *anicca*, *dukkha* and *anattā*—impermanence, sorrow and soullessness. The yogi gains insight into the true nature of the world he has clung to for so long. He breaks through the eggshell of ignorance to the hypercosmic. With that final catharsis

29. MN 27.

he reaches the state where dawns for him the light of Nibbāna, the calm beyond words, the unshakable deliverance of the mind (*akuppā cetovimutti*);[30] and the world holds nothing more for him.

Says the Dhammapada (v. 373):

> "To the monk who has retired to a secluded spot, whose mind is calmed, and who clearly discerns the dhamma, there comes unalloyed joy and happiness transcending that of humans."

VII

The seventh and last factor of enlightenment is *upekkhā*, equanimity. In the Abhidhamma, *upekkhā* is indicated by the term *tatramajjhattatā*, neutrality. It is mental equipoise and not hedonic indifference Equanimity is the result of a calm concentrative mind. It is hard, indeed, to be undisturbed when touched by the vicissitudes of life, but the man who cultivates this difficult quality of equanimity is not upset.

Amidst the welter of experience (*aṭṭha-lokadhammā*), gain and loss, good repute and ill repute, praise and censure, pain and happiness, he never wavers. He is firm as a solid rock. Of course, this is the attitude of the arahat, the perfect one. Of them it is said: "Truly the good give up longing for everything. The good prattle not with thoughts of craving. Touched by happiness or by pain, the wise show neither elation nor depression."[31]

Refraining from intoxicants and becoming heedful, establishing themselves in patience and purity, the wise train their minds, and it is through such training that a quiet mind is achieved. Can we also achieve it? Lord Horder answers the question thus: "Yes. But how? Well, not by doing some great thing. 'Why were the saints saints?' someone asked. And the answer came: 'Because they were cheerful when it was difficult to be cheerful; patient when it was difficult to be patient. They pushed on when they wanted to stand still, and kept silent when they wanted to talk' That was all. So simple, but so difficult. A matter of mental hygiene..."

---

30. MN 30.
31. Dhp 83.

The poet says:

It is easy enough to be pleasant,
When life flows along like a song,
But the man worthwhile
Is the man who can smile
When everything goes dead wrong.

Mention is made in our books of four wrong paths (*cattāro agati*): the paths of greed (*chanda*), of hate (*dosa*), of cowardice (*bhaya*), of delusion (*rnoha*). People commit evil, being enticed along one or more of these wrong paths; but the man who has reached perfect neutrality through the cultivation of equanimity always avoids such wrong paths. His serene neutrality enables him to see all beings impartially. A certain understanding of the working of *kamma* (actions), and how *kamma* comes into fruition (*kammavipāka*), is very necessary for one who is genuinely bent on cultivating equanimity. In the light of *kamma* one will be able to have a detached attitude toward all beings, nay even inanimate things. The proximate cause of equanimity is the understanding that all beings are the results of their actions (*kamma*).

Śāntideva writes in his *Bodhicaryāvatāra*:

Some there be that loathe me; then why
Shall I, in being praised, rejoice?
Some there be that praise me; then why
Shall I brood over blaming voice?

Who master is of self, will ever bear
A smiling face; he puts away all frowns;
Is first to greet another, and to share
His all. This friend of all the world, Truth crowns.[32]

I have here made an attempt to give a glimpse of the seven enlightenment factors, expounded over 2500 years ago by the Supreme Buddha, for the attaining of full realization and perfect wisdom, of Nibbāna, the deathless. The cultivation or the neglect of these factors of enlightenment is left to each one of us. With the aid of the teaching of the Buddha each one of us

32. Translation by Kassapa Thera.

has the power to detect and destroy the cause of suffering. Each one individually can put forth the necessary effort to work out his deliverance.

The Buddha has taught us the way to know life as it is, and has furnished the directions for such a research by each of us individually. Therefore, we owe it to ourselves to find out for ourselves the truth about life, and to make the best of it. We cannot say justifiably that we do not know how to proceed. There is nothing vague in the teaching of the Buddha. All the necessary indications are clear as clear could be. Buddhism from beginning to end is open to all those who have eyes to see, and minds to understand. "So clear is his teaching that it can never be misunderstood."[33] The only thing necessary on our part for the full realization of the truth is firm determination, endeavour, and earnestness to study and apply the teaching, each working it out for himself to the best of his ability. The Dhamma yet beckons the weary pilgrim to the happy haven of Nibbāna's security and peace. Let us, therefore, cultivate the seven enlightenment factors with zest and unflagging devotion, and advance:

> Remembering the saints of other days,
> And recollecting how it was they lived,
> Even though today be but the after-time,
> One yet may win the ambrosial path of peace.[34]

May All Living Beings Be Well and Happy!

33. Fielding Hall, *The Soul of a People.*
34. *Psalms of the Brethren* (Theragāthā), 947.

Vedānta and Buddhism

A Comparative Study

by

Helmuth von Glasenapp

WHEEL PUBLICATION NO. 02

Preface

The present treatise by Prof. Dr. H. von Glasenapp has been selected for reprint particularly in view of the excellent elucidation of the *anattā* doctrine which it contains. The treatise, in its German original, appeared in 1950 in the Proceedings of the Akademie der Wissenschaften and Literatur (Academy of Sciences and Literature). The present selection from that original is based on the abridged translation published in *The Buddhist*, Vol.XXI, No. 12 (Colombo 1951). Partial use has also been made of a different selection and translation which appeared in *The Middle Way*, Vol. XXXI, No. 4 (London 1957).

The author of this treatise was an eminent Indologist of Western Germany, of the University of Königsberg. He also occupied the indological chair of the University of Tübingen. Among his many scholarly publications are books on Buddhism, Hinduism, Jainism and on comparative religion.

Buddhist Publication Society

Vedānta and Buddhism

Vedānta and Buddhism are the highlights of Indian philosophical thought. Since both have grown in the same spiritual soil, they share many basic ideas: both of them assert that the universe shows a periodical succession of arising, existing and vanishing, and that this process is without beginning and end. They believe in the causality which binds the result of an action to its cause (*karma*), and in rebirth conditioned by that nexus. Both are convinced of the transitory, and therefore sorrowful character, of individual existence in the world; they hope to attain gradually to a redeeming knowledge through renunciation and meditation, and they assume the possibility of a blissful and serene state, in which all worldly imperfections have vanished forever. The original form of these two doctrines shows however strong contrasts. The early Vedānta, formulated in most of the older and middle Upanishads, in some passages of the Mahābhārata and the Purāṇas, and still alive today (though greatly changed) as the basis of several Hinduistic systems, teaches an *ens realissimum* (an entity of highest reality) as the primordial cause of all existence, from which everything has arisen and with which it again merges, either temporarily or forever.

With the monistic metaphysics of the Vedānta contrasts the pluralistic Philosophy of Flux of the early Buddhism of the Pāli texts which up to the present time flourishes in Ceylon, Burma and Siam. It teaches that in the whole empirical reality there is nowhere anything that persists; neither material nor mental substances exist independently by themselves; there is no original entity or primordial Being in whatsoever form it may be imagined, from which these substances might have developed. On the contrary, the manifold world of mental and material elements arises solely through the causal cooperation of transitory factors of existence (*dharma*) which depend functionally upon each other; that is, the material and mental universe arises through the concurrence of forces that, according to the Buddhists, are not reducible to something else. It is therefore obvious that deliverance from *saṃsāra*, i.e., the sorrow-laden round of existence, cannot consist in the re-absorption into an eternal Absolute which is at the root of all manifoldness, but can only be achieved by a complete extinguishing of all factors which condition the processes constituting life and world. The Buddhist Nirvāna is, therefore, not the primordial ground, the eternal essence, which is at the basis of everything and from which the whole world has arisen (the Brahman of the Upanishads), but the reverse of all that we know, something altogether different which must be characterized as a nothing in relation to the world, but which is experienced as highest bliss by those who have attained to it (AN 9:34). Vedāntists and Buddhists have been fully aware of the gulf between their doctrines, a gulf that cannot be bridged over. According to Majjhima Nikāya Sutta 22 a doctrine that proclaims "The same is the world and the self. This I shall be after death; imperishable, permanent, eternal!" (see Bṛhadāranyaka Upaniṣad 4:4.13), was styled by the Buddha a perfectly foolish doctrine. On the other side, the Katha Upaniṣad (4.14) does not see a way to deliverance in the Buddhist theory of dharmas (impersonal processes): He who supposes a profusion of particulars gets lost like rain water on a mountain slope; the truly wise man, however, must realize that his Ātman is at one with the Universal Atman, and that the former, if purified from dross, is being absorbed by the latter, "just as clear water poured into clear water becomes one with it, indistinguishably."

Vedānta and Buddhism have lived side by side for such a long time that obviously they must have influenced each other. The strong predilection of the Indian mind for a doctrine of universal unity (monism) has led the representatives of Mahayana to conceive Saṃsāra and Nirvāna as two aspects of the same and single true reality. For Nāgārjuna the empirical world is a mere appearance, as all dharmas manifest in it are perishable and conditioned by other dharmas, without having any independent existence of their own. Only the indefinable "Voidness" (*sūnyatā*) to be grasped in meditation, and realized in Nirvāna, has true reality.

This so-called Middle Doctrine of Nāgārjuna remains true to the Buddhist principle that there can be nowhere a substance, in so far as Nāgārjuna sees the last unity as a kind of abyss, characterized only negatively, which has no genetic relation to the world. Asaṅga and Vasubandhu, however, in their doctrine of Consciousness Only, have abandoned the Buddhist principle of denying a positive reality which is at the root all phenomena, and in doing so, they have made a further approach to Vedānta. To that mahayanistic school of Yogācāras, the highest reality is a pure and undifferentiated spiritual element that represents the non-relative substratum of all phenomena. To be sure, they thereby do not assert, as the (older) Vedānta does, that the *ens realissimum* (the highest essence) is identical with the universe; the relation between the two is rather being defined as "being neither different nor not different." It is only in the later Buddhist systems of the Far East that the undivided, absolute consciousness is taken to be the basis of the manifold world of phenomena. But in contrast to the older Vedānta, it is never maintained that the world is an unfoldment from the unchangeable, eternal, blissful Absolute; suffering and passions, manifest in the world of plurality, are rather traced back to worldly delusion.

On the other hand, the doctrines of later Buddhist philosophy had a far-reaching influence on Vedānta. It is well known that Gaudapada, and other representatives of later Vedānta, taught an illusionistic acosmism, for which true Reality is only "the eternally pure, eternally awakened, eternally redeemed" universal spirit whilst all manifoldness is only delusion; the Brahman has therefore not developed into the world, as asserted by the older Vedānta, but it forms only the world's unchangeable background, comparable to the white screen on which appear the changing images of an unreal shadow play.

In my opinion, there was in later times, especially since the Christian era, much mutual influence of Vedānta and Buddhism, but originally the systems are diametrically opposed to each other. The Atman doctrine of the Vedānta and the Dharma theory of Buddhism exclude each other. The Vedānta tries to establish an Atman as the basis of everything, whilst Buddhism maintains that everything in the empirical world is only a stream of passing Dharmas (impersonal and evanescent processes) which therefore has to be characterized as *anattā*, i.e., being without a persisting self, without independent existence.

Again and again scholars have tried to prove a closer connection between the early Buddhism of the Pāli texts and the Vedānta of the Upanishads; they have even tried to interpret Buddhism as a further development of the Atman doctrine. There are, e.g., two books which show that tendency: *The Vedāntic Buddhism of the Buddha,* by J.G. Jennings (Oxford University Press, 1947), and in German language, *The Soul Problem of Early Buddhism,* by Herbert Guenther (Konstanz, 1949).

The essential difference between the conception of deliverance in Vedānta and in Pāli Buddhism lies in the following ideas: Vedānta sees deliverance as the manifestation of a state which, though obscured, has been existing from time immemorial; for the Buddhist, however, Nirvāna is a reality which differs entirely from all dharmas as manifested in *Saṃsāra,* and which only becomes effective if they are abolished. To sum up: the Vedāntin wishes to penetrate to the last reality which dwells within him as an immortal essence, or seed, out of which everything has arisen. The follower of Pāli Buddhism, however, hopes by complete abandoning of all corporeality, all sensations, all perceptions, all volitions, and all acts of consciousness, to realize a state of bliss which is entirely different from all that exists in the *Saṃsāra.*

After these introductory remarks we shall now discuss systematically the relation of original Buddhism and Vedānta.

(1) First of all we have to clarify to what extent a knowledge of Upanishadic texts may be assumed for the canonical Pāli scriptures. The five old prose Upanishads are, on reasons of contents and language, generally held to be pre-Buddhistic. The younger Upanishads, in any case those beginning from *Maitrāyaṇa,* were certainly written at a time when Buddhism already existed.

The number of passages in the Pāli Canon dealing with Upanishadic doctrines, is very small. It is true that early Buddhism shares many doctrines with the Upanishads (*karma,* rebirth, liberation through insight), but these tenets were so widely held in philosophical circles of those times that we can no longer regard the Upanishads as the direct source from which the Buddha has drawn. The special metaphysical concern of the Upanishads, the identity of the individual and the universal Atman, has been mentioned and rejected only in a few passages in the early Buddhist texts, for instance in the saying of the Buddha quoted earlier. Nothing shows better the great distance that separates the Vedānta and the teachings of the Buddha than the fact that the two principal concepts of Upanishadic wisdom, Ātman and Brahman, do not appear anywhere in the Buddhist texts, with the clear and distinct meaning of a "primordial ground of the world, core of existence, *ens realissimum* (true substance)," or similarly. As this holds likewise true for the early Jaina literature, one must assume that early Vedānta was of no great importance in Magadha, at the time of the Buddha and the Mahāvīra; otherwise the opposition against it would have left more distinct traces in the texts of these two doctrines.

(2) It is of decisive importance for examining the relation between Vedānta and Buddhism, clearly to establish the meaning of the words *attā* and *anattā* in Buddhist literature.

The meaning of the word *attan* (nominative: *attā,* Sanskrit: *ātman,* nominative: *ātmā*) divides into two groups. (A) In daily usage, *attan* ("self") serves for denoting one's own person, and has the function of a reflexive pronoun. This usage is, for instance, illustrated in the 12th Chapter of the Dhammapada. (B) As a philosophical term, *attan* denotes the individual soul as assumed by the Jainas and other schools, but rejected by the Buddhists. This individual soul was held to be an eternal unchangeable spiritual monad, perfect and blissful by nature, although its qualities may be temporarily obscured through its connection with matter. Starting from this view held by the heretics, the Buddhists further understand by the term "self" (*ātman*) any eternal, unchangeable individual entity, in other words, that which Western metaphysics calls a "substance": "something existing through and in itself, and not through something else; nor existing attached to, or inherent in, something else." In the philosophical usage of the Buddhists, *attan* is, therefore, any entity of which the heretics wrongly assume that it exists independently of everything else, and that it has existence on its own strength.

The word *anattan* (nominative: *anattā*) is a noun (Sanskrit: *anātmā*) and means "not-self" in the sense of an entity that is not independent. The word *anātman* is found in its meaning of "what is not the Soul (or Spirit)," also in brahmanical Sanskrit sources (*Bhagavadgīta,* 6.6; Śaṃkara to *Brahmasūtra* I.1.1, *Bibl. Indica*, p. 76; *Vedāntasāra* § 158). Its frequent use in Buddhism is accounted for by the Buddhists' characteristic preference for negative nouns. Phrases like *rūpaṃ anattā* are therefore to be translated "corporeality is a not-self," or "corporeality is not an independent entity," or similarly.

As an adjective, the word *anattan* changes from the consonantal to the *a*-declension; *anattā* (see Sanskrit *anātmaka, anātmya*), e.g., SN 22:57/S III 56), *anattaṃ rūpaṃ* ... *anattā saṅkhāre* ... *na pajānāti* ("he does not know that corporeality is without self ... that the mental formations are without self"). The word *anattā* is, therefore, to be translated here by "not having the nature of a self, not independent, without a (persisting) self, without an (eternal) substance," etc. The passage "*anattaṃ rūpaṃ anattā rūpan' ti yathābhutaṃ na pajānāti*" has to be rendered: "With regard to corporeality having not the nature of a self, he does not know according to truth, 'Corporeality is a not-self (not an independent entity).'" The noun *attan* and the adjective *anattā* can both be rendered by "without a self, without an independent essence, without a persisting core," since the Buddhists themselves do not make any difference in the use of these two grammatical forms. This becomes particularly evident in the case of the word *anattā*, which may be either a singular or a plural noun. In the well-known phrase *sabbe saṅkhārā aniccā* ... *sabbe dhammā anattā* (Dhp 279), "all conditioned factors of existence are transitory ... all factors existent whatever (Nirvāna included) are without a self," it is undoubtedly a plural noun, for the Sanskrit version has "*sarve dharmā anātmānaḥ.*"

The fact that the *anattā* doctrine only purports to state that a *dharma* is "void of a self," is evident from the passage in the Saṃyutta Nikāya (SN 35:85/S IV 54) where it is said *rūpā suññā attena vā attaniyena vā*, "forms are void of a self (an independent essence) and of anything pertaining to a self (or 'self-like')."

Where Guenther has translated *anattan* or *anattā* as "not the self," one should use "*a* self" instead of "*the* self," because in the Pāli Canon the word *attā* does not occur in the sense of "universal soul."

(3) It is not necessary to assume that the existence of indestructible monads is a necessary condition for a belief in life after death. The view that an eternal, immortal, persisting soul substance is the *condition sine qua non* of rebirth can be refuted by the mere fact that not only in the older Upanishads, but also in Pythagoras and Empedocles, rebirth is taught without the assumption of an imperishable soul substance.

(4) Guenther can substantiate his view only through arbitrary translations which contradict the whole of Buddhist tradition.

This is particularly evident in those passages where Guenther asserts that "the Buddha meant the same by Nirvāna and Ātman" and that "Nirvāna is the true nature of man." For in Udāna 8.2, Nirvāna is expressly described as *anattaṃ,* which is rightly rendered by the commentator Dhammapāla's commentary to the Udāna (Ud 21) as *atta-virahita* (without a self), and in Vinaya V p. 86, Nirvāna is said to be, just as the conditioned factors of existence (*saṅkhata*), "without a self" (p. 151).

Neither can the equation Ātman = Nirvāna be proved by the well-known phrase "*attadīpā viharatha dhammadīpā,*" for whether *dīpa* here means "lamp" or "island of deliverance," this passage can, after all, only refer to the monks taking refuge in themselves and in the doctrine (*dhamma*), and *attan* and *dhamma* cannot possibly be interpreted as Nirvāna. In the same way, too, it is quite preposterous to translate Dhammapada 160, "*attā hi attano nātho,*" as "Nirvāna is for a man the leader" (p. 155), for the chapter is concerned only with the idea that we should strive hard and purify ourselves. Otherwise Guenther would have to translate in the following verse 161, *attanā va kataṃ pāpaṃ attajaṃ attasambhavaṃ*, "By Nirvāna evil is done, it arises out of Nirvāna, it has its origin in Nirvāna." It is obvious that this kind of interpretation must lead to manifestly absurd consequences.

(5) As far as I can see there is not a single passage in the Pāli Canon where the word *attā* is used in the sense of the Upanishadic Ātman.[1] This is not surprising, since the word *ātman,* current in all Indian philosophical systems, has the meaning of "universal soul, *ens realissimum,* the Absolute," exclusively in the pan-entheistic and theopantistic Vedānta, but, in that sense, it is alien to all other brahmanical and non-Buddhist doctrines. Why, then, should it have a Vedāntic meaning in Buddhism? As far as I know, no one has ever conceived the idea of giving to the term *ātman* a Vedāntic

1. Except in a few passages rejecting it, as the one quoted by the author: "The same is the world and the self"; see also, Suttanipāta verse 477; and one of the six ego-beliefs rejected in MN 2: 'Even by the self I perceive the self': this view occurs to him as being true and correct" *(attanā va attānaṃ sañjānāmī'ti).* Cf. Bhagavadgīta VI.19 *Yatra caiv' ātmanā ātmānaṃ pasyann-ātmani tusyati.*—The BPS Editor

interpretation, in the case of Nyaya, Vaisesika, classical Śāṅkhya, Yoga, Mīmāṃsā, or Jainism.

(6) The fact that in the Pāli Canon all worldly phenomena are said to be *anattā* has induced some scholars of the West to look for an Ātman in Buddhism. For instance, the following "great syllogism" was formulated by George Grimm: "What I perceive to arise and to cease, and to cause suffering to me, on account of that impermanence, cannot be my ego. Now I perceive that everything cognizable in me and around me, arises and ceases, and causes me suffering on account of its impermanence. Therefore nothing cognizable is my ego." From that Grimm concludes that there must be an eternal ego-substance that is free from all suffering, and above all cognizability. This is a rash conclusion. By teaching that there is nowhere in the world a persisting Ātman, the Buddha has not asserted that there must be a transcendental Ātman (i.e., a self beyond the world). This kind of logic resembles that of a certain Christian sect which worships its masters as "Christs on earth," and tries to prove the simultaneous existence of several Christs from Mark (13.22), where it is said: "False Christs and false prophets shall arise"; for if there are false Christs, there must also be genuine Christs!

The denial of an imperishable Ātman is common ground for all systems of Hinayana as well as Mahayana, and there is, therefore, no reason for the assumption that Buddhist tradition, unanimous on that point, has deviated from the original doctrine of the Buddha. If the Buddha, contrary to the Buddhist tradition, had actually proclaimed a transcendental Ātman, a reminiscence of it would have been preserved somehow by one of the numerous sects. It is remarkable that even the Pudgalavādins, who assume a kind of individual soul, never appeal to texts in which an Ātman in this sense is proclaimed. He who advocates such a revolutionary conception of the Buddha's teachings, has also the duty to show evidence how such a complete transformation started and grew, suddenly or gradually. But none of those who advocate the Ātman-theory has taken pains to comply with that demand which is indispensable to a historian.

(7) In addition to the aforementioned reasons, there are other grounds too, which speak against the supposition that the Buddha has identified Ātman and Nirvāna. It remains

quite incomprehensible why the Buddha should have used this expression which is quite unsuitable for Nirvāna and would have aroused only wrong associations in his listeners. Though it is true that Nirvāna shares with the Vedāntic conception of Ātman the qualification of eternal peace into which the liberated ones enter forever, on the other hand the Ātman is in brahmanical opinion something mental and conscious, a description which does not hold true for Nirvāna. Furthermore, Nirvāna is not, like the Ātman, the primordial ground or the divine principle of the world (Aitareya Up. 1.1), nor is it that which preserves order in the world (Bṛhadāraṇyaka Upaniṣad 3.8.9); it is also not the substance from which everything evolves, nor the core of all material elements.

(8) Since the scholarly researches made by Otto Rosenberg (published in Russian 1918, in German trs. 1924), Th. Stcherbatsky (1932), and the great work of translation done by Louis de la Vallee Poussin on the *Abhidharmakoṣa* (1923–31), there cannot be any doubt about the basic principle of Buddhist philosophy. In the light of these researches, all attempts to give to the Ātman a place in the Buddhist doctrine, appear to be quite antiquated. We know now that all Hinayana and Mahayana schools are based on the *anātma-dharma* theory. This theory explains the world through the causal co-operation of a multitude of transitory factors (*dharma*), arising in mutual functional dependence. This theory maintains that the entire process of liberation consists in the tranquillization of these incessantly arising and disappearing factors. For that process of liberation however, is required, apart from moral restraint (*sīla*) and meditative concentration (*samādhi*), the insight (*prajña*) that all conditioned factors of existence (*saṃskāra*) are transitory, without a permanent independent existence, and therefore subject to grief and suffering. The Nirvāna which the saint experiences already in this life, and which he enters forever after death, is certainly a reality (*dharma*), but as it neither arises nor vanishes, it is not subject to suffering, and is thereby distinguished from all conditioned realities. Nirvāna being a *dharma*, is likewise *anattā*, just as the transitory, conditioned dharmas of *saṃsāra*, which, as caused by volitions—that is, karma-producing energies (*saṃskāra*)—are themselves also called *saṃskāra*. Like them, Nirvāna is no individual entity which could will or act independently. For it is

the basic idea of the entire system that all dharmas are devoid of Ātman, and without cogent reasons we cannot assume that the Buddha himself has taught something different from that which, since more than two thousand years, his followers have considered to be the quintessence of their doctrine.

Buddhism and Science

Collected Essays

by

K. N. Jayatilleke
Robert F. Spencer
Wu Shu

WHEEL PUBLICATION NO. 03

Buddhism and the Scientific Revolution

Prof. K. N. Jayatilleke, B.A. (Lond.), B.A. (Ceylon), M.A. (Cantab.), Ph.D. (Lond.)

It is a historical fact that the scientific revolution which took its rise in the seventeenth century in the West was largely responsible for upsetting the earlier religious conception of the universe. Not only did science controvert the specific dogmas of Western religion, but it seemed to have undermined the foundations as well as the fundamental concepts implicit in the religious outlook on things.

The new cosmology of Copernicus, Galileo and their successors altered the geocentric picture of the universe although it was pronounced to be "contrary to the Holy Scriptures." The new biology (the theory of evolution) upset the doctrines of the special creation and the fall of man. And the new psychology seemed to show that man's mind like his physical body worked on a pattern of causal law and that however deep one plumbed into its depths there was not discoverable in it an unchanging soul which governed its activities entirely.

But much more serious was the effect of the scientific outlook on the general religious attitude which involved a belief in a personal God, in purpose, and in the objectivity of moral values. Science made its discoveries and progressed quite comfortably on the assumption of universal causation without the necessity for teleological explanations or divine intervention. It dealt with an amoral universe indifferent to the aspirations of men. As among men, moral values like economic values were subjective since they were dependent on the needs and desires of men, and an ethical humanism was the best that could be hoped for. Even such an ethics need not be universal, for, as anthropologists discovered, different societies seem to have followed different moral codes which suited them and ethical relativism was the scientific truth about the nature of moral values.

Of course, there are those who still cling to the dogmas in the face of science or believe in them in a non-literal sense. But the position remains very much the same although people are no longer optimistic (after two world wars and in the throes of a third) about the ability of science to usher in a brave new world of peace and plenty. It has also been granted that mechanistic explanations of the universe need not necessarily rule out teleological ones. Science too has given up the crude materialism of the eighteenth century and scientists no longer attempt to explain the universe on machine models, while some scientists have denied that strict determinism holds in the sphere of the atom. But all this is still a far cry from religion.

What place would Buddhism occupy in such a context? Are its dogmas and attitudes no better or no worse than those of any other religion? Some Western writers on religion seem to have assumed that this was so, but if one reads through the Buddhist texts, one begins to wonder whether the scientific revolution would have at all affected religion adversely if it had taken place in the context of early Buddhism.

I say this because I find that early Buddhism emphasises the importance of the scientific outlook in dealing with the problems of morality and religion. Its specific dogmas are said to be capable of verification. And its general account of the nature of man and the universe is one that accords with the findings of science rather than being at variance with them.

To take this last point first, we find for instance that the early Buddhist conception of the cosmos is in essence similar to the modern conception of the universe. In the Pali texts that have come down to us we are literally told that hundreds and thousands of suns and moons, earths, and higher worlds, constitute the minor world system, that a hundred thousand times this is the middling world system, and a hundred thousand times the middling world system is the major world system. In modern terminology it would seem as if a minor world system (*cūḷanikā-loka-dhātu*) is a galaxy of which we observe about a hundred million through our best telescopes. The Buddhist conception of time is equally immense.

There is, of course, no theory of biological evolution as such mentioned in the Buddhist texts, but man and society as well as worlds are pictured as changing and evolving in accordance with causal laws.

Then in psychology we find early Buddhism regarding man as a psychophysical unit whose "psyche" is not a changeless soul but a dynamic continuum composed of a conscious mind as well as an unconscious in which is stored the residua of emotionally charged memories going back to childhood as well as into past lives. Such a mind is said to be impelled to act under the influence of three types of desires—the desire for sense-gratification (*kāma-taṇhā*), the desire for self-preservation (*bhava-taṇhā*), and the desire for destruction (*vibhava-taṇhā*). Except for the belief in rebirth, this conception of the mind sounds very modern, and one cannot also fail to observe the parallel between the threefold desire in Buddhism and the Freudian conceptions of the *eros*, *libido*, and *thanatos*.

I have brought out these similarities not with the intention of showing that Buddhism teaches modern science, but that the scientific revolution does not have the same adverse effect on Buddhism as it had on another religious traditions.

Now let us turn to the content of Buddhism as a theory about the nature and destiny of man. First of all it holds that the honest impartial search for truth even in matters moral and religious is no bar to one's spiritual progress. On more than one occasion the Buddha has admonished honest seekers after the truth in the following words: "You have raised a doubt in a situation in which you ought to be uncertain. Do not accept anything because it is rumoured so, because it is the traditional belief, because the majority hold to it, because it is found in the scriptures, because it is the product of metaphysical argument and speculation, or after a superficial investigation of facts, or because it conforms with one's inclinations, because it is authoritative, or because of the prestige value of your teacher." Critical investigation and personal verification was to be the guide to true morality and religion. "If anyone were to speak ill of me, my doctrine and my order," says the Buddha, "do not bear any ill-will towards him, be upset or perturbed at heart, for if you were to be so it will only cause you harm. If on the other hand anyone were to speak well of me, my doctrine and my order, do not be overjoyed, thrilled or elated at heart, for if so it will only be in your way of forming a correct judgement as to whether the qualities praised in us are real and actually found." A scientific outlook was thus considered necessary not only for discovering the truly moral and religious life but even for the continual self-examination which such an outlook demands.

The field of moral and religious phenomena is, again, not a realm of mystery but one in which the law of cause and effect holds. The principle of causal determination, namely that A is the cause of B if "whenever an event A occurs an event B occurs, and B does not occur unless A has occurred" is laid down by the Buddha in these very terms, and he further states that he "speaks only of causes and of things which arise from causes." Thus all phenomena, including moral and spiritual experience (with the sole exception of Nibbāna, which is not a conditioned phenomenon) are said to be conditioned by causal laws. Such laws are classified according to their sphere of operation as physical laws (*utu-niyāma*), biological laws (*bīja-niyāma*), psychological laws (*citta-niyāma*), and moral and spiritual laws (*dhamma-niyāma*).

Now there are three laws which are said to govern the life and destiny of the individual. They are the law of continuity, which makes for the persistence of individuality (*bhava*), the law of moral retribution (*kamma*) whereby morally good acts tend to result in pleasant consequences for the individual and morally evil acts in unpleasant consequences, and finally, the law of causal genesis (*paṭiccasamuppāda*) which is intended to explain the above two laws.

The law of continuity, popularly known as rebirth, ensures the persistence of the dynamic unconscious of the individual with the death of the physical body. If this unconscious is not attuned to higher worlds by the moral and spiritual development of the individual, it is said generally to persist in the spirit-sphere (*petti-visaya*) as a discarnate spirit, and subsequently gets reborn as a human. Critics of Buddhism often suggest that this theory of rebirth is dogmatically accepted or taken for granted in Buddhism, but a careful study of the texts would show that this is not the case.

Buddhism arose at a time when there was intense speculation on the problem of survival. There were also several schools of materialism, all of which denied survival altogether, and there were the sceptics who merely doubted the possibility of survival. Even experiments such as the weighing of the body immediately before and after death were performed in order to discover any evidence of survival. One of the materialist theories mentioned and dismissed by the Buddha was that consciousness was a by-product of the material elements being mixed up in certain proportions to form the organic body—in the same way in which the red colour is produced by suitable mixtures of betel, arecanut and lime (none of which is red). Several such materialistic theories, as well as a number of one-life-after-death-theories, some of which held that the soul was conscious after death, others that it was unconscious (but existing), and yet others that it was super-conscious after death, are examined and disposed of by the Buddha. The theory of rebirth is offered as one capable of being verified by developing the faculty of seeing our former births, a potentiality which is said to be within the reach of all of us.

Rebirth is therefore not a dogma to be accepted on faith but a hypothesis capable of being scientifically verified. The available evidence for rebirth today is roughly of two sorts.

There is the spontaneous evidence of numerous people from both East and West who have claimed to remember their past lives, in some cases of which the memories have been confirmed by further investigation (e.g., the case of Shanti Devi, *Illustrated Weekly of India*, December 15, 1935; the case of Nellie Horster, *Milwaukee Sentinel*, September 25, 1892). There is also the more reliable and more abundant evidence of psychiatrists and psychologists who have discovered that under hypnotic trance the subject's memories can be traced back not only to childhood but to prior earth lives as well, in some cases of which the facts have been verified (e.g., A. de Rochas, *Les Vies Successives*, Bibilotheque Charcomac, Paris; Ralph Shirley, *The Problem of Rebirth*, Rider & Co., London; Professor Thedore Flournoy, *Des Inde a la planete Mars*; Professor Charles E. Cory, "A Divided Self", article in *Journal of Abnormal Psychology*, Vol. XIV, 1919).

The law of moral retribution or *kamma* as taught in Buddhism has also been criticised on the grounds that it amounts to fatalism. This again is due to ignorance of the Buddhist teaching. Causation in Buddhism is carefully distinguished by the Buddha on the one hand from strict determinism and on the other from indeterminism. The Buddha argues that if everything was determined, then there would be no free will and no moral or spiritual life would be possible and we would be slaves of the past; and on the other hand, if everything was undetermined (*adhicca-samuppanna*) or fortuitous, then again the moral and spiritual life would not be possible, for the cultivation of moral and spiritual values would not result in moral and spiritual growth. It is because the world is so constituted that everything is not strictly determined or completely undetermined that the religious life is possible and desirable, according to the Buddha.

In order to explain rebirth and *kamma*, some of the Upanishadic thinkers who accepted these doctrines had to resort to the concept of *ātman* or a changeless soul. The individual continued to be the same because he had a permanent soul which was the agent of all the actions of the individual as well as the experiencer of their fruits. The Buddha was quick to see that such metaphysical entities explained nothing and that it was meaningless to assert or deny an unverifiable entity. He therefore rejected the concept of soul while maintaining the doctrine of the observable continuity of the individuality, and explained the above two laws of continuity and moral retribution in terms of all the verifiable phenomenal factors which determine the continued genesis and growth of the individual. This is too elaborate to be set out in detail. In brief, it describes how the individual is conditioned by his psychological past (going back to past lives which set the general tone of his character) and the genetic constitution of his body derived from his parents, and continues to act in and react with his environment accumulating the experiences of this life in his evolving consciousness (*saṃvaṭṭanika-viññāṇa*), which continues after the death of the body if the threefold desires in it be still active.

Personal and direct knowledge of the operation of these three laws constitutes the threefold knowledge (*tisso vijjā*) which the Buddha and his disciples claimed to have. The awareness of the fact that and the way in which one is being conditioned is said to result in one ceasing to be conditioned, a state which corresponds to the attainment of the unconditioned and supreme felicity of Nibbāna. This is salvation in Buddhism which is literally salvation from the bondage of finite conditioned existence.

Strictly, Nibbāna is said to be beyond description or conception, the reason given being that it is a state so radically different from the type of existent things which we can conceive of that no meaningful description or definition of it can be given in conceptual terms. It is said that to say that one "exists" in Nibbāna is wrong, for existence is a concept that applies to phenomenal things and has reference to space and time. Nibbāna is "timeless, in that one cannot speak of it as being in the past, present or future," is not located in space, and is not causally conditioned unlike all phenomenal things. But it is also said to be equally wrong to say that one "does not exist" in Nibbāna since this implies a state of oblivion and annihilation. Nevertheless both positive as well as negative descriptions are given though they are not to be taken as exact definitions, as Nibbāna is beyond the scope of logic.

Negatively, Nibbāna is the absence of all unhappiness, and all phenomenal existence is said to be infected with unhappiness; we are unhappy either because we experience mental or physical pain and have forebodings for the future, or because the pleasant experiences that we have are insecure and never lasting. This is to take a realistic view of life even in the face of the fact that as the Buddha says "human beings enjoy on the whole more pleasant experiences than unpleasant ones," and therefore it would not be correct to call it pessimism since it has nothing to do with wishful thinking. Positively, Nibbāna is described as a state of "supreme felicity" (*paramaṃ sukhaṃ*).

The way of salvation is described as an eightfold path in which the first step is that of right understanding and living in accordance with the true philosophy of life, and as a result having right aspirations, right speech, right actions, right mode of living, and right mindfulness, culminating in the growth of religious joy and the spiritual and intuitive awareness of right meditation or contemplation. The full fruit of right contemplation, however, can be reaped by those giving up the active social life for the contemplative life. This meditative life is characterized by the stages of personal mystical consciousness (*rūpa-jhāna*) and impersonal mystical consciousness (*arūpa-jhāna*) culminating in the attainment of Nibbāna. With the growth of his mind and spirit there are said to emerge certain faculties latent in him, such as telepathy and clairvoyance and the ability to see his past lives. These cognitive faculties, as explained earlier, make it possible for the individual to realise the conditioned state in which he is, and thereby to attain the Unconditioned. Considering the requirements of the path, the Way to Nibbāna is therefore described as the culmination of a person's moral development (*sīla*), intuitional or spiritual development (*samādhi*), and intellectual or cognitive development (*paññā*). The Buddha was once asked "whether he hoped to save one-third of the world, one-half of the world or the whole world by offering this Way of Salvation," to which he replied that he did not claim to save one-third of humanity, but that just as a skilful doorkeeper guarding the only entrance to the palace knows that all those who seek the haven of this palace must enter by this door, even so all those in the past who were saved, who in the present are being saved and who in future will be saved, have entered, are entering and will enter by this door.

Such is the teaching of early Buddhism which is offered as a self-consistent scientific hypothesis touching the matters of religion and morality which each person can verify for himself. In fact, not being based on revelation, the fact that it has been verified by him and hundreds of his disciples and is capable of being verified by every earnest seeker is put forward as the criterion of its truth by the Buddha. The empirical and pragmatic test of science is, for the Buddha, the test of true religion. The faith that he requires is the trust that is required to put to the test a certain philosophy of life by devoting one's entire being to living it every moment of one's life. And its worth is to be realised by its fruits by each person for himself. Like the scientists working in other fields, the Buddhas or the Perfect Ones have merely discovered these truths which are there for all time and have preached them for the good of the world. Each one has to seek and work out his own salvation; no one can save another and the Perfect Ones do merely point the way.

It would be seen that such a religion is in accord with the temper and the findings of science, so that Buddhism is not likely to be at variance with science so long as scientists confine themselves to their methodology and their respective fields without making a dogma of materialism.

As for purpose, the Buddhist view is that the world as such has no purpose to accomplish though individuals in it may choose their own ends and thus make their lives purposeful, the end recommended by Buddhism being Nibbāna. The Buddha would argue that if the world had a purpose to be attained in a final consummation, then either salvation would be assured for all or some would be fore-doomed and damned for eternity; but according to the Buddha there is no necessity or inevitability in progress; no one is destined to attain Nibbāna unless he wishes to. But as for moral values Buddhism upholds their objectivity, for according to the Law of Kamma, a drunkard, for instance, unless he repents (i.e. changes his ways) tends to be reborn as a moron whatever the opinions or wishes of the drunkard or the members of his society may be.

The Relation of Buddhism to Modern Science

Robert F. Spencer M.A., Ph.D.

There can be no question that Buddhism is the one system, excepting perhaps science itself, which achieves an objective and detached view toward the nature and destiny of man. This striking objectivity divorces the Buddhist system from the realm of religion and allies it at once with the kind of scientific search for truth which characterized India in the Gupta and other early periods of its civilization and which affords a major preoccupation to most of the intellectual world—both east and west—of today. Buddhism, this writer contends, is not properly a religion; it is a system for life and living in a world which is circumscribed with difficulty and beset with suffering. Buddhism is not a religion, if, in scientific terms, we define religion as the mystic experience, the psychic thrill. It is not a religion because it de-emphasizes faith in the unknown and unknowable and it rejects dogmatism. However much these latter features may obtrude themselves in Buddhist lands, no serious student can regard them as other than superfluous growths, digressions from the scientifically conceived Dharma of the founder. This paper holds that in the strictest sense, Buddhism as a system and scientific endeavour as a comparable system are one.

But there is also a difference: the Buddhist thinker is clear as to his aims; if he uses science and its methods, he does so with the realization that science is a means to an end and not an end in itself. In other words, the Buddhist sees in science reflections of principles expressed and reiterated by the Lord Buddha at a time when there was no absolute methodology of science as such. Since today the world is wedded to the methods of science, we have only to note how wholly compatible with science is the system founded in India over 2,500 years ago. Modern scientific achievement serves merely to lend added perspective to the concepts of impermanence, of the illusory quality, and of *anattā* which were put forth so long ago. As an end in itself, science may solve immediate problems; it feeds more people so that there are more people to feed; it prolongs life and finds more effective means of destroying life. Science as viewed today, is a method, no more, and to make a cult of it, to find in it the answer to problems and questions of the ultimate forms of human destiny is rank error. It is making a dogma of science where no religious emotion or attitude is ever intended. This indeed was the fallacy of some of the sectarian forms of ancient Hinduism: in seeking to explain the universe by means of an atomic theory, however correctly conceived, the Brahmins of India of the past stopped dead and found human salvation, if such it may be called, in science and sciencing. Nor is the contemporary world too different despite the fact that the scientific goal is material rather than spiritual. The method of science admits primarily the formulation of an hypothesis, the testing of that hypothesis, and the stating of new hypothesis, predicated on knowledge obtained by such experimentation. The Lord Buddha experimented with ideas, not with things—he employed the crucible of life in which to measure human experience and he came up with a detached and tested answer.

Science is characterized by its tough-mindedness. The search for truth is not always easy, nor indeed, always pleasant. It has been said that the truth may hurt. It does, but it remains truth for all that. Pristine Buddhism offers an attempt, a successful one, it may be added, to come to grips with truth in an objective way. To those of us who, now living, are seeking a few moments of respite, of surcease from worry, in short, what might be called happiness, the Buddha says in effect: "All right, just remember, it doesn't last; it may be here today but it is never permanent." Just as science seeks to define its answers, objectively, without emotion, so also does Buddhism hit squarely at the target and, free from emotional stress, informs us concisely what is what. We may not like it and we may have to toughen ourselves to take it, but it is proven.

An example of the kind of scientific "tough-mindedness" which the Buddhist has to take is seen in the concept of *kamma*. What indeed could be simpler and yet what could be more scientifically conceived? If one chooses, one may take on faith, to be sure, the *saṃsāra* principle. Objectively, however, previous existences, however envisioned in time or space, remain a matter of complete indifference. What is significant is that "I" am not the same individual that "I" was yesterday, a year ago, or even a moment ago. Ego has changed, physical form has changed, however imperceptibly. Moreover, the "I" of the individual, having volition, free will, can and does act. Acts, however, are pre-conditioned by foregoing acts. A deed of today begets its effects of tomorrow, effects of future action and thought. To the view of this writer, this is the karmic principle with meaning and application. It is scientific; there is nothing esoteric about it.

So much has been said regarding the relations between Buddhism and the natural sciences that it is scarcely worth belabouring the point further here. The nature of matter, the nature of physical reality, problems of space and time are all implicit in Buddhist teachings. This writer must confess that he cannot care less about such mystical relationships as are conceived as between mind and matter. His interests lie in the connections between Buddhism and the social sciences, that wide area which seeks to understand the relation between man and man, not that between atom and unpopulated universe.

In such social sciences as anthropology and sociology, an attempt is made to understand how men behave in groups and why they act as they do. A related aspect is seen in economics and in its handmaiden, political science. Still further, may be added, the discipline which seeks to evaluate the individual, psychology. In all of these fields, one thought becomes paramount: human beings act because of their conditioning; the anthropologist would say because of their cultural heritage. We come to realize that what one people regards as right, another may view as wholly wrong. The social sciences teach the relativism of human behaviour.

Granted that human behaviour be relative, it follows that there are no absolutes of good or evil. Indeed, good and evil, as concepts, are likewise wholly relative. As a trained social scientist, one who has information regarding the differing ways of the peoples of the world, the writer believes this. Only in Buddhism is some order restored from the resulting chaos. Note that the Buddha does not say: "Thou shalt not ...". He does say that it is a good idea to avoid certain kinds of behaviour and he issues a series of wholly positive injunctions on his followers. Regardless of background, regardless of belief, regardless of economic or political systems, Buddhism has application. It makes sense as nothing else can to restore balance to men. Not that it is even desirable to effect a balance from the Buddhist point of view. To realize the concept of *anicca* is unquestionably for all men enough.

But the Buddhist could assist his own goals by a realization of the objectivity of the social scientist. Here the scientist takes the view of detachment toward his fellow man. He does not seek amelioration. The Buddhist can and should do the same; by so doing, he may achieve by indirection solutions to the problem of human suffering. The Lord Buddha realized that the man who helped himself would inevitably help others. He comes concretely to grips with problems of society and personality. Psychoanalysis may in some measure be compared with enlightenment, but the enlightened man does not need to be told how to live with his fellows. The nature of enlightenment brings this inevitably about. The Buddhist can adopt the contemplative detachment of the scientist. In so doing, he makes himself a better Buddhist and follows infinitely more closely the basic precepts. Objectivity in human affairs remains his watchword.

Science and Buddhism

Upāsaka Wu Shu (Loo Yung Tsung)

New theories in physics reveal the following facts:

The simplest part of matter is, at present, supposed to consist of protons and electrons. Around the electrons there are lines of magnetic force. The influence of these lines is theoretically universal. This may be expressed in another way: the constituents of the universe interact on one another and are inseparable. Thus, the concept of the individual existence of any single object is based on illusion. This is the first fact.

In "reality" things do not exist in a 3-dimensional state, as the majority including some scientists believe. Rather, things exists in a 4-dimensional state where to the side of space is introduced time, an important element. Continuum is a new unit of measurement in reality: Even space and time are interdependent! This is the second fact.

From these facts one can see straightway that the properties of nature, reality, are definitely beyond our imagination.

In spite of these facts scientists and philosophers are still trying unabatedly to solve the problem of reality with their same old instrument: the power of imagination and reasoning.

It is certain that they will be disappointed. The only success possible to them is the putting of those conceptual properties of reality into mathematical expressions.

Let us consider the source of our knowledge. It can be shown that the knowledge obtained through the process of thinking or reasoning is relative and indirect. One can only think of space and time being independent and not interdependent. Thus one is unable to get rid of one's unreal 3-dimensional universe, that is, one's conflict with the properties of reality.

The writer believes that the 3-dimensional universe is actually the projection or projections of reality, the 4-dimensional state, viewed by different observers from different angles, and is analogous to a 2-dimensional plan or elevation which is a projection of a 3-dimensional building. Scientists and philosophers are only modifying the projections in order to minimize the error and get nearer to the profiles of reality. They are only designing but not constructing the building. It is obvious that no matter however full of details and however accurate their designs may be the building cannot become actual without construction.

It is equally obvious that to a seeker of truth the theories of scientists and philosophers are only helpful to a certain extent but are not at all vital. What is more important to him than all theories of science and philosophy is to construct the building of reality, with material and labour, so that he could live happily in this building and then see every part clearly.

If one should turn one's direction of observation a hundred and eighty degrees, that is, look back at the direct source of knowledge—consciousness—one would find a lot of data of an invaluable kind concerning reality. But the process of introspection is difficult to master. In order to minimize erroneous and false "intuition," preparatory training, moral and mental, is essential.

Things are cognized in the process of experiencing them. Experience is preserved in the deepest part of our mind. The function of this part of the mind is so fine and subtle that it is scarcely perceptible to ordinary people. Experience undergoes modification little by little from moment to moment. The principle of causality rules these modifications.

In all experience with oneself, the ego, as centre, and material and spiritual elements taken wrongly as individual objects, as environment, a 3-dimensional universe is suggested.

This false concept produces a centripetal tendency drawing one's attention to the self and individuality. It resembles a free-moving element with initial stress in a structure. Although there is no external stress yet the element itself is always under strain. The initial stress represents the force of *kamma*. The strain, the illusive life with suffering. Should this centripetal tendency be properly removed, one would readily be in a universe of 4 dimensions.

This is actually the Buddhist way of interpreting reality. It agrees with modern scientific theories and gives light to the truth seeker to attain true knowledge. The Buddha, the Sakyamuni, is the first saint in this world who was able to gain insight into the Truth. He termed the Real Universe, Nibbāna, the 4-dimensional state of reality. Nibbāna, though it has been explained in many ways, is itself beyond the reach of our speculation.

Using the same parable, one finds that the Teaching of the Buddha is a workable or practical design of reality, drawn on a transitory map. The details of moral and mental training have incomparable value. They are of greater importance than the philosophic side of the Teaching.

The Sakyamuni assures that every living being, and above all the human being, has the chance and a sufficiency of material to obtain Nibbāna. The way of attainment is through moral training and psychological reform.

The Principles of the Buddha lead one to the way of right living, the way that is without contradictions of thought, fallacies of reason and suffering of any kind. This very way may be called Genuine Living. By treading that way one truly lives and denies death.

The foregoing paragraphs may be summarized as follows:

1. Things exist in a state of relation to one another and not independently.
2. Things interact on one another and are changing at every instant.
3. 1 and 2 show that the state of reality is 4-dimensional and that its properties are beyond our imagination.
4. Scientific and philosophical theories give us only projections of reality.
5. The direct source of knowledge is experience. Subjective experience with the ego as centre of observation gives us a false conception of reality. The motive force which causes this seemingly irresistible tendency to misunderstand is called *kamma* in Buddhism.
6. The illusive perception of the universe and especially of a self that is independent causes suffering to every creature. The variation of suffering is governed by the law of cause and effect, and works naturally, as a matter of course. The belief in a God or any supernatural being who governs this world, all anthropomorphizing, is just a phantasm.
7. The way to get rid of kammical disturbance is the "Path to Nibbāna," which consists of moral training:

observance of precepts, etc., and psychological training: concentration, meditation, contemplation, etc., as taught in Buddhism.

8. True knowledge, the aim of philosophy, and virtuous conduct, the aim of ethics, are merely two branches of the one tree of reality. Or they may be compared to the two wheels of the chariot that takes a man to Nibbāna.
9. To the truth seeker right knowledge is the microscope, training is the experiment, and the whole universe the perfect laboratory.
10. The teaching of the Buddha furnishes all that a seeker of truth needs to learn and to follow.

Atom and Anattā

Upāsaka Wu Shu (Loo Yung Tsung)

Everybody should agree in saying that science is the leading factor that creates modern civilization. The recent discovery of the release of nuclear energy brings mankind to a new age—the so-called Atomic Age. But unfortunately the first sign that served as an announcement of the opening of this new era was the explosion of a new lethal weapon called the atomic bomb. Men began to worry that they are living in an atomic age where total annihilation of the whole civilized races is actually possible. They generally cannot but think that men are going along the wrong track, and feel that it would be better to give up the deadly energy and enjoy a peaceful though simpler life like their ancestors. But history does not allow events to go backwards. As Mr. Arthur H. Compton, an authoritative American scientist, said in *One World or None*, "No group of men had the power to prevent the coming of the atomic age." So the only right thing for men to do is to be aware of the serious position where mankind now stands and adjust their thinking and their mode of living in such a way so that they may make the best possible use of this new force that has been put into their hands. As a matter of fact there is nothing wrong with the bomb; what's wrong is with man himself. Furthermore, the truth revealed as to the inside nature of the atom has undoubtedly invaluable influence not only upon the field of science itself but upon all other branches of knowledge: psychology, philosophy and even theology. It is the aim of this talk to introduce the important facts and new conceptions disclosed by the scientists of today and to compare these analogically with the fundamental principles of reality unveiled and preached by Sakyamuni, the Buddha, some two thousand five hundred years ago.

In 1808 John Dalton propounded the atomic theory. He believed that an element actually consisted of separate invisible and indivisible atoms. He thought of atoms as things having the properties of a billiard ball. In the later part of that century great scientists like Michael Faraday, James Maxwell and Lord Kelvin began their work in the development of electrical science. The electric nature of an atom was partly disclosed. In 1913 Niels Bohr of Copenhagen produced a theory stating that an atom consisted of two parts, a small heavy nucleus surrounded by a large empty region in which electrons move somewhat like planets about the sun. Around the electrons there are lines of magnetic force; the influence of these lines is theoretically universal. Faraday symbolized an atom as a starfish with a small body and comparatively long limbs which entangle things the limbs contact. This might be put thus: the constituents of the material universe interact with one another and are really inseparable. This concept of the atom has important philosophical significance.

Things do not exist individually. The existence of a single object is therefore nothing more than a mental illusion. The universe is simply a process, a system of interconnected activities in which nothing moves independently of the rest and where all is in ceaseless motion. This is exactly the same in principle, though different in words, as the Buddha's preaching of *anicca*, which means the impermanent or transient nature of things.

Until the release of nuclear energy men still had a shady belief in the existence of ninety-four elements, whose atoms were visualized to be indestructible. Yet as early as 1905 Scientist Albert Einstein had already foreseen the fact that mass and energy were convertible, and he gave the neat equation: $E = mc^2$, where E = energy, c = the velocity of light, m = mass. It is apparent from the equation that a small piece of matter, if converted entirely into energy, would give an enormous amount of energy. And this equation has been verified to be principally correct by the atomic bombs which exploded over New Mexico, Hiroshima, Nagasaki, and near Bikini Atoll in the Pacific. Thus matter or the atom can be described as a highly concentrated form of energy. The reaction which occurs in an exploding atomic bomb can be expressed in the following:

U-235 + neutron = I = Y = N neutrons (U = uranium, I = iodine, Y = yttrium, N = a number); thus an Uranium atom breaks up and transforms into atoms of Iodine and Yttrium.

The atom, the original meaning of which is "indivisible," had been finally proven to be divisible. But in ordinary chemistry the conventional theory of the atom still holds good for most practical purposes. Paradoxically it might be put in the following way: An atom is not (really) an atom; it is called an atom for the sake of convenience. One might notice the startling resemblance here of science with Buddhism if one ever had read the Diamond Sutra in which it is said: "When the Tathāgata speaks of universes he does not mean really universes; he calls them universes only nominally."

Let us now turn to a field to which scientists pay comparatively little attention, that is, to our mental faculties. Though the psychic functions are much more complicated and subtle than physical phenomena, yet every sentient being has enough instruments, and material of his own, if he only cares to observe and to do his experiment on himself. Our mental or psychic faculties can be divided into two fields: those which function within the field of consciousness, and those beyond the field of consciousness. Different psychologists give different terms and definitions to the latter, some call it subconsciousness, while others call it unconsciousness, yet they generally agree to mean that part of our psychic activities which is beyond the perception and control of our conscious mind. As to the content of this field of subconsciousness or unconsciousness, psychologists suggest various terms, such as: primitive inherited impulse and desire, original nature, impulse, drive, urge, instinct, etc. As a matter of fact science in this particular branch is still in its infancy.

It is a strange fact that the field of subconsciousness, which is in a large part obscure to the men of the atomic age, can be found clearly and repeatedly in various Buddhist writings. In these writings not only is the theory of mind given but also the physical and mental trainings are shown: for getting hold of the seemingly uncontrollable impulses and desires, for uprooting them entirely, and for attaining to the state called Enlightenment where one experiences things as they really are and finally proves the principle of *anatta* which means that there is nothing called a personal ego.

It is not possible to mention here with any detail the Buddhist philosophy and training of mind but it might be of interest to you perhaps if I explain briefly the philosophy of the Dharmalakshana school (the consciousness-only or perception-only school). According to the philosophy of this school, the constituents of the universe are divided into eight faculties (or eight consciousnesses). The first five are the five sensual faculties i.e., the faculty to see, to hear, to smell, to taste, and to feel. The sixth faculty is the most active one. It consists of practically all the mental functions within the field of consciousness. The seventh faculty is the instinctive grasp or attachment of ego. And the eighth one is the most important of all. It is sometimes termed the "reservoir faculty"[1], where the tendencies and energies of all our previous actions and experiences are kept. The seventh and eighth faculties function continuously as the centre of the psychic system no matter whether a man is in the state of awareness or of sleep or is even in the state we commonly call death. When all the above-mentioned six faculties cease to function the force of the seventh faculty or attachment of ego is tremendous; it is like the nuclear binding energy of an atom. It causes the arising of the superficial layer, indifferent forms, in the instinctive desire to live, to propagate, to possess, etc.

As a matter of fact the ego-instinct originates and directs almost all the superficial functions such as volition, emotion, etc., and even affects our system of reasoning. It distorts our conscious mind and hence creates the illusory picture of the individual existence of "I," "Being," "Things," etc., thus overshadowing the real nature of impermanence and egolessness. Since all the faculties of the conscious mind are more or less affected by the blind attachment of the ego, it might be said, figuratively, that the field of subconsciousness is the nucleus in which the ego-attachment is the binding force. The other mental faculties move around it like the electrons revolving round the nucleus of an atom. The arrangement of electrons in the orbits of an atom determines its chemical properties; so do the conscious faculties like volition, emotion, intellect, etc., of a certain individual determine his personality or character.

It is worthwhile to mention especially the intellectual power of a human being. It has the power of reasoning, understanding and generalizing all the events occurring in experience; thus through this faculty men are able to transmit and interchange their ideas and thoughts, just as the electrons in the outermost orbit make possible the flow of electric current. Another

1. *Ālaya-vijñāṇa*—a Mahayana concept (Editor).

important feature of the intellect is that it is the least affected by the influence of the ego-instinct. On the contrary, through reasoning and contemplation it even possesses the power of self-realizing the truth of egolessness. It is actually by means of this delicate faculty that the detachment of the ego, figuratively speaking the breaking of a psychic atom, is possible.

Induced, perhaps, by the newly disclosed scientific ideas and theories, a scientist and philosopher like William James declared that consciousness was only a function, and one like Bertrand Russell said that such a term as "mental" does not belong to a single entity in its own right (that is, the imaginary ego), but only to a system of entities. The revival of egolessness foreshadows the possible recovery of their faith in reality, which is built upon a rational philosophy closely related to modern science.

But to understand the emptiness of the ego is one thing; to practice, to realise and to live an egoless life is quite another. Einstein visualized the probable release of nuclear energy but the actual bomb came into existence some forty years later. There were people like Sakyamuni and his *arahat*-followers, though with aim quite different from the scientists, who declared their attainment to the state of full enlightenment and annihilation of the ego; yet compared with billions of sentient beings they are just as rare as the self-radiating elements uranium, radium, actinium, and thorium on this earth. It is also interesting to notice that in the Buddhist teaching, everywhere, the principle of the so-called "Middle Path" or "Middle Way" can be seen. This principle essentially teaches one to refrain from going to extremes in both physical and mental practices. And it is believed that this principle effectively leads one to penetration and enlightenment. In the process of penetrating into the nature of an atom, scientists found that an atom consisted of a complex system of negatively charged electrons widely spaced around a positively charged nucleus. Charged particles (such as protons, electrons, or alpha particles) and electromagnetic radiations (such as gamma rays) lose energy and thus slow down in passing through that field. They discovered finally a new particle which they called the neutron, having no electric charge, able to penetrate through the orbits and go its way unchecked until it makes a "head on" collision with an atomic nucleus.

Though atomic science and Buddhism seem to be entirely different yet they are really tackling the same problem of energy and release of energy by breaking a highly concentrated form of energy called the atom in one case, and the ego in the other. And their direction is the same, namely, "inward". Therefore we should not be astonished by the close resemblance between the two. The energy released through the breaking of an ego is not so evident as in the atomic bomb yet the Buddha's highest wisdom and infinite compassion are very much like the light and heat released from the natural source of atomic energy of the sun.

Briefly I have mentioned two of the three fundamental principles of Buddhism, namely *anicca* (impermanence) and *anattā* (egolessness). The other important principle is called *dukkha* (suffering) or the consequence of an egoistic life. These three principles are so important that they are actually considered as the testing stone of Buddhism. Any theory or philosophy which is completely in accordance with these three principles is justified to be called Buddhist; and anything not in accordance with the three is not Buddhist. From this fact the rational character of Buddhism can be easily felt.

Science and the Common Understanding

An Extract

J. Robert Oppenheimer (New York 1954)

"If we ask, for instance, whether the position of the electron remains the same, we must say 'no'; if we ask whether the electron's position changes with time, we must say 'no'; if we ask whether the electron is at rest, we must say 'no'; if we ask whether it is in motion, we must say 'no.' The Buddha has given such answers when interrogated as to the conditions of a man's self after his death; but they are not familiar answers for the tradition of seventeenth and eighteenth century science."

Editor's Note

The statement of the Buddha mentioned by Oppenheimer, is frequently met with in the Buddhist scriptures, for instance in the following passage from the 72nd discourse of the Majjhima Nikāya (Middle Length Discourses):

"To think that 'the Perfect One[2] exists after death'; that 'the Perfect One does not exist after death'; that 'the Perfect One both exists and does not exist after death'; that 'the Perfect One neither exists nor does not exist after death'—these, Vaccha, are the assumptions of speculative views; it is a jungle of views, a wilderness of views, a juggling of views, a writhing of views, a fetter of views; it is coupled with misery, distress, despair and agony; it does not conduce to turning away, to dispassion, cessation, quiescence, direct knowledge, awakening, nor to Nibbāna. Perceiving this as a peril, Vaccha, I did not approach any of these speculative views.

---

2. These statements apply not only to the concept of a perfect one (*tathāgata*, i.e. a Buddha) and a saint (arahat), but, according to the commentaries, also to the concept of a being (*satta*) in general.

"As to the assumption of theories, Vaccha, the Perfect One has discarded it. But this has been seen by the Perfect One: 'Such is corporeality, such is the arising of corporeality, such is the disappearing of corporeality; such is feeling ...such is perception... such are mental formations... such is consciousness, such is the arising of consciousness, such is the disappearing of consciousness.' Therefore I say that the Perfect One is free without clinging from all imaginings, all confusions, all assertive tendencies concerning 'I' and 'mine.'"

The Greatest Adventure

A Presentation of the Buddha's Teaching to the Youth of the World

by

David Maurice

WHEEL PUBLICATION NO. 04

Chapter I

Adventure

Men have always sought adventure and some look for it in very curious ways. Sometimes adventure comes to men when they are not seeking it and most of us have had thrilling adventures of this kind that have been pleasant or very much the reverse.

In the early days before history, men lived together in large families, each family related to the other and forming a small tribe and it was man who was the hunter and therefore the adventurer, and woman's place was to guard the camp and to make secure what the men had won. That was also an adventurous life for women of those days; but while men went out after adventure and so made adventure part of their lives, women for the most part feared adventure as something likely to destroy the security necessary for building a home and rearing a family.

In those early days of civilization, men ventured from the small patches of forest-land which they lived in, to explore wider areas of the country. They met with hostile tribes and animals and with fire and flood and famine, and overcame these enemies or were overcome by them. They learnt which fruits were edible and which were poisonous and they learnt better ways of tilling the soil to produce more food, and better ways of building houses, villages, towns and finally cities.

They conquered the land and in time they began to conquer the rivers, using logs of wood which they later learned to hollow out, and finally they found out how to build ships. Then they began to conquer the sea and to sail to far-off places on great adventures. Later they began to conquer the air and now we find men attempting to conquer space, to fly to other worlds that are millions of miles away.

Now notice that word "conquer." It means to vanquish or to overcome and is used in warfare between nations. The word is associated with adventure and unfortunately many adventures have been attempts to overcome other people in warfare.

Sometimes that has seemed very necessary to the fighters; they have thought that they could live better if they took more land and more cattle from others. On the other hand this has not always been the case. Some wars have been fought by adventurous men just for the thrill of the adventure itself.

There is something exciting in adventure that appeals to men and that quite often brings out the best in men and incites them to do great deeds. Courage and determination, selflessness and fortitude are virtues that are part of the spirit of adventure, but they are virtues only when they are combined with the greatest of virtues, with loving-kindness.

In the modern world much of the adventure has gone out of life and only a few people can set out to climb high mountains or to explore deep caves or to fit themselves to travel in spaceships. There are cinemas and storybooks and the football field to give some sense of adventure to the others.

There is a greater adventure than any we have mentioned and that is also a conquest, the adventure found in the pursuit of science. There is as much a thrill in finding a new breed of plant, especially if a man has created that plant, as there is in finding a new country. There is a wonderful thrill in conquering disease and bringing health to one's country and to the world.

In fighting death and disease there is all the thrill of battle and all the excitement of war and some of the risks as well. In the development of X-rays, for instance, many a scientist has lost a limb and some have lost their lives due to these rays. When the flesh is exposed repeatedly for a long period to X-rays, the exposed part is destroyed and affects neighbouring parts and the only remedy is to amputate the limb. When the case is such that the part cannot be amputated, the man dies. Knowing this, many brave men and women have taken great risks to make ray treatment possible, and the work of making it safer still goes on.

In other fields of medicine and science similar risks are taken daily. They are taken not in order to kill but in order to cure. In this is greater adventure and higher service to the world.

Chapter II

The Supreme Scientist

We have just read of the realms of adventure where there is still room for adventurers who can give service to the world. It is very interesting to note the word "adventurer" because that is a good example of how words can change their meaning. The word is still used in praise of a man and we may still say of Tensing and Hillary, who conquered Mt. Everest, "They were great adventurers."

Four hundred years ago the people of Europe began to explore the world and to travel to far countries and they greatly praised the brave men who endured many perils in such adventures. Then they began looking for countries which they could conquer and from which they could get gold and raw material for manufacture as they began to invent machines. Using superior weapons they took many countries and then in their greed they began to fight among themselves and to rob one another's ships. The successful men who fought against other countries and against the pirates who lay in wait for their ships carrying the wealth of Asia and America back to Europe, were called great adventurers. But since many of these men were no better than pirates themselves and used force and fraud to gain their fortunes the word began to acquire a bad meaning. Today the word may be used either in praise or blame. In business when a man does not follow the rules but takes great risks, sometimes with the money of other people, he may be called "just an adventurer."

But if we take the word in its best and highest sense, meaning one who has courage, determination, fortitude and selflessness, we can see that some of the medical workers and scientists have been great adventurers.

Of all such scientists, he who renounced the whole world and gave up everything to undertake the greatest adventure of all was the supreme scientist.

He was born in India nearly two thousand six hundred years ago, the son of Suddhodana, head of the Sakya clan and ruler of Kapilavatthu and his queen Mahāmāyā, and was named Siddhattha

Gotama. Twenty-nine years later he gave up all his sheltered life, all the luxuries which his father had surrounded him with, to enter on the most difficult search that man has undertaken. That might seem to the unthinking man just the beginning of the adventure that was to last six years until he attained "Buddhahood" or Supreme Enlightenment. Actually this greatest of adventures had begun many millions of years before, with the vow of a determined man to find a way out of all suffering.

That you may read about elsewhere. This is not so much to tell you of the beginning of the adventure, but of the last stages and of the end of it, and of the result that opens the way for you to undertake the greatest of all adventures. But where Siddhattha Gotama had to find a way for himself with no one to guide him, you may start off with a well-marked map and a way that has been well pointed out. Even so it is still the greatest adventure that you can undertake.

Before his birth his mother had a strange dream: she dreamt that a small white elephant had entered into her body. Since the white elephant has always been the symbol of power and leadership, this dream was interpreted, by those men who were skilled in such things, as a favourable omen. The child, they said, would be a great man of outstanding ability. When he was born he had also all the signs of health and vigour and intelligence above the ordinary. The wise men predicted that he would be a conqueror and that there were two courses open to him: either he would conquer the world in battle or he would conquer the world in an entirely different way, the peaceful way of giving up the material world in order to find that which is beyond the world.

His mother died when he was a few days old and his aunt, Pajāpati, cared for him and brought him up.

The Sakyans were brave warriors, and their clan was of the Khattiya caste. At that time there were four castes in India. The Khattiyas were the leading class, the rulers and great warriors; the Brahmins or priestly class were the teachers and religious men; the Vessas were the trading class; and the Sudda caste provided the workmen. People were proud of their castes, especially those who could claim to be Khattiyas, the highest caste; so King Suddhodana determined that his son should not become a mere religious man but should be a great warrior, leader of the clan, conqueror of other clans and finally ruler of the world.

He taught his son archery and all the war-like sports, and the young Siddhattha excelled in all of these. His father surrounded him with luxury and comfort and tried to shield him from even the sight of sorrow and suffering. Already, however, there were signs in the young prince of loving-kindness and compassion and freedom from the things of the world. At an early age, we are told, while watching his father perform the ceremonial ploughing of the fields, a custom of that time requiring the king to do the first ploughing so that the fields would be fertile, Siddhattha sat apart and meditated. He had a glimpse of another world and of higher things and never really forgot this.

Siddhattha was married at an early age to his beautiful and charming cousin, Yasodharā, and although for some years they had no children they were very happy together. Finally a son was born to them. He loved his wife very dearly and at that time every man looked forward eagerly to having a son to love also, and in the eyes of the world a woman was counted as nothing unless she had borne a son. A woman with no children was never completely happy.

Siddhattha now realized that he could not easily leave his home and family; but on the other hand he had no wish to live the luxurious life of a household man. Neither did he wish to make himself a great man by killing others as a conqueror in battle. Later, after he had become the Buddha, when he was asked why the Sakyans were called warriors, though so many were his followers, the Buddha answered, "Warriors are we called, and wherefore warriors? For lofty endeavour." He also said, "Though he should conquer a thousand times a thousand men in the field of battle, yet he who conquers himself is the noblest victor."

His preparation during previous lives had given him extraordinary powers of intelligence and made him a deep thinker. Although he had led a protected life and had never seen sickness, old age and death, yet he felt unsatisfactoriness behind all the carefree court life. His father had planned for him a sheltered, luxurious life with the thought that only pleasant things should meet the eye of the young prince; no sign of sickness, suffering or death should be visible. He had three palaces, one for each season of the Indian year, and the king had ordered that when the young prince went out, the roads should be cleared and that nothing unpleasant was to be allowed to disturb Siddhattha.

However, the prince went out one day accompanied only by his faithful charioteer and saw a sick man, weak and pale. It was the first time he had seen such sickness and he was shocked to realize that this was the common lot of all men. After that he saw an old man, shaking and withered and with eyes dim and teeth missing. He then understood that this, too, was to be his fate and that of all his friends. Then he saw a dead man, something also that was new to him. This was something else that was a misfortune all men must meet. Finally he saw a calm person in the robes of a monk, an ascetic who had given up the pleasures of the world. His charioteer explained that there were such men who sought the way out of suffering that none had yet found.

He felt that death was not the end of everything but that there was continual rebirth, life after life. That was the general belief and there were those who knew it for certain, just as there are today some who know it for certain. What nobody knew was the way to prove it; and nobody knew for certain the way out of this continual circle of rebirth. Most people believed either that there was no way out or that by "uniting with God" as they thought of it, they would end their long struggle. Siddhattha Gotama wanted to discover if there were really a way out and, if so, how to show that way to others, so that all who wished could win freedom from suffering. He and his beloved wife and son and his father, his aunt and his close friends could not stay together for ever, that he knew well. One by one they would be snatched away by death. Maybe they would be reborn in states of greater suffering.

Siddhattha pondered upon all this and now that a son was born he saw that to seek this ending of sorrow and to find the remedy was the greatest gift he could give to his wife, to his child and to the world. His mind was made up and he renounced all the years of comfort and happiness with wife and child and friends, to set out to find the deathless.

With one last, lingering look at his sleeping wife and child he left the palace and mounted his great horse, Kaṇṭhaka, and with his charioteer, Channa, went outside the city gates. There he cut off his hair and changed from his rich dress to the robes of an ascetic, and sending back his faithful friend and follower, left on his great quest.

At that time the world was very different from the world you are used to. There was no steam or electricity and the only machinery was the primitive spinning wheel turned by hand or the wood-working tools operated by hand. The only way of travelling on land was by ox-cart or chariot or on horseback, although there were sailing ships which went to countries far away. There were no books, only stone slabs with writing sculptured on them or clay plates on which people wrote with sticks and then baked in a kiln or oven. That made it difficult to write and difficult to read, so writing was used for the sake of keeping records and there was no reading for pleasure, and no education by book. Most of the teaching was by word of mouth and most of the learning by heart. There were two great and famous teachers who claimed to have a method of teaching which would lead a man to union with God. That, they said, was the final end which men should seek. To these in turn the Bodhisatta (the Buddha-to-be) went for study and he quickly mastered their systems. Each in turn begged him to stay as a teacher but he saw that these systems did not lead to the deathless.

He set out anew with five companions who acknowledged him to be their leader. At that time there were people who believed that there was a way out of the constant round of rebirth. They believed that the way was to conquer the body by inflicting suffering on it and so they tortured themselves. They lived on as little food as they possibly could, and endured great hardships. Siddhattha and his companions tried this way for some years and he starved himself until he almost died. Eventually he realized that to follow his present course was to die with the goal not yet won. Then he remembered the experience of his early boyhood when he had had a glimpse of higher things. At that time, he remembered, his body was comfortable and his mind free. He decided to try this way and sat under a tree, now known as the Bodhi tree or tree of enlightenment, determined not to rise until he had attained full enlightenment. He succeeded and when he did rise up from his seat next morning it was as an Omniscient Buddha.

Chapter III

The Teaching

In attaining full enlightenment the Buddha attained omniscience. The word means "knowledge of everything." He knew all the past and all the present and had only to turn His mind towards a thing to see and understand it. He had become a different being, a Buddha, greater than any man and greater than the highest god, with powers far surpassing those of any other being, man or god, whomsoever. Looking round with this superior power, he saw men lost in greed and craving (*lobha*), in hate and dislike (*dosa*), and in dullness and delusion (*moha*). There, he saw, are the roots of all action. Although they have their opposites—disinterestedness (*alobha*), amity (*adosa*) and wisdom (*amoha* or *paññā*)—the latter three were, and still are, very rare in the world. He hesitated to give so deep a teaching to the ordinary men of the world who were bent only on pleasure, but on looking over the world with his superior understanding he realized that there were some men "whose eyes were only lightly covered with dust," who would awaken and understand. Such men, with more intelligence and more kindness than their fellow human beings, would accept the Teaching and follow it.

It is interesting to note that it was not always the learned men who understood the Teaching quickly. Learning is, at times, a great help to understanding, but it is simplicity and earnestness and clarity of mind that are required above all for understanding. The Buddha then set out to teach those in the world who would listen to his teaching, and could understand it. He knew that his former teachers, under whom he had studied, would be most likely to understand the teaching. Then he saw by his superior powers that they had already died. So he decided to teach first his former companions who had practised with him a life of asceticism.

In gaining enlightenment he had gained an appearance of great calmness and majesty and appeared as truly splendid as only a Buddha can appear. On the way to these former companions he met a wandering ascetic who was surprised at the wonderful appearance of the Buddha and asked him, "Friend, who is your teacher?" The Buddha replied that he was the Buddha, a fully enlightened one, conqueror of the world and teacher of gods and men, and that there was no one among men or gods whom he could regard as a teacher. There was at that time in India a sect of ascetics who had the strange belief that by owning nothing at all, not even clothes, they would be nearer to some supposed god. Therefore they went about quite naked and dirty. There are a very few of such people in India even today. This ascetic was one of that sect and he was not able to grasp such a teaching as that of the Buddha. He said, "May be!" and nodded and went on his way.

When the Buddha arrived at the place where his former companions were, they saw him coming and determined not to accept him as a friend and teacher. They thought that he had betrayed all their ideas by giving up the strict ascetic life of torture, and was living what was, to them, a comparatively luxurious life. As he approached nearer, they were struck by his majestic and calm presence, just as was the naked ascetic, and their resolution to treat him coldly could not be kept up. They could not at first accept his Teaching but when he had spoken for some time they saw part of the truth and then, one by one, they perceived the full truth and became *arahats*.

What is the difference between an *arahat* and a Buddha? In one way there is none, since both on the death of the body attain full Nibbāna, never to be reborn in any of the worlds again. However, a *Sammā Sambuddha* (a Fully Enlightened Buddha) has, by his long preparation through many lives, superior powers; and while still living in the world is able to find the Truth as no one else can and is able to teach this Truth as no one else can.

You may read elsewhere the story of the forty-five years of life of the Buddha, how all sorts of men became His followers. Many of these became *arahats*, some from rich families of high caste and some from the families of the poorest people and the lowest caste, and even those "out-castes" who were regarded by others as the lowest of men; some were mere children and others old men. Here we shall read of the Teaching of the Buddha.

Today men of science are beginning to make wonderful discoveries. They are now beginning to understand much of the truth taught by the Buddha so many centuries ago. The Buddha was omniscient and knew everything that ordinary men were able to do. He knew all the natural laws, those known to ordinary men and those unknown to ordinary men. In his teachings you will find that he knew all about atoms, for instance. But he did not teach how to use atomic power. He said that the truths he had taught his followers were like a handful of leaves in number while the truths that could be known were like the leaves in a great forest. "Why," he asked, "have I not taught you the other truths? Because they would not be helpful to you. Only those truths which will help you to attain calm and happiness and freedom from this round of rebirth have I taught you."

He taught the six roots of action of which we read in the last chapter and he taught also the three signs of being. That means the three conditions which govern everything that exists in the world. To put it more simply, everything is subject to *anicca, dukkha* and *anattā*. These three Pāli words may be translated into English as follows: *anicca* is impermanence, that is, everything is continually changing and is in what we call a state of flux. From moment to moment nothing is the same. Things may appear to be the same, just as a river flowing towards the sea may seem to keep the same form. The river, however, is not composed of the same drops of water at one moment as it was the moment before or will be the next moment. In addition the river is slowly eating out its banks at some places and building them up at other places. Similarly your body and your mind are changing all the time, every part of your mind. Even such seemingly solid things as chairs and tables and houses and stones are all the time in motion. This was shown by the Buddha more than 2500 years ago and in the last fifty years western science has at last found this to be true.

Dukkha is sorrow and suffering. Whether it is deep sorrow and great suffering or just an uneasy feeling or a feeling of "unsatisfactoriness," it is all contained in the word *dukkha*. If you think deeply you will see that even in what we think are happy moments, the shadow of sorrow is always present. Since we cannot stay with our happy friends always and since we are always changing and always having to leave happiness behind, nothing is permanently happy and so happiness itself changes to sorrow.

The third fact of being is *anattā*, absence of any permanent unchanging self or soul. When you say "I" you are speaking of something that has already changed and is still changing. It is impossible that such an unsatisfactory compound or mixture, a bundle of feelings, changing from moment to moment can be thought of as a "Soul" which doesn't change. Take away from yourself all thoughts and all feelings and what is left? Nothing is left at all that is able to be recognized as yourself or part of yourself or anything to do with yourself.

So having in mind these facts that can be proved, the Buddha gave the further Teaching of the Four Noble Truths and the Eightfold Noble Path.

Chapter IV

The Four Noble Truths and the Precepts

All of the Buddha's Teachings are true and one part follows another very clearly. Following on the teaching of the Three Signs of Being, are the Four Noble Truths. These are:

1. That all in the world is, in its inner essence, suffering.
2. That there is a cause of suffering and that cause is desire or craving.
3. That if we can get rid of our craving and ignorance we can get rid of suffering.
4. That there is a way to get rid of ignorance and craving and that way is the Noble Eightfold Path.

It is put in the Scriptures in a longer way. "This is the Noble Truth of Suffering:

> birth is suffering;
> growth and decay are suffering;
> death is suffering;
> to be bound to what we do not love is suffering;
> to be parted from what we love is suffering;
> not to obtain that for which we long is suffering;
> all the Elements of Being are suffering.

"This is the Noble Truth of the Arising of Suffering: it is that craving which leads from birth to birth, joined with lusts and longings which, now here, now there, continually seek satisfaction; it is the desire for the gratification of passion; it is craving for eternal life; it is longing for enjoyment here in this present life.

"This is the Noble Truth of the Ceasing of Suffering: it is the utter and complete annihilation of this craving (*taṇhā*); separation from it, freedom from it, deliverance from it.

"This is the Noble Truth of the Way that leads to the Ceasing of Suffering: it is that Noble Eightfold Path which consists of:

1. Right Understanding
2. Right Thought
3. Right Speech
4. Right Bodily Action
5. Right Livelihood
6. Right Effort
7. Right Attentiveness
8. Right Concentration"

We call it an "Eightfold" path because each part is not separate. The whole eight parts of the path have to be followed at one time and not one after the other. It can be seen that, as we follow this path, the path itself will become clearer to us the farther we go.

Thus the first step "Right Understanding" is, at the beginning, the right understanding of all we have learnt about the Four Noble Truths. Later on we get right understanding of these Noble Truths in a fuller and deeper sense.

"Right Thought" means a mind free from selfish desire, from ill-will and from cruelty. At the beginning we can only commence to make our minds clean and good. Later we can make them ever cleaner and clearer.

"Right Speech" is speaking only what is good and useful and kind. It is refraining from saying harsh and rough things and from telling lies, tale-bearing and from speaking foolishly.

"Right Bodily Action" is abstaining from taking life, from killing and from stealing and from dirty and immoral sexual acts.

"Right Livelihood" is to make a living in ways that do not harm others.

"Right Effort" is putting forth energy to make evil and nasty thoughts leave the mind and to put forth energy to keep the mind on good and wholesome things. It is right effort to follow the good and right effort to stay away from the bad. It takes a good deal of effort to be attentive and to concentrate and this is right effort.

"Right Attentiveness" is being aware of the body, the feelings, the mind and of mental objects.

"Right Concentration" is keeping the mind firmly fixed on an object. This we shall mention fully in Chapter VI.

The Teaching of the Buddha is something to be and something to do. The something to do is our great adventure and we shall deal with it in Chapter VI also. The something to be is just to be good and decent. It is to follow at least the Five Precepts, and when and where possible, the Eight or the Ten.

Most Buddhists recite the Five Precepts in Pāli and so we give them here in Pāli with the English translations.

Pāṇātipāta veramaṇī—sikkhāpadaṃ samādiyāmi
I undertake to abide by the rule of training to refrain from taking life.

Adinnādāna veramaṇī—sikkhāpadaṃ samādiyāmi
I undertake to abide by the rule of training to refrain from taking that which is not given.

Kāmesu micchācārā veramaṇī—sikkhāpadaṃ samādiyāmi
I undertake to abide by the rule of training to refrain from sexual immorality.

Musāvādā veramaṇī—sikkhāpadaṃ samādiyāmi
I undertake to abide by the rule of training to refrain from telling lies.

Surāmeraya-majjapamādaṭṭhānā veramaṇī—sikkhāpadaṃ samādiyāmi
I undertake the rule of training to refrain from all intoxicants.

There are three further rules to make the eight precepts. They are:

I undertake to abide by the rule of training to refrain from eating after midday.

I undertake the rule of training to refrain from attending dancing, singing, musical and such shows and from the use of garlands, scents, cosmetics and adornments.

I undertake the rule of training to refrain from using luxurious beds.

For the Ten Precepts, the first five rules are used and the next are very like the last three of the eight. They are:

I undertake the rule of training to refrain from eating after midday.

I undertake the rule of training to refrain from attending dancing, singing, musical and such shows.

I undertake the rule of training to refrain from the use of garlands, scents, cosmetics and adornments.

I undertake the rule of training to refrain from the use of luxurious beds.

I undertake the rule of training to refrain from accepting gold and silver.

The layman who undertakes the eight or the ten rules of training should follow them very seriously and very strictly. For instance he must preserve absolute chastity as the third rule.

Monks can follow the Ten Precepts all the time and laymen can follow them on special days when they have no work or classes. Monks must follow all the above rules very strictly and further rules as well. Monks have in all 227 rules to follow and that is why we should respect monks, since a true monk follows all the rules very strictly.

Now there is a question that an intelligent man may ask. That is: "Why should I keep all these rules?" He may think that there should be a reason, and there is indeed a reason. The Buddha gave a very good reason for his Teaching.

The first five precepts are plain to everyone. They are just the basic morality that all should follow. It requires very little common sense to understand that by keeping these simple rules you will earn a good name in this world as well as building a character that will be to your benefit after death. But the question may occur to you, "Why should a layman, especially a young man, keep the other five rules of training for a time?" You might also ask, "What harm am I doing to others if I never keep them?" You are not doing harm if you do not keep them, but you can gain a lot of good for yourself if you do keep them sometimes. The Buddha said that it is good for a layman to keep them on special fasting days as it will help him to think of the *arahats* who keep them always, and it will improve his mind.

By undertaking this voluntary discipline, your mind will be clean and clear and united. Many people have divided minds. A man wants to do a thing with part of his mind and wants to do something else, maybe the opposite, with another part of his mind. His mind is not steady and in a way is fighting itself. Just as in a country if the citizens are fighting among themselves that country becomes poor and weak, so if a man's mind is not united, it becomes poor and weak. You do not have to believe that without thinking about it, but if you think about it, then you will see for yourself that it is true. The Buddha taught that men should think for themselves. They should consider what they see or hear or are taught and neither believe it blindly nor disbelieve it blindly. Only after thinking it over deeply should they believe or disbelieve. When they see that a thing is not good and not reasonable they should reject it. When they see that a thing is good and in accord with reason, then they should accept it.

The Teaching of the Buddha has been preserved and enshrined in the Pāli language. In the days of the Buddha there were monks who knew his teachings by heart and could recite them. There are still some who can do this. After the Buddha died and thus attained *Mahāparinibbāna* (complete Nibbāna without any remainder) a Great Council was called and Reciting Monks were appointed who, in groups, recited the Teachings to one another daily. As new members came into the Sangha, which is the name for the Noble Order of Monks, they took the "Yoke of Learning" or the "Yoke of Development," that is, they decided to specialize on development of insight or on learning the Teachings so that the Teachings could be handed down exactly as the Buddha gave them.

Those who learnt the teachings joined one of the groups of reciting monks and so, though individuals have died, the groups remain as living bodies right through the centuries to the present day. That is why we can rely on the Pāli Canon, or collection of teachings as being true. They are divided into three sections, called *piṭakas*, and the whole is called the *Tipiṭaka*.

There is the Vinaya Piṭaka, or Collection of Rules for Monks, with the stories of how those rules came to be promulgated; there is the Sutta Piṭaka or Sermons to Monks and Laymen; and there is the Abhidhamma Piṭaka or Philosophical Collection.

The Buddha did not teach a dogma, that is, something that must be believed merely because some person in authority has said it. In the Kālāma Sutta, or sermon to the people of the clan of Kālāma, he said, "Do not accept views merely from hearsay or from what you have been told. Do not accept them merely because they are mentioned in scriptures, or merely because of argument, or because the reasoning seems to be plausible. Do not believe because the speculations about a thing appear possible, and do not believe merely because your teacher is venerable.

"When you realize by yourself that these views are unwholesome, faulty, censured by the wise, and they lead to harm and misery when practised, you should reject them. When you realize by yourselves that these views are good, faultless, praised by the wise, and when carried out and practised lead to good and happiness, then after acquiring them you should abide in them."

The Buddha then questioned the Kālāmas, "What do you think, Kālāmas? When generosity (*alobha*) arises in a man, does it arise for his good or his harm?"

"For his good, Lord."

"This person free from greed, O Kālāmas, not being overcome by covetousness, with his mind totally uninfluenced by it, does not take life, does not commit theft and adultery, does not tell lies, and does not urge others to do so, and this leads him to good and happiness for a long time."

"Quite so, Lord."

"What do you think, Kālāmas? When goodwill arises in a person, does it arise for his good or harm?"

"For his good, Lord."

"O Kālāmas, a man who is free from ill-will, not being overcome by it, and his mind not being under its influence does not take life, does not commit theft and adultery, does not tell lies, and does not urge others to do so, and this leads him to good and happiness for a long time."

"'Quite so, Lord."

"What do you think, O Kālāmas? When knowledge arises in a man, does it arise for his good or for his harm?'"

"For his good, Lord."

"O Kālāmas, this person who is free from delusion, not being overcome by it, and his mind not being under its influence, does not take life, does not commit theft and adultery, does not tell lies, and does not urge others to do so, and this leads him to good and happiness for a long time."

"Quite so, Lord."

The Buddha thus showed the people of the Kālāma clan what is true virtue and that nothing is to be believed unless it is investigated and seen by reason to be good and true.

Buddhism and other Teachings

The Buddha taught that we should rely on ourselves and that we should live a life of virtue and that by our own efforts we can and should attain Nibbāna. He also said, however, that if a teacher of another sect speaks that which is Dhamma (truth and purity) we should salute him with joined hands. A Buddhist respects all truth and all good and realizes that many great teachers have taught this. Therefore a good Buddhist respects other teachings while holding fast to the truth, and respects all who live a life of purity and loving-kindness. There is no competition between Buddhism and other sects.

Chapter V

Mind and Body and the Roots of Action

The Buddha taught loving-kindness and compassion, and reason. That we have seen in the previous chapters. He did not teach something to be believed in without a reason. He taught that we should be good and he gave good reasons for being good. That is not his greatest teaching, however. As well as teaching something to be, he taught something to do. "Who sees the Dhamma (the good law)," he said "sees me." He was not a God to be worshipped merely, but a man who became greater than any God, a being to be followed.

The evil caste system was beginning to rise in India and he taught:

"Not by birth is one an outcaste,
Not by birth is one a noble;
But by deeds is one an outcaste,
And by deeds is one a noble."

He also said on another occasion:

"This two-footed dirty body
Which carries about a bad odour
And which is full of impurities
Which pour out from different places;
With a body of this sort
If one thinks highly of oneself
And looks down upon others
Due to what can it be except ignorance?"

This was to show that what we call the "Self" is not important and we cannot think of ourselves as being great and wonderful.

Do you ever look at yourself in a mirror? You will not see there exactly what other people see when they look at you. You will see an image of your body but it will be changed by your mind at the very moment the image reaches your mind. You cannot see anything at all exactly as it is and, as the Buddha said, "Self is dear to self." Your idea of yourself will be made grander than it is by your wishes for yourself, so you do not see yourself clearly and truly. This self that is changing like a flowing river, this mind that is jumping about like a fish that has just been pulled out of the water, cannot be clearly perceived, cannot be fully understood. Only when the mind becomes completely clear and calm can it see itself. Only then can you really see yourself.

The Buddha, shortly after attaining Full Enlightenment, met a party of thirty young men who were in a very disturbed state. They had gone out on a picnic with their wives, and one young man, having no wife, had taken along a girl he had met by chance. This young woman was a cheat and a swindler and she had pretended to be very tired and had suggested that the young people should keep their valuable jewels and ornaments with her, where she sat at the foot of a tree, while they enjoyed themselves by running races. When they agreed, she had taken charge of all the valuables, but stole away with them when the friends were busy with their games.

Now the young men were running here and there looking for the thief, and they told the Buddha that they were looking for a woman who had stolen their property.

"Is it more important to find this woman or to find yourself?" asked the Buddha.

The intelligent young men realized the deep truth behind the Buddha's question and agreed that the most important thing in life is to seek for one's self, for unless and until one begins to search for and to find and to understand this changing "Self," one cannot gain that freedom, the only freedom worth having, which we call Nibbāna.

What is the thing that is closest to you? The "Self" is closest to you, since, in a sense, it is "you," and yet you are not a single indivisible whole. Sometimes you laugh at yourself and sometimes you blame yourself. Do you ever try to think what it is that blames "itself"; or what the "self" blames? If you do that for one minute you will realize that what you call the "Self" is a changing bundle of feelings, never for one moment quite the same.

To find your "Self" and to know your "Self" is the most important thing in the world for you and it is certainly the greatest adventure you can undertake.

How are we to set about this search for that which is so near and yet so far? Men have been trying and failing since the beginning of civilization, since the very earliest times. No god or spirit can help one and yet alone and unaided the task is almost an impossible one, though it may seem simple at first glance.

Alone and unaided the Buddha solved this great problem of existence, of life and death and of what lies beyond both life and death. Luckily for us he left a way which we can follow clearly. He called it *ekāyano,* "the only way." This way is open to all men and the chart is clearly drawn, but it is not a way to be followed by fools or by sots or by cowards; it is a way for the brave, the resolute and the good.

It is a way that can be followed by the learned and by the uneducated and although the educated man has something of an advantage in all things, if learning causes pride, that can be a handicap.

The story is told of the very learned monk, Poṭhila, who was the teacher of other monks but had never found the way himself because he was too proud of his learning to follow the path. When the Buddha called him "Poṭhila, the Empty-head," he realized that it was because he had not practised Development of Insight and had not really understood the changing self.

He went to a company of monks who had reached the end of the Path and had become *arahats* and asked for instruction. They, in order to humble his pride, sent him successively to younger and younger members of their community until he reached the youngest, a mere child. This youngster told Poṭhila, "You, Sir, are a great teacher of the three *piṭakas*, all of the Buddha's teachings. I have something to learn from you," but Poṭhila was now humble and promised to do anything the young boy commanded if he would only show him the way. Finally the lad said to him, "Venerable Sir, if there are six holes in a certain anthill and a lizard enters the anthill through one of these holes, and if you wish to catch the lizard you must stop up five of the six holes, leaving the sixth hole open, and catch the lizard in the hole through which he entered. Just so, you must deal with the six doors of the senses;

close five of the six doors, and devote your attention to the door of the mind." There, and there only can you seize and understand the "Self." The method will be explained in the next chapter.

When you perform any action you are moved by one or more of the six roots or springs of action. These are *lobha, dosa, moha,* and *alobha, adosa,* and *amoha*, which we mentioned in Chapter III. It is important for you to know and understand when and how these six roots of action play in your mind. When you are lustful or greedy or desirous, you should be truthful with yourself and aware that you are lustful, greedy or desirous. When you are angry or irritable or feel even a slight aversion to anything, you should be fully aware of the feeling. When your mind is "dark" and perplexed and ignorant, you should be fully aware of that. Similarly when your mind is full of loving-kindness and well-wishing to all, when your mind is keen and alert but peaceful and poised, you should be fully aware of these states.

Chapter VI

Something to Do

Now, then, we come to the greatest adventure, which you are ready to set out on. It is a discipline, but a discipline that you impose on yourself, not one imposed on you by others. It is a training, and you are the trainer. If you can find a teacher to help you, you are more sure of success and success will come the more quickly.

You may take some preliminary exercises, just as a man who intends to climb mountains, first practises by walking long distances, and by climbing hills, or just as a man who intends to conquer some disease that endangers humanity, first fits himself by study and laboratory work. Something of this preliminary training has been mentioned earlier. You must take a few exercises in knowing your mind, in practising awareness. You watch for the arising of feelings of anger or of kindness or joy or sorrow and are aware that they are rising, that they are there and that they are dying away. Then you think to yourself, "These feelings change my mind and they are not permanent it seems, nor is my mind always the same. These feelings arise without my will and against my will. How would it be if I could become complete master of my feelings and make them arise when I will and vanish when I will?"

A thought of lust or hate or just black dullness comes to your mind. You think, "I did not call you, get out!" But sometimes the thought stays and grows even as you think this and if you have not practised being aware of your thoughts and feelings, you will be overwhelmed like a weak swimmer in a stormy sea. Struggling is sure to end in disaster. You remain calm and cool. You do not struggle negatively. You are positive. You have a plan and you put that plan into operation. Just as a general in battle makes his plans beforehand, as an inventor or scientist makes his plans beforehand, so do you. Here is your plan, one given by the Buddha:

This practise has been given by the Buddha in the Vitakkasaṇṭhāna Sutta of the Majjhima Nikāya.[1] It consists in taking one's mind from the evil thought to an associated thought which is not evil. The modern psychologists call it "sublimation." If that is not successful there is a second step, the consideration of the wretchedness of such evil thoughts. Then, if the thoughts are not by this means driven away there is a third step, the turning of the mind away to other thoughts that are not associated at all with the evil thoughts, but are thoughts good in themselves. If they still persist, the thoughts may be lessened by degrees, by taking thought that they may be made less violent: "Just as a man running swiftly might say to himself, 'But what am I going so hurriedly for? How if I were to go more gently…?'. Thus as a man might slow down from more vigorous postures until he has finally stopped, then sat, then lain down, so evil, unbeneficial thoughts that arise may be gradually slowed down if other methods of banishing such thoughts fail altogether."

"But if," said the Omniscient Buddha, "O disciples, bringing these considerations to subsidence by degrees, evil unbeneficial considerations connected with desire and hate and delusion should still persist in arising, then with teeth clenched and tongue pressed against palate, the monk by main force must constrain his mind and coerce it; and thus with clenched teeth and taut tongue, constraining and coercing his mind, those evil, unbeneficial considerations will disappear and go to decay; and with their disappearance, the mind of the disciple within him will become settled, subdued, unified, concentrated."

Then there is the positive practise of *mettā-bhāvanā*. This is an actual, intense, creative force which is a protecting tenderness that vibrates long after it is sent forth. It is a sort of mental electrical impulse.

This is a Buddhist practise laid down by the Buddha in very many of his sermons as something that can be done by both laymen and bhikkhus alike.

While its practise, which can be undertaken for a few minutes each night and morning by anyone at all, has the effect of

1. *The Removal of Distracting Thoughts* (*Vitakkasaṇṭhāna Sutta*) transl. by Soma Thera. *The Wheel* No. 21, B.P.S.

"loosening the heart," improving the health, guarding against the worries and ulcers of modern men, improving the concentration and mental ability generally, this practise is not laid down for solely those reasons.

The force released, depending on its increasing purity and intensity, is able to build a new world, to change oneself and to change others for the better and to bring peace, tranquillity and calm happiness to a distracted universe. The practise is a positive radiation of loving-kindness to every being, whether insect or reptile or bird or animal or man or ghost or demon; to those who are unfriendly to us and attack us as well as to those who are friendly to us and help us.

The practise is as follows:

The person who practises prepares himself by putting away, taking out of the mind, all thoughts of temper, enmity, envy, grudging, cunning and other evil thoughts. He takes up a suitable sitting position, comfortable but not too relaxed, keeping the body erect and the intelligence alert and intent. Then putting away the canker of ill-will, he abides with heart free from enmity, benevolent and compassionate towards every living thing, and purifies his mind of malevolence. Putting away sloth and torpor, he abides clear of both; conscious of light, mindful and self-possessed, he purifies his mind of sloth and torpor. Putting away flurry and worry, he abides free from excitement; with heart serene within, he purifies his mind of flurry and worry. Putting away doubt, he abides as one who has passed beyond perplexity; no longer in suspense as to what is good, he purifies his mind of doubt.

He, having put away these Five Hindrances, and to weaken by insight the strength of the things that defile the heart, abides letting his mind, fraught with loving-kindness, pervade one quarter of the world, that in front of him, and so too, the second quarter, to his right, and so the third, behind him, and so the fourth, to his left. Then he so pervades all below him and lastly all above him. And thus the whole wide world, above, below, around and everywhere, and altogether does he continue to pervade with love-burdened thought, abounding, sublime, and beyond measure, free from hatred and ill-will. Then he lets his mind, fraught with compassion, pervade the world, and he lets his mind, fraught with sympathetic joy in the achievement of others, pervade the world. And he lets his mind, fraught with equanimity, pervade one quarter of the world, and so the second quarter, and so the third, and so the fourth. And thus the whole wide world—above, below, around and everywhere, and altogether—does he continue to pervade with heart fraught with equanimity, abounding, sublime, and beyond measure, free from hatred and ill-will.

This practise will help to change the world and it will certainly help to change you and help you to know yourself, but it is only the beginning; just as in climbing a high mountain, the more easy ascent of the foothills takes you part of the way and fits you better for the steep climb before you.

The real ascent now begins. Just as in climbing a high mountain, difficulties and dangers may be met and only a brave and resolute man can complete his task, so also in this practise. One may meet obstacles and seem at times to be losing ground, but the determined man is not defeated, he begins again and again with confidence that as the way has been followed by others, he, too, can follow it if he summons up all his energies and turns temporary defeat into future victory. Even his defeats, since they have been preceded by struggles, have firmed his muscles and his mind for the next assault, if he realizes it.

In mountaineering, just as a capable and experienced guide is necessary, so is it necessary in following this Path to have a capable and experienced guide who has himself trodden the path, who knows the surest trails and how to avoid the dangers.

If you have practised all that has been mentioned above, you are better in morals and more poised and intelligent already. You are like a man who has climbed above the malarial swamps and jungle to higher and healthier ground. You have accomplished a great thing and you are all the better for it in every way, but still you have not found the "Self," and still you are not entirely out of danger. You are more ready for the great adventure, but it is at this point that many stop. They have gained something with no very great effort and what lies ahead is to be gained only by the expenditure of a great deal of effort.

The ascent to the heights, to complete freedom, to complete liberation, to the position where one can help others is by that Right Concentration taught in the Noble Eightfold Path.

The method at first sounds very simple, and you may think it is easier than it is in reality. Later, when you find it difficult you may think it is harder than it is in reality. We have to try to avoid both feelings of elation and feelings of depression and go ahead with the practise.

Try this exercise first. Think of some one thing, perhaps a book in front of you. Think just of the idea of the book, not all about its size and colour, just of the idea "book." Keep your mind on this idea and do not let any other idea enter your mind. After a minute you will find that you are no longer thinking of the book, you have probably thought of twenty or even a hundred other things. The mind is not under your control, is it? The reason is that although you have had some practise in concentration, more than the ordinary individual if you are a real student, your mind is far from being a fully concentrated mind.

In the special practise you have to take a subject for concentration and practise holding it in the mind with just bare attention. That means that you are to keep your mind on that particular subject and not let the mind wander. You do not think about the subject but actually of the subject. Naturally your mind will wander. The Buddha said that it was like a wild calf that was caught in the jungle and tied to a post. The calf struggles to get free and wanders as far as it can. But if it is tied firmly to the post it will be brought back every time and finally will lie down quietly. The calf is like the mind, the rope is attention or mindfulness and the post is the subject of concentration you have chosen. If without flurry and worry you bring your mind back every time to the subject of concentration, gradually you will discipline the mind and you will be your own master.

The Omniscient Buddha gave forty different subjects of concentration, some suitable for certain types of men and others suitable for others, while some are suitable for any kind of man, for the dull as well as for the bright, for the irritable as well as for the calm.

This is often called "meditation" and in our thinking and speaking and writing, we must always remember that a word may mean different things to different people. "Meditation" means to some people "reflecting upon, thinking about and pondering, i.e. weighing in the mind." To others it means "observing with alertness." Our concentration practise is something more than this, it is exactly the opposite of "pondering'; it is keeping the attention strictly on the subject and holding the attention there so that the mind does not wander.

Here we shall not discuss the forty subjects of concentration but shall mention only one that is suitable to all persons. That is concentration on in-breathing and out-breathing. This calms the body and the mind, by regular breathing, and focuses the mind-power just as a magnifying glass can focus the rays of the sun so that they are gathered into one point where they are then strong enough to set fire to paper or leaves.

The state of mind is then exactly the opposite of hypnosis. In hypnotism, part of the mind is lulled to sleep, leaving another part free to work. Sometimes, especially in the case of a mind that is fighting against itself, this makes the free part of the mind stronger, and in the absence of opposition, better able to do its work. Indeed the part of the mind, since it is not fighting against itself, can do exceedingly more than the whole mind if that whole mind is disunited. Nevertheless there is still only a portion of the mind at work when a person is hypnotised. On the other hand, in the practise of Buddhist concentration the whole mind is awake, aware, alert and working in unity, once it has gained the mastery that is given by this practise.

The practise can be very dangerous if one attempts it with an impure mind. Virtue is the necessary beginning of the practise. The highest virtue is not just the repeating of precepts nor even the keeping of precepts. It is the mental attitude of an absence of greed, of a mind full of loving-kindness and of alertness and knowledge.

Concentration to the point of clear insight is the peak of Buddhist endeavour and sets Buddhism apart from all other teachings. If you learn more about Buddhist concentration and practise it, you will really know yourself.

You will know yourself and you will master yourself, if you persist and if you have a wise guide.

This is the greatest adventure that you can imagine. It is also the most interesting adventure that you can think of. You are, to yourself, the most important being in the whole universe. Yet you do not know who or what you are in reality. In finding out the fact, you will find out the truth about the world and the beginning of the world and the end of the world. You will win serene and unshakable happiness if you succeed.

No one can carry you on the adventure. "You yourself must make the effort, even Buddhas only point out the way."

As the Buddha said with his last breath, "Decay is inherent in all component things! Work out your own salvation with diligence."

It is possible that you may live to a great age or die in middle age or die tonight, but die, some day, you must. If you die while on the great adventure, the supreme quest, it is certain that the new being which will arise because of you, will be happier and stronger. If you reach the end of your adventure before you die, then you will have attained "the deathless" and there will be no more death for you.

The Buddha

His Life and Teaching

by

Piyadassi Thera

WHEEL PUBLICATION NO. 05

The Buddha

Introduction

"The ages roll by and the Buddha seems not so far away after all; his voice whispers in our ears and tells us not to run away from the struggle but, calm-eyed, to face it, and to see in life ever greater opportunities for growth and advancement. Personality counts today as ever, and a person who has impressed himself on the thought of mankind as the Buddha has, so that even today there is something living and vibrant about the thought of him, must have been a wonderful man—a man who was, as Barth says, 'the finished model of calm and sweet majesty of infinite tenderness for all that breathes and compassion for all that suffers, of perfect moral freedom and exemption from every prejudice.'"[1]

"His message old and yet very new and original for those immersed in metaphysical subtleties, captured the imagination of the intellectuals; it went deep down into the hearts of the people."[2]

Buddhism had its birth at Sārnāth near the city of Vārānasi (Benares), India. With only five followers at the beginning, it penetrated into many lands, and is today the religion of more than 600 million. Buddhism made such rapid strides chiefly due to its intrinsic worth and its appeal to the reasoning mind. But there were other factors that aided its progress: never did the *dhammadūtas*, the messengers of the Dhamma, the teaching, use any iniquitous methods in spreading the Dhamma. The only weapon they wielded was that of universal love and compassion.

Furthermore, Buddhism penetrated to these countries peaceably, without disturbing the creeds that were already there. Buddhist missions, to which the annals of religious history scarcely afford a parallel, were carried on neither by force of arms nor by

---

1. Jawaharlal Nehru, *The Discovery of India* (Calcutta: Signet Press, 1946 p.143.)
2. Ibid., p.137.

the use of any coercive or reprehensible methods. Conversion by compulsion was unknown among the Buddhists, and repugnant to the Buddha and his disciples. No decrying of other creeds has ever existed in Buddhism. Buddhism was thus able to diffuse itself through a great variety of cultures throughout the civilized world.

"There is no record known to me," wrote T.W. Rhys Davids, "in the whole of the long history of Buddhism throughout the many centuries where its followers have been for such lengthened periods supreme, of any persecution by the Buddhists of the followers of any other faith."

The Birth

The Buddha, the founder of Buddhism, lived over 2,500 years ago and is known as Siddhattha Gotama.[3] His father, Suddhodana, the kshatriya[4] king, ruled over the land of the Sakyans at Kapilavatthu on the Nepalese frontier. As he came from the Gotama family, he was known as Suddhodana Gotama. Mahāmāyā, princess of the Koliyas, was Suddhodana's queen.

In 623 BCE on a full-moon day of May—Vasanta-tide, when in India the trees were laden with leaf, flower, and fruit, and man, bird, and beast were in joyous mood—Queen Mahāmāyā was travelling in state from Kapilavatthu to Devadaha, her parental home, according to the custom of the times, to give birth to her child. But that was not to be, for halfway between the two cities, in the beautiful Lumbini Grove, under the shade of a flowering Sal tree, she brought forth a son.

Lumbini, or Rummindei, the name by which it is now known, is one hundred miles north of Vārānasi and within sight of the snow-capped Himalayas. At this memorable spot where Prince Siddhattha, the future Buddha, was born, Emperor Asoka, 316 years after the event, erected a mighty stone pillar to mark the holy spot. The inscription engraved on the pillar in five lines consists of ninety-three Asokan characters, among which occurs the following: "*hida budhe jāte sākyamuni*" (Here was born the Buddha, the sage of the Sakyans).

3. In Sanskrit, Siddhattha Gautama.
4. The warrior class.

The mighty column is still to be seen. The pillar, as crisp as the day it was cut, had been struck by lightning even when Hiuen Tsiang, the Chinese pilgrim, saw it towards the middle of the seventh century CE. The discovery and identification of Lumbini Park in 1896 is attributed to the renowned archaeologist, General Cunningham.

On the fifth day after the birth of the prince, the king summoned eight wise men to choose a name for the child and to speak of the royal babe's future. He was named Siddhattha, which means one whose purpose has been achieved. The brahmins deliberated and seven of them held up two fingers each and declared: "O King, this prince will become a *cakravarti*, a universal monarch, should he deign to rule, but should he renounce the world, he will become a *sammā-sambuddha*, a Supremely Enlightened One, and deliver humanity from ignorance." But Koṇḍañña, the wisest and the youngest, after watching the prince, held up only one finger and said: "O King, this prince will one day go in search of truth and become a Supremely Enlightened Buddha."

Queen Mahāmāyā, the mother, passed away on the seventh day after the birth of her child, and the babe was nursed by his mother's sister, Pajāpatī Gotamī. Though the child was nurtured till manhood in refinement amid an abundance of material luxury, the father did not fail to give his son the education that a prince ought to receive. He became skilled in many branches of knowledge, and in the arts of war easily excelled all others. Nevertheless, from his childhood the prince was given to serious contemplation.

The Four Significant Visions

When the prince grew up, the father's fervent wish was that his son should marry, bring up a family, and be his worthy successor; for he often recalled to mind with dread the prediction of the sage Koṇḍañña, and feared that the prince would one day give up home for the homeless life of an ascetic. According to the custom of the time, at the early age of sixteen the prince was married to his cousin, the beautiful Princess Yasodharā, the only daughter of King Suppabuddha and Queen Pamitā of the Koliyas. The princess was of the same age as the prince.

His father provided him with the greatest comforts. He had, so the story tells, three palaces, one for each of the Indian year's three seasons. Lacking nothing of the earthly joys of life, he lived amid song and dance, in luxury and pleasure, knowing nothing of sorrow. Yet all the efforts of the father to hold his son a prisoner to the senses and make him worldly-minded were of no avail. King Suddhodana's endeavours to keep away life's miseries from his son's inquiring eyes only heightened Prince Siddhattha's curiosity and his resolute search for truth and Enlightenment. With the advance of age and maturity, the prince began to glimpse the woes of the world.

On one occasion, when the prince went driving with his charioteer Channa to the royal gardens, he saw to his amazement what his eyes had never beheld before: a man weakened with age, and in the last stage of ageing, crying out in a mournful voice: "Help master! lift me to my feet; oh, help! Or I shall die before I reach my house!"[5]

This was the first shock the prince received. The second was the sight of a man, mere skin and bones, supremely unhappy and forlorn, "smitten with some pest. The strength is gone from ham, and loin, and neck, and all the grace and joy of manhood fled."[6] On a third occasion he saw a band of lamenting kinsmen bearing on their shoulders the corpse of one beloved for cremation. These woeful signs, seen for the first time in his life, deeply moved him. From the charioteer he learned that even he, his beloved Princess Yasodharā, and his kith and kin—all, without exception, are subject to ageing, disease, and death.

Soon after this the prince saw a recluse moving with measured steps and down-cast eyes, calm and serene, aloof and independent. He was struck by the serene countenance of the man. He learned from Channa that this recluse was one who had abandoned his home to live a life of purity, to seek truth and answer the riddle of life. Thoughts of renunciation flashed through the prince's mind and in deep contemplation he turned homeward. The heart throb of an agonized and ailing humanity found a responsive echo in his own heart. The more he came in contact with the world outside

5. Edwin Arnold, *The Light of Asia.*

6. Ibid.

his palace walls, the more convinced he became that the world was lacking in true happiness. But before reaching the palace he was met by a messenger with the news that a son had been born to Yasodharā. "A fetter is set upon me," uttered the prince and returned to the palace.

The Great Renunciation

In the silence of that moonlit night (it was the full-moon day of July, *Āsāḷha*) such thoughts as these arose in him: "Youth, the prime of life, ends in old age and man's senses fail him at a time when they are most needed. The hale and hearty lose their vigour and health when disease suddenly creeps in. Finally death comes, sudden perhaps and unexpected, and puts an end to this brief span of life. Surely there must be an escape from this unsatisfactoriness, from ageing and death."

Thus the great intoxication of youth (*yobbana-mada*), of health (*ārogya-mada*), and of life (*jīvita-mada*) left him. Having seen the vanity and the danger of the three intoxications, he was overcome by a powerful urge to seek and win the Deathless, to strive for deliverance from old age, illness, misery, and death not only for himself, but for all beings (including his wife and child) that suffer.[7] It was his deep compassion that led him to the quest ending in enlightenment, in Buddhahood. It was compassion that now moved his heart towards the great renunciation and opened for him the doors of the golden cage of his home life. It was compassion that made his determination unshakeable even by the last parting glance at his beloved wife asleep with the baby in her arms.

Thus at the age of twenty-nine, in the flower of youthful manhood, on the day his beautiful Yasodharā had given birth to his only son, Rāhula, Prince Siddhattha Gotama, discarding and disdaining the enchantment of the royal life, scorning and spurning joys that most young men yearn for, tore himself away, renouncing wife and child, and a crown that held the promise of power and glory.

He cut off his long locks with his sword, doffed his royal robes, and putting on a hermit's robe retreated into forest

---

7. A I 146.

solitude to seek a solution to those problems of life that had so deeply stirred his mind. He sought an answer to the riddle of life, seeking not a palliative, but a true way out of suffering—to perfect enlightenment and Nibbāna. His quest for the supreme security from bondage—Nibbāna (Nirvāna)—had begun. This was the great renunciation, the greatest adventure known to humanity.

First he sought guidance from two famous sages, from Ālāra Kālāma and Uddaka Rāmaputta, hoping that they being masters of meditation, would teach him all they knew, leading him to the heights of concentrative thought. He practised concentration and reached the highest meditative attainments possible thereby, but was not satisfied with anything short of Supreme Enlightenment. These teachers' range of knowledge, their ambit of mystical experience, however, was insufficient to grant him what he so earnestly sought, and he saw himself still far from his goal. Though both sages, in turn, asked him to stay and succeed them as the teacher of their following, the ascetic Gotama declined. Paying obeisance to them, he left them in search of the still unknown.

In his wanderings he finally reached Uruvelā, by the river Nerañjarā at Gayā. He was attracted by its quiet and dense groves, and the clear waters of the river were soothing to his senses and stimulating to his mind. Nearby was a village of simple folk where he could get his alms. Finding that this was a suitable place to continue his quest for enlightenment, he decided to stay. Soon five other ascetics who admired his determined effort joined him. They were Koṇḍañña, Bhaddiya, Vappa, Mahānāma, and Assaji.

Self-Mortification

There was, and still is, a belief in India among many of her ascetics that purification and final deliverance can be achieved by rigorous self-mortification, and the ascetic Gotama decided to test the truth of it. And so there at Uruvelā he began a determined struggle to subdue his body in the hope that his mind, set free from the shackles of the body, might be able to soar to the heights of liberation. Most zealous was he in these practises. He lived on leaves and roots, on a steadily reduced pittance of food; he wore rags from dust heaps; he slept among corpses or on beds of thorns. The utter paucity of nourishment left him a physical wreck. Says the Master: "Rigorous have I been in my ascetic discipline. Rigorous have I been beyond all others. Like wasted, withered reeds became all my limbs." In such words as these, in later years, having attained to full enlightenment, did the Buddha give his disciples an awe-inspiring description of his early penances.[8]

Struggling thus for six long years, he came to death's very door, but he found himself no nearer to his goal. The utter futility of self-mortification became abundantly clear to him by his own experience. He realized that the path to the fruition of his ardent longing lay in the direction of a search inward into his own mind. Undiscouraged, his still active mind searched for new paths to the aspired for goal. He felt, however, that with a body so utterly weakened as his, he could not follow that path with any chance of success. Thus he abandoned self-torture and extreme fasting and took normal food.

His emaciated body recovered its former health and his exhausted vigour soon returned. Now his five companions left him in their disappointment, for they thought that he had given up the effort and had resumed a life of abundance. Nevertheless, with firm determination and complete faith in his own purity and strength, unaided by any teacher, accompanied by none, the Bodhisatta resolved to make his final effort in complete solitude.

On the forenoon of the day before his enlightenment while the Bodhisatta was seated in meditation under a banyan tree, Sujātā, the daughter of a rich householder, not knowing whether the ascetic was divine or human, offered milk-rice to him saying: "Lord, may your aspirations be crowned with success!" This was his last meal prior to his enlightenment.

The Final Triumph

Cross-legged he sat under a tree, which later became known as the Bodhi Tree, the "Tree of Enlightenment" or "Tree of Wisdom," on the bank of the river Nerañjarā, at Gayā (now known as

8. For a detailed account see MN 36, trans. by I.B. Horner in *Middle Length Sayings*, Vol. I (PTS). See also R. Abeysekara, *The Master's Quest for Light* (Kandy, BPS) BL A7.

Buddhagayā), making the final effort with the inflexible resolution: "Though only my skin, sinews, and bones remain, and my blood and flesh dry up and wither away, yet will I never stir from this seat until I have attained full enlightenment (*sammā-sambodhi*)." So indefatigable in effort, so unflagging in his devotion was he, and so resolute to realize truth and attain full enlightenment.

Applying himself to the "mindfulness of in-and-out breathing" (*ānāpānasati*), the Bodhisatta entered upon and dwelt in the first meditative absorption (*jhāna*; Skt. *dhyāna*). By gradual stages he entered upon and dwelt in the second, third, and fourth jhānas. Thus cleansing his mind of impurities, with the mind thus composed, he directed it to the knowledge of recollecting past births (*pubbenivāsānussatiñāṇa*). This was the first knowledge attained by him in the first watch of the night. Then the Bodhisatta directed his mind to the knowledge of the disappearing and reappearing of beings of varied forms, in good states of experience, and in states of woe, each faring according to his deeds (*cutūpapātañāṇa*). This was the second knowledge attained by him in the middle watch of the night. Next he directed his mind to the knowledge of the eradication of the taints (*āsavakkhayañāṇa*).[9]

He understood as it really is: "This is suffering (*dukkha*); this is the arising of suffering; this is the cessation of suffering; this is the path leading to the cessation of suffering." He understood as it really is: "These are defilements (*āsavas*); this is the arising of defilements; this is the cessation of defilements; this is the path leading to the cessation of defilements."

Knowing thus, seeing thus, his mind was liberated from the defilements of sense pleasures (*kāmāsava*), of becoming (*bhavāsava*), and of ignorance (*avijjāsava*).[10] When his mind was thus liberated, there came the knowledge "liberated", and he understood: "Destroyed is birth, the noble life (*brahmacariya*) has been lived, done is what was to be done, there is no more of this to come" (meaning, there is no more continuity of the mind and body, no more becoming, rebirth). This was the third knowledge

9. Mahā Saccaka Sutta, MN 36.

10. Elsewhere we see the defilement of false view (*diṭṭhāsava*) added to these as the fourth taint.

attained by him in the last watch of the night. This is known as *tevijjā* (Skt. *trividyā*), threefold knowledge.[11]

Thereupon he spoke these words of victory:

"Seeking but not finding the house builder,
I hurried through the round of many births:
Painful is birth ever and again.

O house builder, you have been seen;
You shall not build the house again.
Your rafters have been broken up,
Your ridgepole is demolished too.

My mind has now attained the unformed Nibbāna
And reached the end of every sort of craving."[12]

Thus the Bodhisatta[13] Gotama at the age of thirty-five, on another full moon of May (*vesākha, vesak*), attained Supreme Enlightenment by comprehending in all their fullness the Four Noble Truths, the Eternal Verities, and he became the Buddha, the Great Healer and Consummate Master-Physician who can cure the ills of beings. This is the greatest unshakeable victory.

The Four Noble Truths are the priceless message that the Buddha gave to suffering humanity for their guidance, to help them to be rid of the bondage of *dukkha*, and to attain the absolute happiness, that absolute reality—Nibbāna.

These truths are not his creation. He only re-discovered their existence. We thus have in the Buddha one who deserves our

11. MN 36/M I 249.

12. Dhp 153–154. Trans. by Ñāṇamoli Thera.

13. A *bodhisatta* (Skt. *bodhisattva*) is one who adheres to or is bent on (*satta*) the ideal of enlightenment, or knowledge of the Four Noble Truths (*bodhi*). In this sense, the term may be applied to anyone who is bent on supreme enlightenment (*sammā-sambodhi*). A Bodhisatta fully cultivates ten perfections or *pāramī*, which are essential qualities of an extremely high standard initiated by compassion, and ever tinged with understanding, free from craving, pride, and false views (*taṇhā, diṭṭhi*, and *māna*) that qualify an aspirant for Buddhahood. They are: *dāna, sīla, nekkhamma, paññā, viriya, khanti, sacca, adhiṭṭhāna, mettā*, and *upekkhā*—generosity, morality, renunciation, wisdom, effort, forbearance, truthfulness, determination, loving-kindness, and equanimity.

respect and reverence not only as a teacher but also as model of the noble, self-sacrificing, and meditative life we would do well to follow if we wish to improve ourselves.

One of the noteworthy characteristics that distinguishes the Buddha from all other religious teachers is that he was a human being having no connection whatsoever with a God or any other "supernatural" being. He was neither God nor an incarnation of God, nor a prophet, nor any mythological figure. He was a man, but an extraordinary man (*acchariya manussa*), a unique being, a man par excellence (*purisuttama*). All his achievements are attributed to his human effort and his human understanding. Through personal experience he understood the supremacy of man.

Depending on his own unremitting energy, unaided by any teacher, human or divine, he achieved the highest mental and intellectual attainments, reached the acme of purity, and was perfect in the best qualities of human nature. He was an embodiment of compassion and wisdom, which became the two guiding principles in his Dispensation (*sāsana*).

The Buddha never claimed to be a saviour who tried to save "souls" by means of a revealed religion. Through his own perseverance and understanding he proved that infinite potentialities are latent in man and that it must be man's endeavour to develop and unfold these possibilities. He proved by his own experience that deliverance and enlightenment lie fully within man's range of effort.

"Religion of the highest and fullest character can coexist with a complete absence of belief in revelation in any straightforward sense of the word, and in that kernel of revealed religion, a personal God. Under the term personal God I include all ideas of a so-called superpersonal god, of the same spiritual and mental nature as a personality but on a higher level, or indeed any supernatural spiritual existence or force." (Julian Huxley, *Religion Without Revelation*, pp. 2 and 7.)

Each individual should make the appropriate effort and break the shackles that have kept him in bondage, winning freedom from the bonds of existence by perseverance, self-exertion, and insight. It was the Buddha who for the first time in the world's history taught that deliverance could be attained independently of an external agency, that deliverance from suffering must be wrought and fashioned by each one for himself upon the anvil of his own actions.

None can grant deliverance to another who merely begs for it. Others may lend us a helping hand by guidance and instruction and in other ways, but the highest freedom is attained only through self-realization and self-awakening to truth and not through prayers and petitions to a Supreme Being, human or divine. The Buddha warns his disciples against shifting the burden to an external agency, directs them to the ways of discrimination and research, and urges them to get busy with the real task of developing their inner forces and qualities.

Misconceptions

There are some who take delight in making the Buddha a non-human. They quote a passage from the Aṅguttara Nikāya (A II 37), mistranslate it, and misunderstand it. The story goes thus:

Once the Buddha was seated under a tree in the meditation posture, his senses calmed, his mind quiet, and attained to supreme control and serenity Then a Brahmin, Doṇa by name, approached the Buddha and asked:

> "Sir, will you be a god, a *deva*?"
> "No, brahmin."
> "Sir, will you be a heavenly angel, a *gandhabba*?"
> "No, brahmin."
> "Sir, will you be a demon, a *yakkha*?"
> "No, brahmin."
> "Sir, will you be a human being, a *manussa*?"
> "No, brahmin."
> "Then, sir, what indeed will you be?"

Now, understand the Buddha's reply carefully:

> "Brahmin, whatever defilements (*āsavas*) there be owing to the presence of which a person may be identified as a god or a heavenly angel or a demon or a human being, all these defilements in me are abandoned, cut off at the root, made like a palm-tree stump, done away with, and are no more subject to future arising.

"Just as, brahmin, a blue or red or white lotus born in water grows in water and stands up above the water untouched by it, so too I, who was born in the world and grew up in the world, have transcended the world, and I live untouched by the world. Remember me as one who is enlightened (*Buddho ti maṃ dhārehi brāhmaṇa*)."

What the Buddha said was that he was not a god or a heavenly angel or a demon or a human being full of defilements. From the above it is clear that the Buddha wanted the brahmin to know that he was not a human being with defilements. He did not want the brahmin to put him into any of those categories. The Buddha was in the world but not of the world. This is clear from the simile of the lotus. Hasty critics, however, rush to a wrong conclusion and want others to believe that the Buddha was not a human being.

In the Aṅguttara Nikāya (A I 22), there is a clear instance in which the Buddha categorically declared that he was a human being:

> "Monks, there is one person (*puggala*) whose birth into this world is for the welfare and happiness of many, out of compassion for the world, for the gain and welfare and happiness of gods (*devas*) and humanity. Who is this one person (*eka puggala*)? It is the Tathāgata, who is a Worthy One (*arahat*), a Supremely Enlightened One (*sammā-sambuddho*)... Monks, one person born into the world is an extraordinary man, a marvellous man (*acchariya manussa*)."

Note the Pāli word *manussa*, a human being. Yes, the Buddha was a human being but not just another man. He was a marvellous man.

The Buddhist texts say that the Bodhisatta (as he is known before he became the Buddha) was in the Tusita heaven (*devaloka*) but came down to the human world to be born as a human being (*manussatta*). His parents, King Suddhodana and Queen Mahāmāyā, were human beings.

The Bodhisatta was born as a man, attained enlightenment (Buddhahood) as a man, and finally passed away into *parinibbāna* as a man. Even after his Supreme Enlightenment he did not call himself a God or Brahmā or any "supernatural being," but an extraordinary man.

Dr. S. Radhakrishnan, a Hindu steeped in the tenets of the Vedas and Vedanta, says that Buddhism is an offshoot of Hinduism, and even goes to the extent of calling the Buddha a Hindu. He writes: "The Buddha did not feel that he was announcing a new religion. He was born, grew up, and died a Hindu. He was restating with a new emphasis the ancient ideals of the Indo-Aryan civilization."[14]

But the Buddha himself declares that his teaching was a revelation of truths discovered by himself, not known to his contemporaries, not inherited from past tradition. Thus, in his very first sermon, referring to the Four Noble Truths, he says: "Monks, with the thought 'This is the noble truth of suffering, this is its cause, this is its cessation, this is the way leading to its cessation,' there arose in me vision, knowledge, wisdom, insight, and light concerning things unheard of before (*pubbesu ananussutesu dhammesu*)."[15]

Again, while making clear to his disciples the difference between a Fully Enlightened One and the arahats, the consummate ones, the Buddha says: "The Tathāgata, O disciples, while being an arahat is fully enlightened. It is he who proclaims a way not proclaimed before, he is the knower of a way, who understands a way, who is skilled in a way (*maggaññū, maggavidū, maggakovido*). And now his disciples are wayfarers who follow in his footsteps."[16]

The ancient way the Buddha refers to is the Noble Eightfold Path and not any ideals of the Indo-Aryan civilization as Dr. Radhakrishnan imagines.

However, referring to the Buddha, Mahatma Gandhi, the architect of Indian independence, says: "By his immense sacrifice, by his great renunciation and by the immaculate purity of his life, he left an indelible impress upon Hinduism, and Hinduism owes an eternal debt of gratitude to that great teacher." (Mahādev Desai, *With Gandhiji in Ceylon*, Madras, 1928, p.26.)

14. *2500 Years of Buddhism*, Foreword, p. ix, Government of India, 1971.
15. Vin I 10; V 420.
16. S III 66.

Dependent Arising

For a week, immediately after the enlightenment, the Buddha sat at the foot of the Bodhi Tree, experiencing the supreme bliss of emancipation. At the end of the seven days he emerged from that concentration (*samādhi*) and in the first watch of the night thought over the dependent arising (*paṭicca-samuppāda*) as to how things arise (*anuloma*) thus:

> "When this is, that comes to be; with the arising of this, that arises; namely: dependent on ignorance, volitional or kamma formations; dependent on volitional formations, (rebirth or rebecoming) consciousness; dependent on consciousness, mentality-materiality (mental and physical combination); dependent on mentality-materiality, the sixfold base (the five physical sense organs with consciousness as the sixth); dependent on the sixfold base, contact; depend on contact, feeling; dependent on feeling, craving; dependent on craving, clinging; dependent on clinging, the process of becoming; dependent on the process of becoming, there comes to be birth; dependent on birth arise ageing and death, sorrow, lamentation, pain, grief, and despair. Thus does this whole mass of suffering arise."

In the second watch of the night, the Buddha thought over the dependent arising as to how things cease (*paṭiloma*) thus:

> "When this is not, that does not come to be; with the cessation of this, that ceases; namely: with the utter cessation of ignorance, the cessation of volitional formations; with the cessation of formations, the cessation of consciousness... (and so on). Thus does this whole mass of suffering cease."

In the third watch of the night, the Buddha thought over the dependent arising both as to how things arise and cease thus:

> "When this is, that comes to be; with the arising of this, that arises; when this is not, that does not come to be; with the cessation of this, that ceases; namely: dependent on ignorance, volitional formations ... (and so on). Thus does this whole mass of suffering arise. With the utter cessation of ignorance,

the cessation of volitional formations (and so on). Thus does this whole mass of suffering cease."[17]

The Buddha now spent six more weeks in lonely retreat at six different spots in the vicinity of the Bodhi Tree. At the end of this period two merchants, Tapassu and Bhallika, who were passing that way, offered rice cake and honey to the Master, and said: "We go for refuge to the Buddha and to the Dhamma.[18] Let the Blessed One receive us as his followers."[19] They became his first lay followers (*upāsakas*).

The First Sermon

Now, while the Blessed One dwelt in solitude this thought occurred to him: "The Dhamma I have realized is deep, hard to see, hard to understand, peaceful and sublime, beyond mere reasoning, subtle, and intelligible to the wise. But this generation delights, revels, and rejoices in sensual pleasures. It is hard for such a generation to see this conditionality, this dependent arising. Hard too is it to see this calming of all conditioned things, the giving up of all substance of becoming, the extinction of craving, dispassion, cessation, Nibbāna. And if I were to teach the Dhamma and others were not to understand me, that would be a weariness, a vexation for me."[20]

Pondering thus he was first reluctant to teach the Dhamma, but on surveying the world with his mental eye, he saw beings with little dust in their eyes and with much dust in their eyes, with keen faculties and dull faculties, with good qualities and bad qualities, easy to teach and hard to teach, some who are alive to the perils hereafter of present wrongdoings, and some who are not. The Master then declared his readiness to proclaim the Dhamma in this solemn utterance:

17. Ud 1. See too the author's *Dependent Origination* (Wheel No. 15).
18. At this time there was as yet no Order (*saṅgha*).
19. Vin I 4.
20. MN 26; MI 167-68.

Apārutā tesaṃ amatassa dvārā
Ye sotavanto pamuñcantu saddhaṃ.

"Open are the doors of the Deathless.
Let those that have ears repose trust."

When considering to whom he should teach the Dhamma first, he thought of Ālāra Kālāma and Uddaka Rāmaputta, his teachers of old; for he knew that they were wise and discerning. But that was not to be; they had passed away. Then the Blessed One made up his mind to make known the truth to those five ascetics, his former friends, still steeped in the fruitless rigours of extreme asceticism. Knowing that they were living at Benares in the Deer Park at Isipatana, the Resort of Seers (modern Sārnāth), the Blessed One left Gayā for distant Benares, walking by stages some 150 miles. On the way not far from Gayā the Buddha was met by Upaka, an ascetic who, struck by the serene appearance of the Master, inquired: "Who is your teacher? Whose teaching do you profess?"

The Buddha replied: "I have no teacher, one like me does not exist in all the world, for I am the Peerless Teacher, the Arahat. I alone am Supremely Enlightened. Quenching all defilements, Nibbāna's calm have I attained. I go to the city of Kāsi (Benares) to set in motion the Wheel of Dhamma. In a world where blindness reigns, I shall beat the Deathless Drum."

"Friend, you then claim you are a universal victor," said Upaka. The Buddha replied: "Those who have attained the cessation of defilements, they are, indeed, victors like me. All evil have I vanquished. Hence I am a victor."

Upaka shook his head, remarking sarcastically, "It may be so, friend," and took a bypath. The Buddha continued his journey, and in gradual stages reached the Deer Park at Isipatana. The five ascetics, seeing the Buddha from afar, discussed among themselves: "Friends, here comes the ascetic Gotama who gave up the struggle and turned to a life of abundance and luxury. Let us make no kind of salutation to him." But when the Buddha approached them, they were struck by his dignified presence and they failed in their resolve. One went to meet him and took his alms-bowl and robe, another prepared a seat, still another brought him water. The Buddha sat on the seat prepared for him, and the five ascetics then addressed him by name and greeted him as an equal, saying, *āvuso* (friend).

The Buddha said, "Address not the Tathāgata (Perfect One) by the word *āvuso*. The Tathāgata, monks, is a Consummate One (Arahat), a Supremely Enlightened One. Give ear, monks, the Deathless has been attained. I shall instruct you, I shall teach you the Dhamma; following my teaching you will know and realize for yourselves even in this lifetime that supreme goal of purity for the sake of which clansmen retire from home to follow the homeless life." Thereupon the five monks said: "Friend Gotama, even with the stern austerities, penances, and self-torture you practised, you failed to attain the superhuman vision and insight. Now that you are living a life of luxury and self-indulgence, and have given up the struggle, how could you have reached superhuman vision and insight?"

Then replied the Buddha: "The Tathāgata has not ceased from effort and reverted to a life of luxury and abundance. The Tathāgata is a Supremely Enlightened One. Give ear, monks, the Deathless has been attained. I shall instruct you. I shall teach you the Dhamma."

A second time the monks said the same thing to the Buddha who gave the same answer a second time. A third time they repeated the same question. In spite of the assurance given by the Master, they did not change their attitude. Then the Buddha spoke to them thus: "Confess, O monks, did I ever speak to you in this way before?" Touched by this appeal of the Blessed One, the five ascetics submitted and said: "No, indeed, Lord." Thus did the Supreme Sage, the Tamed One, tame the hearts of the five ascetics with patience and kindness, with wisdom and skill. Overcome and convinced by his utterances, the monks indicated their readiness to listen to him.

The Middle Path

Now, on a full moon day of July, 589 years before Christ, in the evening, at the moment the sun was setting and the full moon simultaneously rising, in the shady Deer Park at Isipatana, the Buddha addressed them:

> "Monks, these two extremes ought not to be cultivated by the recluse. What two? Sensual indulgence, which is low, vulgar, worldly, ignoble, and conducive to harm; and self-mortification, which is painful, ignoble, and conducive to harm. The middle path, monks, understood by the Tathāgata, avoiding the extremes, gives vision and knowledge and leads to calm, realization, enlightenment, and Nibbāna. And what, monks, is that middle path? It is this Noble Eightfold Path, namely: right understanding, right thought, right speech, right action, right livelihood, right effort, right mindfulness, right concentration."

Then the Buddha explained to them the Four Noble Truths: the noble truth of suffering, the noble truth of the arising of suffering, the noble truth of the cessation of suffering, and the noble truth of the way leading to the cessation of suffering.[21]

Thus did the Supreme Buddha proclaim the truth and set in motion the Wheel of the Dhamma (*dhamma-cakka-pavattana*). This first discourse, this message of the Deer Park, is the core of the Buddha's Teaching. As the footprint of every creature that walks the earth could be included in the elephant's footprint, which is preeminent for size, so does the doctrine of the Four Noble Truths embrace the entire teaching of the Buddha.

Explaining each of the Four Noble Truths, the Master said: "Such, monks, was the vision, the knowledge, the wisdom, the insight, the light that arose in me, that I gained about things not heard before. As long as, monks, my intuitive knowledge, my vision in regard to these Four Noble Truths was not absolutely clear to

---

21. For a comprehensive explanation of these truths, see the author's *The Buddha's Ancient Path*; Bhikkhu Ñāṇamoli, *Three Cardinal Discourses of the Buddha* (Wheel No. 17); Francis Story, *The Four Noble Truths* (Wheel No. 34/35); Nyanatiloka Thera, *The Word of the Buddha*. All published by BPS.

me, I did not claim that I had gained the incomparable Supreme Enlightenment. But when, monks, my intuitive knowledge, my vision, in regard to these Four Noble Truths was absolutely clear to me, then only did I claim that I had gained the incomparable Supreme Enlightenment. And there arose in me insight and vision: unshakeable is the deliverance of my mind (*akuppā me cetovimutti*), this is my last birth, there is no more becoming (rebirth)."[22] Thus spoke the Buddha, and the five monks, glad at heart, applauded the words of the Blessed One.

On December 2, 1930, at the royal dinner at the King's Palace, Sweden, when it was his turn to speak, Sir C. Venkata Raman, the Nobel Prize winning physicist, left aside science and, to the surprise of the renowned guests, delivered a most powerful address on the Buddha and India's past glories. "In the vicinity of Benares," said Sir Venkata Raman, "there exists a path which is for me the most sacred place in India. This path was one day travelled over by the Prince Siddhattha, after he had gotten rid of all his worldly possessions in order to go through the world and proclaim the annunciation of love."[23]

The Siṃsapa Grove

The supremacy of the Four Noble Truths in the teaching of the Buddha is abundantly clear from the message of the Siṃsapa Grove as from the message of the Deer Park.

> Once the Blessed One was living at Kosambī (near Allahabad) in the Siṃsapa Grove. Then, gathering a few *siṃsapa* leaves in his hand, the Blessed One addressed the monks:
>
> "What do you think, monks, which is greater in quantity, the handful of *siṃsapa* leaves gathered by me or what is in the forest overhead?"
>
> "Not many, trifling, venerable sir, are the leaves in the handful gathered by the Blessed One; many are the leaves in the forest overhead."
>
> "Even so, monks, many are those things I have fully realized, but not declared to you; few are the things I have

22. Dhammacakkappavattana Sutta, S V 420.
23. *The Bosat* (Vol. 5, No.I, 1942), Vajirarama, Colombo, p 8.

declared to you. And why, monks, have I not declared them? They, monks, are not useful, are not essential to the life of purity, they do not lead to disgust, to dispassion, to cessation, to tranquillity, to full understanding, to full enlightenment, to Nibbāna. That is why, monks, they are not declared by me.

"And what is it, monks, that I have declared? This is suffering—this have I declared. This is the arising of suffering—this have I declared. This is the cessation of suffering—this have I declared. This is the path leading to the cessation of suffering—this have I declared.

"And why, monks, have I declared these truths? They are, indeed, useful, are essential to the life of purity, they lead to disgust, to dispassion, to cessation, to tranquillity, to full understanding, to enlightenment, to Nibbāna. That is why, monks, they are declared by me. Therefore, monks, an effort should be made to realize: 'This is suffering, this is the arising of suffering, this is the cessation of suffering, this is the way leading to the cessation of suffering.'"[24]

The Buddha has emphatically said:

"One thing do I make known: suffering, and the cessation of suffering."[25] (*Dukkhaṃ ceva paññāpemi, dukkhassa ca nirodhaṃ.*)

To understand this unequivocal saying is to understand Buddhism; for the entire teaching of the Buddha is nothing else than the application of this one principle. What can be called the discovery of a Buddha is just these Four Noble Truths. This is the typical teaching of the Buddhas of all ages.

The Peerless Physician

The Buddha is also known as the peerless physician (*bhisakko*), the supreme surgeon (*sallakatto anuttaro*). He indeed is an unrivalled healer.

The Buddha's method of exposition of the Four Noble Truths is comparable to that of a physician. As a physician, he

24. S V 437.
25. MN 22; M I 140.

first diagnosed the illness, next he discovered the cause for the arising of the illness, then he considered its removal, and lastly applied the remedy.

Suffering (*dukkha*) is the illness; craving (*taṇhā*) is the arising or the root cause of the illness (*samudaya*); through the removal of craving, the illness is removed, and that is the cure (*nirodha-nibbāna*); the Noble Eightfold Path (*magga*) is the remedy.

The Buddha's reply to a brahmin who wished to know why the Master is called a Buddha clearly indicates that it was for no other reason than a perfect knowledge of the Four Noble Truths. Here is the Buddha's reply:

> "I knew what should be known,
> What should be cultivated I have cultivated,
> What should be abandoned that have I let go.
> Hence, O brahmin, I am Buddha—
> The Awakened One."[26]

With the proclamation of the Dhamma for the first time, with the setting in motion of the Wheel of the Dhamma, and with the conversion of the five ascetics, the Deer Park at Isipatana became the birthplace of the Buddha's Dispensation (*sāsana*) and of his Community of Monks (*saṅgha*).[27]

---

26. S V 588; MN 92; Vin I 45; Th 828.

27. In 273 BCE Emperor Asoka came on pilgrimage to this holy spot and caused a series of monuments and a commemorative pillar with the lion capital to be erected. This capital with its four magnificent lions upholding the *dharmacakra*, "the Wheel of Dharma," now stands in the museum of Sarnath, Benares, and is today the official crest of India. The *dharmacakra* festival is still held in Sri Lanka.

Jawaharlal Nehru writes: "At Sarnath near Benares, I would almost see the Buddha preaching his first sermon, and some of his recorded words would come like a distant echo to me through two thousand five hundred years. Asoka's pillars of stone with their inscriptions would speak to me in their magnificent language and tell me of a man who, though an emperor, was greater than any king or emperor." (*The Discovery of India*, p 44)

The Spread of the Dhamma

Thereafter the Buddha spent the *vassa*[28] at the Deer Park at Isipatana, sacred this day to over 600 million of the human race. During these three months of "rains" fifty others headed by Yasa, a young man of wealth, joined the Order. Now the Buddha had sixty disciples, all arahats who had realized the Dhamma and were fully competent to teach others. When the rainy season ended, the Master addressed his immediate disciples in these words:

> "Released am I, monks, from all ties whether human or divine. You also are delivered from all fetters whether human or divine. Go now and wander for the welfare and happiness of many, out of compassion for the world, for the gain, welfare, and happiness of gods and men. Let not two of you proceed in the same direction. Proclaim the Dhamma that is excellent in the beginning, excellent in the middle, and excellent in the end, possessed of meaning to the letter and utterly perfect. Proclaim the life of purity, the holy life consummate and pure. There are beings with little dust in their eyes who will be lost through not hearing the Dhamma, there are beings who will understand the Dhamma. I also shall go to Uruvelā, to Senānigama, to teach the Dhamma."[29]

Thus did the Buddha commence his sublime mission, which lasted to the end of his life. With his disciples he walked the highways and byways of India enfolding all within the aura of his boundless compassion and wisdom. Though the Order of Monks began its career with sixty bhikkhus, it expanded soon into thousands, and, as a result of the increasing number of monks, many monasteries came into being. In later times monastic Indian universities like Nālandā, Vikramasilā, Jagaddalā, Vikramapuri, and Odantapuri, became cultural centres which gradually influenced the whole of Asia and through it the mental life of humankind.

After a successful ministry of forty-five years, the Buddha passed away at the age of eighty at the twin Sāla Trees of the Mallas

---

28. The *vassa or* "rains" is the three months of seclusion during the rainy season, i.e. from July to October in India.
29. Vin I 21.

at Kusinārā (in modern Uttar Pradesh about 120 miles northeast of Benares).[30]

The Buddha's Ministry

During his long ministry of forty-five years the Buddha walked widely throughout the northern districts of India. But during the rains retreat (*vassa*), he generally stayed in one place. Here follows a brief sketch of his retreats gathered from the texts:

1st year: Vārānasi. After the first proclamation of the Dhamma on the full moon day of July, the Buddha spent the first *vassa* at Isipatana, Vārānasi.

The 2nd, 3rd, and 4th years: Rājagaha (in the Bamboo Grove, Veḷuvana). It was during the third year that Sudatta, a householder of Sāvatthī known for his bounty as Anāthapiṇḍika, "the feeder of the forlorn," having heard that a Buddha had come into being, went in search of him, listened to him, and having gained confidence (*saddhā*) in the Teacher, the Teaching, and the Taught (the Buddha, Dhamma, and Sangha), attained the first stage of sainthood (*sotāpatti*). He was renowned as the chief supporter (*dāyaka*) of the Master. Anāthapiṇḍika had built the famous Jetavana monastery at Sāvatthī, known today as Sahet-mahet, and offered it to the Buddha and his disciples. The ruins of this monastery are still to be seen.

5th year: Vesāli. The Buddha kept retreat in the Pinnacled Hall (*kūṭāgārasālā*). It was at this time that King Suddhodana fell ill. The Master visited him and preached the Dhamma, hearing which the king attained perfect sanctity (*arahatta*), and after enjoying the bliss of emancipation for seven days, passed away. The Order of Nuns was also founded during this time.

---

30. It is interesting to note that this greatest of Indian *rishis* (seers) was born under a tree in a park, attained enlightenment under the Bodhi Tree, set in motion the Wheel of Dhamma at the Deer Park under trees, and finally passed away under the twin sāla trees. He spent most of his time in the open in forests and in the villages of India. The south branch of the Bodhi Tree was brought to Sri Lanka by the arhat nun Saṅghamittā, daughter of Asoka the Great of India, in the third century BCE. The oldest recorded tree in the world, it still flourishes at Anuradhapura.

6th year: Maṅkula Hill. Here the Buddha performed the "Twin Wonder" (*yamaka pāṭihāriya*). He did the same for the first time at Kapilavatthu to overcome the pride of the Sakyans, his relatives.

7th year: Tāvatimsa (the Heaven of the Thirty-three). Here the Buddha preached the Abhidhamma or the Higher Doctrine to the deities (*devas*) headed by his mother Mahāmāyā, who had passed away seven days after the birth of Prince Siddhattha, and was reborn as a deva in the Tāvatiṃsa.

8th year: Bhesakalā Forest (near Suṃsumāragiri). It was here that Nakulapitā and his wife, a genial couple, came to see the Buddha, told him about their very happy married life, and expressed the wish that they might continue to live together both here and hereafter. These two were placed by the Buddha as chiefs of those that win confidence.

9th year: Kosambī—at the Ghosita Monastery.

10th year: Pārileyyakka Forest. It was in the tenth year that, at Kosambi, a dispute arose between two parties of monks owing to a trivial offence committed by a monk. As they could not be reconciled, and as they did not pay heed to his exhortation, the Buddha retired to the forest. At the end of the *vassa*, their dispute settled, the monks came to Sāvatthī and begged pardon of the Buddha.

11th year: Village of Ekanāla (in the Magadha country). It was here that the Buddha met the brahmin farmer Kasībhāradvāja who spoke to the Buddha somewhat discourteously. The Buddha, however, answered his questions with his characteristic sobriety. Bhāradvāja became an ardent follower of the Buddha. It was on this occasion that the very interesting discourse, Kasībhāradvāja Sutta (Suttanipāta), was delivered. (Read *The Book of Protection* by this author (BPS).)

12th year: Verañja. The introduction of the Vinaya is attributed to the twelfth year. It was also during this retreat that the brahmin Verañja came to see the Buddha, asked a series of questions on Buddhist practises, and being satisfied with the answers, became a follower of the Blessed One. He invited the Master and the Sangha to spend the rainy season (*vassa*) at his village Verañja. At that time there was a famine. The Buddha and his disciples had to be satisfied with very coarse food supplied by horse merchants. As it was the custom of the Buddha to take leave of the inviter before setting out on his journeying, he saw the brahmin at the end of the *vassa*. The latter admitted that though he had invited the Buddha and his disciples to spend the retreat at Verañja, he had failed in his duties towards them during the entire season owing to his being taxed with household duties. However, the next day he offered food and gifts of robes to the Buddha and the Sangha.

13th year: Cāliya Rock (near the city of Cālika). During this time the elder Meghiya was his personal attendant. The elder being attracted by a beautiful mango grove near a river asked the Buddha for permission to go there for meditation. Though the Buddha asked him to wait till another monk came, he repeated the request. The Buddha granted him permission. The elder went, but to his great surprise he was oppressed by thoughts of sense pleasures, ill will, and harm, and returned disappointed. Thereupon the Buddha said: "Meghiya, for the deliverance of the mind of the immature, five things are conducive to their maturing: (1) a good friend; (2) virtuous behaviour guided by the essential precepts for training; (3) good counsel tending to dispassion, calm, cessation, enlightenment and Nibbāna; (4) the effort to abandon evil thoughts; and (5) acquiring of wisdom that discerns the rise and fall of things."[31]

14th year: Jetavana monastery, Sāvatthī. During this time the Venerable Rāhula, who was still a novice (*sāmaṇera*), received higher ordination (*upasampadā*). According to the Vinaya, higher ordination is not conferred before the age of twenty; Ven. Rāhula had then reached that age.

---

31. The whole of this discourse is at A IV 354, Ud 34–37, and in brief at *Dhammapada Commentary*, I, 287. In the elder's verse (66) in *Theragāthā*, it is said that Venerable Meghiya was of a Sakyan Rājā's family. The Dhammapada verses (33, 34) are as follows:

The unsteady fickle mind
Hard to guard and hard to control,
The wise man straightens
Even as a fletcher an arrow.
Like a fish jerked out of its watery abode
And cast on land, this mind quakes;
(Therefore) the realm of Māra
Should be abandoned.

15th year: Kapilavatthu (the birthplace of Prince Siddhattha). It was in this year that the death occurred of King Suppabuddha, the father of Yasodharā.

16th year: City of Āḷavi. During this year Āḷavaka, the demon who devoured human flesh, was tamed by the Buddha. He became a follower of the Buddha. For Āḷavaka's questions and the Master's answers read the Āḷavaka Sutta, in the Suttanipāta.[32]

17th year: Rājagaha, at Veḷuvana Monastery. During this time a well-known courtesan, Sirimā, sister of Jīvaka, the physician, died. The Buddha attended the funeral, and asked the king to inform the people to buy the dead body—the body that attracted so many when she was alive. No one cared to have it even without paying a price. On that occasion, addressing the crowd, the Buddha said in verse:

"Behold this painted image, a body full of wounds,
heaped up (with bones), diseased,
the object of thought of many, in which there is
neither permanence nor stability."[33]

18th year: Cāliya Rock. During this time a young weaver's daughter met the Buddha and listened to his discourse on mindfulness of death (*maraṇānussati*). On another occasion she answered correctly all the four questions put to her by the Master, because she often pondered over the words of the Buddha. Her answers were philosophical, and the congregations who had not given a thought to the Buddha word, could not grasp the meaning of her answers. The Buddha, however, praised her and addressed them in verse thus:

"Blind is this world;
few here clearly see.
Like a bird that escapes from the net,
only a few go to a good state of existence."[34]

She heard the Dhamma and attained the first stage of sanctity (*sotāpatti*). But unfortunately she died an untimely death.[35]

---

32. See *The Book of Protection*, p.81, by this author, publ. by BPS.
33. Dhammapada, 147
34. Dhammapada, 174
35. For a detailed account of this interesting story, and the questions

19th year: Cāliya Rock.

20th year: Rājagaha, at Veḷuvana Monastery.

From the 21st year till the 43rd year: Sāvatthī. Of these twenty-four *vassas*, eighteen were spent at Jetavana Monastery, the rest at Pubbārāma. Anāthapiṇḍika and Visākhā were the chief supporters.

44th year: Beluva (a small village, probably situated near Vesāli), where the Buddha suppressed, by force of will, a grave illness.

In the 45th year of his Enlightenment, the Buddha passed away at Kusinārā in the month of May (*vesākha*) before the commencement of the rains.

During the first twenty years of the Buddha's life, the bhikkhus Nāgasamāla, Nāgita, Upavāna, Sunakkhatta, Sāgata, Rādha, and Meghiya, and the novice (*sāmaṇera*) Cunda attended upon him, though not regularly. However, after the twentieth year, the Buddha wished to have a regular attendant. Thereon all the great eighty arahats, like Sāriputta and Moggallāna, expressed their willingness to attend upon their Master. But this did not meet with his approval. Perhaps the Buddha thought that these arahats could be of greater service to humanity

Then the elders requested Ānanda Thera, who had kept silent all this while, to beg of the Master to be his attendant. Ānanda Thera's answer is interesting. He said, "If the Master is willing to have me as his attendant, he will speak." Then the Buddha said: "Ānanda, let not others persuade you. You on your own may attend upon me."

Buddhahood and Arahatship

Perfect Enlightenment, the discovery and realization of the Four Noble Truths (Buddhahood), is not the prerogative of a single being chosen by divine providence, nor is it a unique and unrepeatable event in human history. It is an achievement open to anyone who earnestly strives for perfect purity and wisdom, and with inflexible will cultivates the *pāramī*, the perfections which are the requisites of Buddhahood, and the Noble Eightfold Path. There have been

and answers, see the *Commentary on the Dhammapada*, Vol. III, p.170, or Burlingame, *Buddhist Legends*, Part 3, p.14.

Buddhas in the dim past and there will be Buddhas in the future when necessity arises and conditions are favourable. But we need not think of that distant future; now, in our present days, the "doors to the Deathless" are still wide open. Those who enter through them, reaching perfect sanctity or arahatship, the final liberation from suffering (Nibbāna), have been solemnly declared by the Buddha to be his equals as far as the emancipation from defilements and ultimate deliverance is concerned:

> "Victors like me are they, indeed,
> They who have won defilements' end."[36]

The Buddha, however, also made clear to his disciples the difference between a Fully Enlightened One and the arahats,[37] the accomplished saints:

> "The Tathāgata, O disciples, while being an arahat, is Fully Enlightened. It is he who proclaims a path not proclaimed before; he is the knower of a path, who understands a path, who is skilled in a path. And now his disciples are wayfarers who follow in his footsteps. That, disciples, is the distinction, the specific feature which distinguishes the Tathāgata, who being an arahat, is Fully Enlightened, from the disciple who is freed by insight."[38]

Salient Features of the Dhamma

There are no dark corners of ignorance, no cobwebs of mystery, no smoky chambers of secrecy; there are no "secret doctrines," no hidden dogmas in the teaching of the Buddha, which is open as daylight and as clear as crystal. "The doctrine and discipline proclaimed by the Buddha shine when open and not when covered, even as the sun and moon shine when open and not when covered" (A I 283).

---

36. Ariyapariyesana Sutta, MN 26/M I 264.
37. The word is applied only to those who have fully destroyed the taints. In this sense the Buddha was the first arahat in the world, as he himself revealed to Upaka.
38. S III 66.

The Master disapproved of those who professed to have "secret doctrines," saying, "Secrecy is the hallmark of false doctrines." Addressing the disciple Ānanda, the Master said: "I have taught the Dhamma, Ānanda, without making any distinction between exoteric and esoteric doctrine; for in respect of the truths, Ānanda, the Tathāgata has no such thing as the closed fist of a teacher who hides some essential knowledge from the pupil."[39]

A Buddha is an extreme rarity, but is no freak in human history. He would not preserve his supreme knowledge for himself alone. Such an idea would be completely ridiculous and abhorrent from the Buddhist point of view, and to the Buddha such a wish is utterly inconceivable. Driven by universal love and compassion, the Buddha expounded his teaching without keeping back anything that was essential for man's deliverance from the shackles of saṃsāra, repeated wandering.

The Buddha's teaching from beginning to end is open to all those who have eyes to see and a mind to understand. Buddhism was never forced upon anyone at the point of the gun or the bayonet. Conversion by compulsion was unknown among Buddhists and repugnant to the Buddha.

Of the Buddha's creed of compassion, H. Fielding Hall writes in *The Soul of a People*: "There can never be a war of Buddhism. No ravished country has ever borne witness to the prowess of the followers of the Buddha; no murdered men have poured out their blood on their hearth-stones, killed in his name; no ruined women have cursed his name to high heaven. He and his faith are clean of the stain of blood. He was the preacher of the Great Peace, of love of charity, of compassion, and so clear is his teaching that it can never be misunderstood."

When communicating the Dhamma to his disciples, the Master made no distinctions whatsoever among them; for there were no specially chosen favourite disciples. Among his disciples, all those who were arahats, who were passion-free and had shed the fetters binding to renewed existence, had equally perfected themselves in purity. But there were some outstanding ones who were skilled in different branches of knowledge and practise, and because of their mental endowments, they gained positions of

39. Mahā Parinibbāna Sutta, DN 16/D II 100.

distinction; but special favours were never granted to anyone by the Master. Upāli, for instance, who came from a barber's family, was made the chief in matters of discipline (*vinaya*) in preference to many arahats who belonged to the class of the nobles and warriors (*khattiya*). Sāriputta and Moggallāna, brahmins by birth, because of their longstanding aspirations in former lives, became the chief disciples of the Buddha. The former excelled in wisdom (*paññā*) and the latter in supernormal powers (*iddhi*).

The Buddha never wished to extract from his disciples blind and submissive faith in him or his teachings. He always insisted on discriminative examination and intelligent inquiry. In no uncertain terms he urged critical investigation when he addressed the inquiring Kālāmas in a discourse that has been rightly called the first charter of free thought:

> "Come, Kālāmas. Do not go by oral tradition, by lineage of teaching, by hearsay, by a collection of scriptures, by logical reasoning, by inferential reasoning, by reflection on reasons, by the acceptance of a view after pondering it, by the seeming competence of a speaker, or because you think, 'The ascetic is our teacher.' But when you know for yourselves, 'These things are unwholesome, these things are blamable; these things are censured by the wise; these things, if undertaken and practised, lead to harm and suffering,' then you should abandon them. And when you know for yourselves, 'These things are wholesome, these things are blameless; these things are praised by the wise; these things, if undertaken and practised, lead to welfare and happiness,' then you should engage in them."

To take anything on trust is not in the spirit of Buddhism, so we find this dialogue between the Master and the disciples: "If now, knowing this and preserving this, would you say: 'We honour our Master and through respect for him we respect what he teaches'?"—"No, Lord." —"That which you affirm, O disciples, is it not only that which you yourselves have recognized, seen, and grasped?"—"Yes, Lord."[40]

40. MN 38/M I 264.

The Buddha faced facts and refused to acknowledge or yield to anything that did not accord with truth. He does not want us to recognize anything indiscriminately and without reason. He wants us to comprehend things as they really are, to put forth the necessary effort and work out our own deliverance with mindfulness.

You should make the effort
The Tathāgatas point out the way.[41]

Bestir yourselves, rise up,
And yield your hearts unto the Buddha's teaching.
Shake off the armies of the king of death,
As does the elephant a reed-thatched shed.[42]

The Buddha, for the first time in the world's history taught that deliverance should be sought independent of a saviour, be he human or divine.

The idea that another raises a man from lower to higher levels of life, and ultimately rescues him, tends to make man indolent and weak, supine and foolish. This kind of belief degrades a man and smothers every spark of dignity from his moral being.

The Enlightened One exhorts his followers to acquire self-reliance. Others may lend us a helping hand indirectly, but deliverance from suffering must be wrought out and fashioned by each one for himself upon the anvil of his own actions.

True Purification

In the understanding of things, neither belief nor fear plays any role in Buddhist thought. The truth of the Dhamma can be grasped only through insight, never through blind faith, or through fear of some known or unknown being.

Not only did the Buddha discourage blind belief and fear of an omnipotent God as unsuitable approaches for understanding the truth, but he also denounced adherence to unprofitable rites and rituals, because the mere abandoning of outward things, such

41. Dhp 276.
42. S I 156.

as fasting, bathing in rivers, animal sacrifice, and similar acts, does not tend to purify a man or make a man holy and noble.

We find this dialogue between the Buddha and the brahmin Sundarika Bhāradvāja: Once the Buddha, addressing the monks, explained in detail how a seeker after deliverance should train himself, and further added that a person whose mind is free from taints, whose life of purity is perfected, and the task done, could be called one who bathes inwardly.

Then Bhāradvāja, seated near the Buddha, heard these words and asked him:

> "Does the Venerable Gotama go to bathe in the river Bāhuka?"
>
> "Brahmin, what good is the river Bāhuka? What can the river Bāhuka do?"
>
> "Indeed, Venerable Gotama, the river Bāhuka is believed by many to be holy. Many people have their evil deeds (*pāpa*) washed away in the river Bāhuka."

Then the Buddha made him understand that bathing in rivers would not cleanse a man of his dirt of evil, and instructed him thus:

> "Bathe just here (in this Doctrine and Discipline, *Dhamma-vinaya*), brahmin, give security to all beings. If you do not speak falsehood, or kill or steal, if you are confident, and are not mean, what does it avail you to go to Gayā (the name of a river in India during the time of the Buddha)? Your well at home is also a Gayā."[43]

Caste Problem

Caste, which was a matter of vital importance to the brahmins of India, was one of utter indifference to the Buddha, who strongly condemned the debasing caste system. In his Order of Monks all castes unite as do the rivers in the sea. They lose their former

43. Vatthūpama Sutta, MN 7. See Nyanaponika Thera, *The Simile of the Cloth* (Wheel No. 61/62).

names, castes, and clans, and become known as members of one community—the Sangha.

Speaking of the equal recognition of all members of the Sangha the Buddha says:

> Just as, O monks, the great rivers Gaṅgā, Yamunā, Aciravatī, Sarabhū, and Mahī, on reaching the ocean, lose their earlier name and identity and come to be reckoned as the great ocean, similarly, O monks, people of the four castes (*vaṇṇa*)... who leave the household and become homeless recluses under the Doctrine and Discipline declared by the Tathāgata, lose their previous names and identities and are reckoned as recluses who are sons of Sākya. (Udāna 5.5)

The Buddhist position regarding racism and racial discrimination made explicit at such an early age is one reflected in the moral and scientific standpoint adopted by UNESCO in the present century (Declaration on Race and Racial Prejudice, UNESCO 1978).[44]

To Sundarika Bhāradvāja, the brahmin who inquired about his lineage, the Buddha answered:

> "No Brahmin I, no prince,
> No farmer, or aught else.
> All worldly ranks I know,
> But knowing go my way
> as simply nobody:
> Homeless, in pilgrim garb,
> With shaven crown, I go
> my way alone, serene.
> To ask my birth is vain."[45]

On one occasion a caste-ridden brahmin insulted the Buddha saying: "Stop, you shaveling! Stop, you outcast!"

The Master, without any feeling of indignation, gently replied:

> "Birth makes not a man an outcast,

---

44. P.D. Premasiri, "The Buddhist Concept of A Just Social and Political Order," *Young Buddhist*, Singapore.

45. Sn 455, 456; Chalmer's translation (Harvard Oriental Series).

Birth makes not a man a brahmin;
Action makes a man an outcast,
Action makes a man a brahmin." (Suttanipāta, 142)

He then delivered a whole sermon, the Vasala Sutta, explaining to the brahmin in detail the characteristics of one who is really an outcast (*vasala*). Convinced, the haughty brahmin took refuge in the Buddha.[46]

The Buddha freely admitted into the Order people from all castes and classes when he knew that they were fit to live the holy life, and some of them later distinguished themselves in the Order. The Buddha was the only contemporary teacher who endeavoured to blend in mutual tolerance and concord those who hitherto had been rent asunder by differences of caste and class.

Upāli, who was the chief authority on the Vinaya—the disciplinary rules of the Order—was a barber, regarded as one of the basest occupations of the lower classes. Sunīta, who later won arahatship, was a scavenger, another base occupation. In the Order of Nuns were Puṇṇā and Puṇṇikā, both slave girls. According to Mrs. C.A.F. Rhys Davids, 8.5% of the number of those nuns who were able to realize the fruits of their training were drawn from the despised castes, which were mostly illiterate.[47]

Chief Disciples

Rājagaha, the capital of the kingdom of Magadha, was one of the first places visited by the Buddha soon after his enlightenment. As a wandering ascetic in the early days of his renunciation, he had promised King Seniya Bimbisāra that he would visit Rājagaha when he achieved the object of his search. King Bimbisāra was overjoyed at the sight of the Buddha, and having listened to his teaching, became a lay follower. His devotion to the Buddha became so ardent that within a few days he offered him his pleasure park, Veluvana, for residence.

---

46. See *The Book of Protection*, p.91.)
47. See G.P Malalasekera and K.N. Jayatilleke, *Buddhism and the Race Question* (Wheel 200/201).

Rājagaha during that time was a centre of great learning where many schools of philosophy flourished. One such school of thought had as its head Sañjaya; and among his retinue of two hundred and fifty followers were Upatissa and Kolita, who were later to become Sāriputta and Mahā Moggallāna, the two chief disciples of the Buddha.

One day when Upatissa was walking through the streets of Rājagaha, he was greatly struck by the serene countenance and the quiet, dignified deportment of one of the first disciples of the Buddha, the arahat Assaji, who was on his alms round.

All the strenuous endeavours to achieve perfection that Upatissa had made through many a birth were now on the verge of being rewarded. Without going back to his teacher, he followed the arahat Assaji to his resting place, eager to know whom he followed and what teaching he had accepted.

"Friend," said Upatissa, "serene is your countenance, clear and radiant is your glance. Who persuaded you to renounce the world? Who is your teacher? What Dhamma (teaching) do you follow?" The Venerable Assaji, rather reluctant to speak much, humbly said: "I cannot expound the Doctrine and Discipline at length, but I can tell you the meaning briefly." Upatissa's reply is interesting: "Well, friend, tell little or much; what I want is just the meaning. Why speak many words?" Then the arahat Assaji uttered a single verse which embraces the Buddha's entire doctrine of causality:

Ye dhammā hetuppabhavā
Tesaṃ hetuṃ tathāgato āha
Tesaṃ ca yo nirodho
Evaṃvādi mahā samaṇo.

"Whatever from a cause proceeds, thereof
The Tathāgata has explained the cause,
Its cessation too he has explained.
This is the teaching of the Supreme Sage."[48]

Upatissa instantly grasped the meaning and attained the first stage of realization, comprehending:

48. Vinaya Mahāvagga

"Whatever is of the nature of arising, all that is of the nature of ceasing."[49]

With a heart full of joy, he quickly went back to his friend Kolita and told him of his meeting with the arahat and of the teaching he had received. Kolita, too, like Upatissa, instantly gained the first stage of realization, having heard the Dhamma from his friend. Thereon both of them approached Sañjaya and asked him to follow the Buddha. But afraid of losing his reputation as a religious teacher, he refused to do so. Upatissa and Kolita then left Sañjaya—much against his protestations—for the Veḷuvana monastery and expressed their wish to become followers of the Buddha. The Buddha gladly welcomed them saying, "Come, monks, well proclaimed is the Dhamma. Live the holy life for the complete ending of suffering." He admitted them into the Order. They attained deliverance and became the two chief disciples.

Another great one who joined the Order during the Buddha's stay at Veḷuvana was the brahmin sage Mahā Kassapa, who had renounced great wealth to find the way to deliverance. It was the Venerable Mahā Kassapa, three months after the Buddha's passing away (*parinibbāna*), who called up the convocation of arahats (the First Council), at the Sattapaṇṇi Cave near Rājagaha under the patronage of King Ajātasattu, to collect and codify the Dhamma and Vinaya.

The Order of Nuns

In the early days of the Order, only men were admitted to the Sangha since the Buddha was reluctant to admit women. But there were many devout women among the lay followers who had a keen desire for a life of renunciation as nuns. Urged by their keenness, Pajāpatī Gotamī, the foster mother of the Buddha, in the company of many ladies of rank, approached the Buddha, beseeching him to grant them ordination. But the Buddha still hesitated to accept them.

Seeing their discomfiture, and urged by their zeal, the Venerable Ānanda took up their cause and pleaded with the Buddha on their behalf. The Buddha finally yielded to this appeal,

49. *Yaṃ kiñci samudayadhammaṃ sabbaṃ taṃ nirodhadhammaṃ.*

placing, however, eight cardinal rules on the ordination of women. Thus was established, in the fifth year after his enlightenment, the Order of Nuns, the Bhikkhunī Sāsana, for the first time in history; for never before this had there been an Order where woman could lead a celibate life of renunciation.

Women from all walks of life joined the Order. Foremost in the Order stood the Therīs Khemā and Uppalavaṇṇā. The lives of quite a number of these noble nuns, their strenuous endeavours to win the goal of freedom, and their paeans of joy at deliverance of mind, are graphically described in the *Therīgāthā*, *The Psalms of the Sisters*.[50]

At Kapilavatthu

While at Rājagaha, the Blessed One heard that his father wished to see him, and he set out for Kapilavatthu. He did not, however, go straight to the palace, but, according to custom, stopped in a grove outside the town. The next day the Buddha, with his bowl, went for his alms from house to house in the streets of Kapilavatthu. King Suddhodana, startled at the news, rushed to the Buddha and said; "Why, Master, why do you put us to shame? Why do you go begging for your food? Not one of our race has ever done so." Replied the Buddha: "You and your family may claim descent from kings; my descent is from the Buddhas of old; and they, begging their food, always lived on alms." Then explaining the Dhamma the Master said, "Be alert, be mindful, lead a righteous life. The righteous live happily both in this world and the next." And so the king became established in the Path, he realized the Dhamma.

The Buddha was then conducted into the palace where all came to pay their respects to him, but not Princess Yasodharā. The Buddha went to her, and the princess, knowing the impassable gulf between them, fell on the ground at his feet and saluted him. Then relating the Candakinnara Jātaka, a story of his previous birth,[51] revealing how great her virtue had been in that former life,

50. *Psalms of the Early Buddhists—The Sisters*, trans. by C.A.F. Rhys Davids (PTS Translation Series).

51. Jātaka No. 485.

he made her an adherent to the Doctrine. Later when the Buddha was induced to establish an Order for women, Yasodharā became one of the first nuns and attained arahatship, highest sanctity.

When the Buddha was in the palace, Princess Yasodharā arrayed her son Rāhula in all his best attire and sent him to the Blessed One, saying, "That is your father, Rāhula, go and ask for your inheritance."

Prince Rāhula went to the Buddha, stood before him, and said, "Pleasant indeed, is your shadow, sage."

And when the Blessed One had finished his meal and left the palace, Prince Rāhula followed him saying, "Give me my inheritance, sage; give me my inheritance." At that the Blessed One spoke to the Venerable Sāriputta: "Well then, Sāriputta, take him into the Order."

Then the Venerable Sāriputta gave Prince Rāhula the ordination.[52] In the Majjhima Nikāya, one of the five original collections in Pāli containing the Buddha's discourses, there are three discourses (Nos. 61, 62, 147) entitled Rāhulovāda or exhortations to Rāhula, delivered by the Blessed One to teach the Dhamma to little Rāhula. The discourses are entirely devoted to advice on discipline and meditation. Here is an extract from the Master's exhortation in the Mahā Rāhulovāda Sutta:[53]

> "Cultivate the meditation on loving-kindness (*mettā*), Rāhula, for by cultivating loving-kindness, ill will is banished. Cultivate the meditation on compassion (*karuṇā*), Rāhula, for by cultivating compassion, cruelty is banished. Cultivate the meditation on appreciative joy (*muditā*), Rāhula, for by cultivating appreciative joy, aversion is banished. Cultivate the meditation on equanimity (*upekkhā*), Rāhula, for by cultivating equanimity, hatred is banished. Cultivate the meditation on impurity (*asubha*), Rāhula, for by meditating on impurity, lust is banished. Cultivate the meditation on the concept of impermanence (*anicca-saññā*), Rāhula, for by meditating on the concept of impermanence, pride of self (*asmi-māna*) is banished. Cultivate the meditation on

52. Vin I 82–83. See Piyadassi Thera and J.F. Dickson, *Ordination in Theravāda Buddhism*, Wheel No.56.

53. MN 62. For a full translation, see *Advice to Rāhula* (Wheel No. 33).

mindfulness of in-and-out-breathing (*ānāpānasati*), Rāhula, for mindfulness of breathing, cultivated and frequently practised, bears much fruit and is of great advantage."

Women in Buddhism

Generally speaking, during the time of the Buddha, owing to brahminical influence, women were not given much recognition. Sometimes they were held in contempt and in servility to man. It was the Buddha who raised the status of women and there were cases of women showing erudition in matters of philosophy. In his large-heartedness and magnanimity he always treated women with consideration and civility, and pointed out to them, too, the path to peace, purity, and sanctity. Said the Blessed One: "A mother is the friend at one's home. A wife is the highest friend of the husband."

The Buddha did not reject the invitation for a meal, though Ambapāli[54] was of bad repute. Whatever food she offered he accepted, and in return, gave her the *Dhammadāna*, the gift of truth. She was immediately convinced by the teaching and leaving aside her frivolous lay life, she entered the Order of Nuns. Ardent and strenuous in her religious practises, she then became an arahat.

Kisāgotamī was another woman to whom the Buddha gave the assistance of his great compassion. Her story is one of the most touching tales recorded in our books. Many more are the instances where the Buddha helped and consoled women who suffered from the vicissitudes of life.

Ministering to the Sick

Great indeed, was the Master's compassion for the sick. On one occasion the Blessed One found an ailing monk, Pūtigatta Tissa, with festering ulcers lying on his soiled bed. Immediately the Master prepared hot water, and with the help of the Venerable Ānanda washed him, tenderly nursed him with his own hands, and taught the Dhamma, thus enabling him to win arahatship before he died. On another occasion, too, the Master tended a

54. C.A.F. Rhys Davids, *Psalms of the Early Buddhists—The Sisters*, p 120.

sick monk and admonished his disciples thus:

> "Whosoever, monks, would follow my admonition (would wait upon me, would honour me), he should wait upon the sick."[55]

When the arahat Tissa passed away, the funeral rites were duly performed and the Buddha caused the relics to be enshrined in a *stūpa*.[56]

The Buddha's *mettā* or loving-kindness was all-pervading and immeasurable. His earnest exhortation to his disciples was:

> "Just as with her own life
> a mother shields from hurt
> her own, her only child,
> let all-embracing thoughts
> for all that lives be thine."[57]

Being one who always acted in constant conformity with what he preached, loving-kindness and compassion always dominated his actions.

While journeying from village to village, from town to town, instructing, enlightening, and gladdening the many, the Buddha saw how superstitious folk, steeped in ignorance, slaughtered animals in worship of their gods. He spoke to them:

> "Of life, which all can take but none can give,
> Life which all creatures love and strive to keep,
> Wonderful, dear, and pleasant unto each,
> Even to the meanest...."[58]

Thus when people who prayed to the gods for mercy were

55. Vin I 302.

56. "To the north-east of the monastery of Jetavana," wrote General Alexander Cunningham in his *Archaeological Report*, 1862–3, "there was a *stūpa* built on the spot where the Buddha had washed the hands and feet of a sick monk...The remains of the *stūpa* still exist in a mass of solid brick work at a distance of 550 feet from the Jetavana Monastery." In General Cunningham's map of Sāvatthī (modern Sahet-Mahet), the site of this *stūpa* is marked H. *Archaeological Survey of India* (Simla 1871), p 341.

57. Mettā Sutta, *Sutta Nipāta*, 149, 149; Chalmer's translation.

58. Edwin Arnold, *The Light of Asia.*

merciless, and India was bloodstained with the morbid sacrifices of innocent animals at the desecrated altars of imaginary deities, and the harmful rites and rituals of ascetics and brahmins brought disaster and brutal agony, the Buddha, the Compassionate One, pointed out the ancient path of the Enlightened Ones, the path of righteousness, love, and understanding.

Mettā or love is the best antidote for anger in oneself. It is the best medicine for those who are angry with us. Let us then extend love to all who need it with a free and boundless heart. The language of the heart, the language that comes from the heart and goes to the heart, is always simple, graceful, and full of power.

Equanimity and Self-Composure

Amid all the vicissitudes of life—gain and loss, repute and ill-repute, praise and censure, pain and happiness[59] the Buddha never wavered. He was firm as a solid rock. Touched by happiness or by pain he showed neither elation nor depression. He never encouraged wrangling and animosity. Addressing the monks he once said: "I do not quarrel with the world, monks. It is the world that quarrels with me. An exponent of the Dhamma does not quarrel with anyone in the world."[60]

He admonished his disciples in these words:

> "Monks, if others were to speak ill of me or ill of the Dhamma or ill of the Sangha (the Order), you should not on that account entertain thoughts of enmity and spite, and be worried. If, monks, you are angry and displeased with them, it will not only impede your mental development but you will also fail to judge how far that speech is right or wrong. You should unravel what is untrue and make it all clear. Also, monks, if others speak highly of me, highly of the Dhamma and the Sangha, you need not on that account be elated; for that too will mar your inner development. You should acknowledge what is right and show the truth of what has been said."[61]

59. These are the *aṭṭha loka-dhamma*, the eight vicissitudes of life.
60. S II 138.
61. D I 3.

There never was an occasion when the Buddha manifested unfriendliness towards anyone—even to his opponents and enemies. There were those who opposed him and his doctrine, yet the Buddha never regarded them as enemies. When others reproached him in strong terms, the Buddha neither manifested anger nor aversion nor uttered an unkind word, but said:

> "As an elephant in the battlefield endures the arrows shot from a bow, even so will I endure abuse and unfriendly expressions of others."[62]

Devadatta

A striking example of this mental attitude is seen in his relation with Devadatta. Devadatta was a cousin of the Buddha who entered the Order and gained supernormal powers of the mundane plane (*puthujjana-iddhi*). Later, however, he began to harbour thoughts of jealousy and ill will toward his kinsman, the Buddha, and his two chief disciples, Sāriputta and Mahā Moggallāna, with the ambition of becoming the leader of the Sangha, the Order of Monks.

Devadatta wormed himself into the heart of Ajātasattu, the young prince, the son of King Bimbisāra. One day when the Blessed One was addressing a gathering at the Veḷuvana Monastery, where the king, too, was present, Devadatta approached the Buddha, saluted him, and said: "Venerable sir, you are now enfeebled with age. May the Master lead a life of solitude free from worry and care. I will direct the Order."

The Buddha rejected this overture and Devadatta departed irritated and disconcerted, nursing hatred and malice toward the Blessed One. Then, with the malicious purpose of causing mischief, he went to Prince Ajātasattu, kindled in him the deadly embers of ambition, and said:

"Young man, you had better kill your father and assume kingship lest you die without becoming the ruler. I shall kill the Blessed One and become the Buddha."

So when Ajātasattu murdered his father and ascended the throne Devadatta suborned ruffians to murder the Buddha, but failing in

62. Dhammapada, 310.

that endeavour, he himself hurled down a rock as the Buddha was climbing up Gijjhakūṭa Hill in Rājagaha. The rock tumbled down, broke in two, and a splinter slightly wounded the Buddha. Later Devadatta made an intoxicated elephant charge at the Buddha; but the animal prostrated himself at the Master's feet, overpowered by his loving-kindness. Devadatta now proceeded to cause a schism in the Sangha, but this discord did not last long. Having failed in all his intrigues, Devadatta retired, a disappointed and broken man. Soon afterwards he fell ill, and on his sick-bed, repenting his follies, he desired to see the Buddha. But that was not to be; for he died on the litter while being carried to the Blessed One. Before his death, however, he uttered repentance and sought refuge in the Buddha.[63]

The Last Days

The Mahā Parinibbāna Sutta,[64] the discourse on the passing away of the Blessed One, records in moving detail all the events that occurred during the last months and days of the Buddha's life.

The Blessed One had now reached the ripe age of eighty; his two chief disciples, Sāriputta and Mahā Moggallāna, had passed away three months earlier. Pajāpatī Gotamī, Yasodharā, and Rāhula were also no more. The Buddha was now at Vesālī, and the rainy season having come, he went together with a great company of monks to Beluva to spend the rains there. There a severe sickness fell upon him, causing him much pain and agony, but the Blessed One, mindful and self-possessed, bore it patiently. He was on the verge of death; but he felt he should not pass away without taking leave of the Order. So with a great effort of will he suppressed that illness and kept his hold on life. His sickness gradually abated, and when quite recovered he called the Venerable Ānanda, his personal attendant, and addressing him said:

> "Ānanda, I am now grown old and full of years, my journey is drawing to a close. I have reached my sum of days, I am turning eighty years of age; and just as a worn out cart, Ānanda, can only with much additional care be made to move along, so the body of the Tathāgata can only be kept

63. *Commentary on the Dhammapada*, Vol. I, p 147.

64. DN 16, translated as *Last Days of the Buddha* (BPS).

going with much infusion of will-power. It is only when the Tathāgata, ceasing to attend to any outward thing and to experience any worldly sensation, attains to the signless (*animitta*) concentration of mind, and dwells in it—it is only then that the body of the Tathāgata is at ease.

"Therefore, Ānanda, be islands unto yourselves. Be your own refuge. Have recourse to none else for refuge. Hold fast to the Dhamma as an island. Hold fast to the Dhamma as a refuge. Resort to no other refuge. Whosoever, Ānanda, either now or after I am gone, shall be islands unto themselves, refuges unto themselves, shall seek no external refuge—it is they, Ānanda, among my disciples who shall reach the very topmost height! But they must be keen to progress."

From Beluva the Buddha journeyed to the Mahāvana, and there calling up an assembly of all the monks residing in the neighbourhood of Vesāli, addressed them saying: "Disciples, the Dhamma realized by me, I have made known to you. Make yourselves masters of the Dhamma, practise it, meditate upon it, and spread it abroad out of pity for the world, for the good and the gain and welfare of gods and men."

The Buddha concluded his exhortation by saying:

"My age is now full ripe, my life draws to its close;
I leave you, I depart, relying on myself alone!
Be earnest then, O disciples, holy, full of thought!
Be steadfast in resolve! Keep watch o'er your own hearts!
Who wearies not but holds fast to this Truth and Law
Shall cross this sea of life, shall make an end of grief."

Worn out with sickness, with feeble limbs, the Blessed One now journeyed on with much difficulty, followed by the Venerable Ānanda and a great company of monks. Even in this last, long, wearisome journey of his, the Buddha never failed in his attention to others. He instructed Cunda, the smith, who offered him his last meal. Then on the way, he stopped for Pukkusa, a disciple of Ālāra Kālāma, replied to all his questions, and so instructed him that Pukkusa offered himself as a follower of the Buddha, the Dhamma, and the Sangha.

The Blessed One now reached the Sāla Grove of the Mallas

at Kusinārā—the journey's end. Knowing that here would be his last resting place, he told the Venerable Ānanda: "I am weary, Ānanda, and would lie down. Spread over for me the couch with its head to the north between the twin sāla trees."

He then lay down on his right side, composed and mindful, with one leg resting on the other. Speaking now to the Venerable Ānanda, the Blessed One said:

> "They who fulfil the greater and lesser duties, they who are correct in life, walking according to the precepts—it is they who rightly honour, reverence, and venerate the Tathāgata, the Perfect One, with the worthiest homage. Therefore, Ānanda, be steady in the fulfilment of the greater and the lesser duties, and be correct in life, walking according to the precepts. Thus, Ānanda, should you train yourselves."

The Last Convert

At that time, a wandering ascetic named Subhadda, who was at Kusinārā, heard the news of the Blessed One's approaching death; and in order to clear up certain doubts that troubled his mind, he hurried to the Sāla Grove to speak to the Buddha. The Venerable Ānanda, however, did not wish the Buddha to be disturbed in his last moments, and though Subhadda made several appeals, access to the Master was refused. The Blessed One overheard the conversation. He knew at once that Subhadda was making his investigations with a genuine desire for knowledge; and knowing that Subhadda was capable of quickly grasping the answers, he desired that Subhadda be allowed to see him.

Subhadda's uncertainty was whether the leaders of the other schools of thought such as Pūraṇa Kassapa, Nigaṇṭha Nātaputta, and others had attained a true understanding. The Blessed One then spoke:

> "In whatsoever Doctrine and Discipline (*dhammavinaya*), Subhadda, the Noble Eightfold Path is not found, neither in it is there found a man of true saintliness of the first, or of the second, or of the third, or of the fourth degree. And in whatsoever Doctrine and Discipline, Subhadda, the Noble Eightfold Path is found, in it is found the man of true

saintliness of the first, and the second, and the third, and the fourth degree.[65] Now, in this Doctrine and Discipline, Subhadda, is found the Noble Eightfold Path, and in it too are found the men of true saintliness of all the four degrees. Void are the systems of other teachers—void of true saints. And in this one, Subhadda, may the brethren live the life that is right, so that the world be not bereft of arahats."

Hearing the words of the Blessed One, Subhadda gained confidence, and took refuge in the Buddha, the Dhamma, and the Sangha. Furthermore, he desired to be admitted into the Order, and the Buddha requested the Venerable Ānanda to receive him. Subhadda thus became the last convert and the last disciple of the Blessed One, and before long by his strenuous effort he attained the final stage of arahatship.

The Last Scene

Now, the Blessed One, addressing the Venerable Ānanda, said:

"I have taught the Dhamma, Ānanda, without making any distinction between exoteric and esoteric doctrine, for in respect of the truth, Ānanda, the Tathāgata has no such thing as the 'closed fist' of a teacher who hides some essential knowledge from the pupil.

"It may be, Ānanda, that in some of you the thought may arise, 'The word of the Master is ended. We have no teacher any more.' But it is not thus, Ānanda, that you should think.

"The Doctrine and the Discipline which I have set forth and laid down for you—let them, after I am gone, be your teacher. It may be, monks, that there may be doubts in the minds of some brethren as to the Buddha, or the Dhamma, or the Sangha, or the path (*magga*) or method (*paṭipadā*). Inquire, monks, freely. Do not have to reproach yourselves afterwards with the thought: 'Our teacher was face to face with us, and we could not bring ourselves to inquire of the Exalted One

65. These four stages are: *sotāpatti* (stream-entry); *sakadāgāmi*, (once-return); *anāgāmi* (non-return); and *arahatta* (the final stage of sainthood). Arahatship is the stage at which fetters are severed and taints rooted out.

when we were face to face with him.'"

When the Buddha had thus spoken the monks were silent.

A second and a third time the Blessed One repeated these words to the monks, and yet the monks were silent. And the Venerable Ānanda said to the Blessed One: "How wonderful a thing is it, Lord, how marvellous! Truly, I believe that in this whole assembly of the monks there is not one who has any doubt or misgivings as to the Buddha or the Dhamma or the Sangha, or the path or the method."

The Blessed One confirmed the words of the Venerable Ānanda, adding that in the whole assembly even the most backward one was assured of final deliverance. And after a short while the Master made his final exhortation to those who wished to follow his teaching now and in the future:

> "Behold now, O monks, I exhort you: impermanent are all compounded things. Work out your deliverance with mindfulness (*vayadhammā saṅkhārā, appamādena sampādetha*)."[66]

These were the last words of the Buddha.

Then the Master entered into those nine successive stages of meditative absorption (*jhāna*) which are of increasing sublimity: first the four fine-material absorptions (*rūpa-jhāna*), then the four immaterial absorptions (*arūpa-jhāna*), and finally the state where perceptions and sensations entirely cease (*saññā-vedayita-nirodha*). Then he returned through all these stages to the first fine-material absorption and rose again to the fourth one. Immediately after having re-entered this stage (which has been described as having "purity of mindfulness due to equanimity"), the Buddha passed away (*parinibbāyi*). He realized Nibbāna that is free from any substratum of further becoming (*parinibbāna*).[67]

In the Mahā Parinibbāna Sutta are recorded, in moving detail, all the events that occurred during the last months and days of the Master's life.

In the annals of history, no man is recorded as having so

66. The Mahā Parinibbāna Sutta (DN 16) records in moving detail all the events that occurred during the last months and days of the Master's life.

67. The passages in quotations are taken with slight alterations from the "Book of the Great Decease" in *Dialogues of the Buddha*, Dīgha Nikāya, Part II.

consecrated himself to the welfare of all beings, irrespective of caste, class, creed, or sex, as the Supreme Buddha. From the hour of his enlightenment to the end of his life, he strove tirelessly and unostentatiously to elevate humanity regardless of the fatigue involved and oblivious to the many obstacles and handicaps that hampered his way. He never relaxed in his exertion for the common weal and was never subjected to moral or spiritual fatigue. Though physically he was not always fit, mentally he was ever vigilant and energetic.

Therefore it is said:

"Ah, wonderful is the Conqueror,
who e'er untiring strives,
for the blessings of all beings,
for the comfort of all lives."

Though twenty-five centuries have gone since the passing away of the Buddha, his message of love and wisdom still exists in its purity, decisively influencing the destinies of humanity. Forests of flowers are daily offered at his shrines and countless millions of lips daily repeat the formula: *Buddhaṃ saraṇaṃ gacchāmi*, "I take refuge in the Buddha." His greatness yet glows today like a sun that blots out lesser lights, and his Dhamma yet beckons the weary pilgrim to Nibbāna's security and peace.

The Four Sublime States

Contemplations on Love, Compassion, Sympathetic Joy, and Equanimity

by

Nyanaponika Thera

WHEEL PUBLICATION NO. 06

Introduction

Four sublime states of mind have been taught by the Buddha:

Love, or loving-kindness (*mettā*)
Compassion (*karuṇā*)
Sympathetic Joy (*muditā*)
Equanimity (*upekkhā*).

In Pali, the language of the Buddhist scriptures, these four are known as *Brahma-vihāra*, a term which may be rendered as excellent, lofty, or sublime states of mind; or alternatively, as Brahma-like, god-like, or divine abodes.

These four attitudes are said to be *excellent* or *sublime* because they are the right or ideal way of conduct towards living beings (*sattesu sammā paṭipatti*). They provide, in fact, the answer to all situations arising from social contact. They are the great removers of tension, the great peacemakers in social conflict, and the great healers of wounds suffered in the struggle of existence. They level social barriers, build harmonious communities, awaken slumbering magnanimity long forgotten, revive joy and hope long abandoned, and promote human brotherhood against the forces of egotism.

The Brahma-vihāras are incompatible with a hating state of mind, and in that they are akin to Brahmā, the divine but transient ruler of the higher heavens in the traditional Buddhist picture of the universe. In contrast to many other conceptions of deities, East and West, who by their own devotees are said to show anger, wrath, jealousy, and "righteous indignation," Brahmā is free from hate; and one who assiduously develops these four sublime states, by conduct and meditation, is said to become an equal of Brahmā (*brahma-samo*). If they become the dominant influence in one's mind, one will be reborn in congenial worlds, the realms of Brahmā. Therefore these states of mind are called *god-like, Brahma-like.*

They are called *abodes* (*vihāra*) because they should become the mind's constant dwelling-places where we feel "at home"; they should not remain merely places of rare and short visits, soon forgotten. In other words, our minds should become thoroughly saturated by them. They should become our inseparable companions, and we should be mindful of them in all our common activities. As the Mettā Sutta, the Song of Loving-Kindness, says:

When standing, walking, sitting, lying down,
Whenever one feels free of tiredness
Let one establish well this mindfulness—
This, it is said, is the Divine Abode.

These four—love, compassion, sympathetic joy, and equanimity—are also known as the *boundless states* (*appamaññā*), because, in their perfection and their true nature, they should not be narrowed by any limitation as to the range of beings towards whom they are extended. They should be non-exclusive and impartial, not bound by selective preferences or prejudices. A mind that has attained to that boundlessness of the Brahma-vihāras will not harbour any national, racial, religious, or class hatred.

But unless rooted in a strong natural affinity with such a mental attitude, it will certainly not be easy for us to effect that boundless application by a deliberate effort of will and to avoid consistently any kind or degree of partiality. To achieve that, in most cases, we shall have to use these four qualities not only as principles of conduct and objects of reflection but also as subjects of methodical meditation. That meditation is called *brahma-vihāra-bhāvanā*, the meditative development of the sublime states. The practical aim is to achieve, with the help of these sublime states, those high stages of mental concentration called *jhāna*, "meditative absorption." The meditations on love, compassion, and sympathetic joy can each produce the attainment of the first three absorptions, while the meditation on equanimity will lead to the fourth only, in which equanimity is the most significant factor.

Generally speaking, persistent meditative practise will have two crowning effects: first, it will make these four qualities sink deep into the heart so that they become spontaneous attitudes not easily overthrown; and second, it will bring out and secure their *boundless* extension, the unfolding of their all-embracing range. In fact, the detailed instructions given in the Buddhist scriptures for the practise of these four meditations are clearly intended to gradually unfold the boundlessness of the sublime states. They systematically break down all barriers restricting their application to particular individuals or places.

In the meditative exercises, the selection of people to whom the thought of love, compassion, or sympathetic joy is directed, proceeds from the easier to the more difficult. For instance, when meditating on loving-kindness, one starts with an aspiration for one's own well-being, using it as a point of reference for gradual extension: "Just as I wish to be happy and free from suffering, so may *that* being ... may *all* beings be happy and free from suffering!" Then one extends the thought of loving-kindness to a person for whom one has a loving respect, as, for instance, a teacher; then to dearly beloved people, to indifferent ones, and finally to enemies, if any, or those disliked. Since this meditation is concerned with the welfare of the living, one should not choose people who have died; one should also avoid choosing people towards whom one may have feelings of sexual attraction.

After one has been able to cope with the hardest task, to direct one's thoughts of loving-kindness to disagreeable people, one should now "break down the barriers" (*sīma-sambheda*). Without making any discrimination between those four types of people, one should extend one's loving-kindness to them equally. At that point of the practise one will have come to the higher stages of concentration: with the appearance of the mental reflex-image (*paṭibhāga-nimitta*), "access concentration" (*upacāra-samādhi*) will have been reached, and further progress will lead to the full concentration (*appanā*) of the first jhāna, then the higher jhānas.

For spatial expansion, the practise starts with those in one's immediate environment such as one's family, then extends to one's neighbours, to the whole street, the town, country, other countries, and the entire world. In "pervasion of the directions," one's thought of loving-kindness is directed first to the east, then to the west, north, south, the intermediate directions, the zenith, and nadir.

The same principles of practise apply to the meditative development of compassion, sympathetic joy, and equanimity, with due variations in the selection of people. Details of the practise will be found in the texts (see *Visuddhimagga*, Chapter IX).

The ultimate aim of attaining the jhānas on the Brahmavihāras is to produce a state of mind that can serve as a firm basis for the liberating insight into the true nature of all phenomena, as being impermanent, liable to suffering, and unsubstantial. A mind that has achieved meditative absorption induced by the sublime states will be pure, tranquil, firm, collected, and free of coarse selfishness. It will thus be well prepared for the final work of deliverance that can be completed only by insight.

The preceding remarks show that there are two ways of developing the sublime states: first by practical conduct and an appropriate direction of thought; and second by methodical meditation aiming at the absorptions. Each will prove helpful to the other. Methodical meditative practise will help love, compassion, joy, and equanimity to become spontaneous. It will help make the mind firmer and calmer in withstanding the numerous irritations in life that challenge us to maintain these four qualities in thoughts, words, and deeds.

On the other hand, if one's practical conduct is increasingly governed by these sublime states, the mind will harbour less resentment, tension, and irritability, the reverberations of which often subtly intrude into the hours of meditation, forming there the "hindrance of restlessness." Our everyday life and thought have a strong influence on the meditative mind; only if the gap between them is persistently narrowed will there be a chance for steady meditative progress and for achieving the highest aim of our practise.

Meditative development of the sublime states will be aided by repeated reflection upon their qualities, the benefits they bestow, and the dangers from their opposites. As the Buddha says, "What a person considers and reflects upon for a long time, to that his mind will bend and incline."

The Basic Passage on the Four Sublime States

From the Discourses of the Buddha

I

Here, monks, a disciple dwells pervading one direction with his heart filled with loving-kindness, likewise the second, the third, and the fourth directions; so above, below, and around; he dwells pervading the entire world everywhere and equally with his heart filled with loving-kindness, abundant, grown great, measureless, free from enmity, and free from distress.

II

Here, monks, a disciple dwells pervading one direction with his heart filled with compassion, likewise the second, the third, and the fourth directions; so above, below, and around; he dwells pervading the entire world everywhere and equally with his heart filled with compassion, abundant, grown great, measureless, free from enmity, and free from distress.

III

Here, monks, a disciple dwells pervading one direction with his heart filled with sympathetic joy, likewise the second, the third, and the fourth directions; so above, below, and around; he dwells pervading the entire world everywhere and equally with his heart filled with sympathetic joy, abundant, grown great, measureless, free from enmity, and free from distress.

IV

Here, monks, a disciple dwells pervading one direction with his heart filled with equanimity, likewise the second, the third, and the fourth directions; so above, below, and around; he dwells pervading the entire world everywhere and equally with his heart filled with equanimity, abundant, grown great, measureless, free from enmity, and free from distress.

Dīgha Nikāya 13

Contemplations on the Four Sublime States

I

Love (Mettā)

Love, without desire to possess, knowing well that in the ultimate sense there is no possession and no possessor: this is the highest love.

Love, without speaking and thinking of "I," knowing well that this so-called "I" is a mere delusion.

Love, without selecting and excluding, knowing well that to do so means to create love's own contrasts: dislike, aversion, and hatred.

Love, embracing all beings: small and great, far and near, be it on earth, in the water, or in the air.

Love, embracing impartially all sentient beings, and not only those who are useful, pleasing, or amusing to us.

Love, embracing all beings, be they noble-minded or low-minded, good or evil. The noble and the good are embraced because love is flowing to them spontaneously. The low-minded and evil-minded are included because they are those who are most in need of love. In many of them the seed of goodness may have died merely because warmth was lacking for its growth, because it perished from cold in a loveless world.

Love, embracing all beings, knowing well that we all are fellow wayfarers through this round of existence—that we all are overcome by the same law of suffering.

Love, but not the sensuous fire that burns, scorches and tortures, that inflicts more wounds than it cures—flaring up now, at the next moment being extinguished, leaving behind more coldness and loneliness than was felt before.

Rather, love that lies like a soft but firm hand on the ailing beings, ever unchanged in its sympathy, without wavering, unconcerned with any response it meets. Love that is comforting coolness to those who burn with the fire of suffering and passion; that is life-giving warmth to those abandoned in the cold desert of loneliness, to those who are shivering in the frost of a loveless world; to those whose hearts have become as if empty and dry by the repeated calls for help, by deepest despair.

Love, that is a sublime nobility of heart and intellect which knows, understands, and is ready to help.

Love, that is strength and gives strength: this is the highest love.

Love, which by the Enlightened One was named "the liberation of the heart," "the most sublime beauty": this is the highest love.

And what is the highest manifestation of love?

To show to the world the path leading to the end of suffering, the path pointed out, trodden, and realized to perfection by Him, the Exalted One, the Buddha.

II

Compassion (Karuṇā)

The world suffers. But most people have their eyes and ears closed. They do not see the unbroken stream of tears flowing through life; they do not hear the cry of distress continually pervading the world. Their own little grief or joy bars their sight, deafens their ears. Bound by selfishness, their hearts turn stiff and narrow. Being stiff and narrow, how should they be able to strive for any higher goal, to realize that only release from selfish craving will effect their own freedom from suffering?

It is compassion that removes the heavy bar, opens the door to freedom, makes the narrow heart as wide as the world. Compassion takes away from the heart the inert weight, the paralyzing heaviness; it gives wings to those who cling to the lowlands of self.

Through compassion the fact of suffering remains vividly present to our mind, even at times when we personally are free from it. It gives us the rich experience of suffering, thus strengthening us to meet it prepared when it does befall us.

Compassion reconciles us to our own destiny by showing us the lives of others, often much harder than ours.

Behold the endless caravan of beings, men and beasts, burdened with sorrow and pain! The burden of every one of them, we also have carried in bygone times during the unfathomable sequence of repeated births. Behold this, and open your heart to compassion!

And this misery may well be our own destiny again! One who is without compassion now will one day cry for it. If sympathy with others is lacking, it will have to be acquired through one's own long and painful experience. This is the great law of life. Knowing this, keep guard over yourself!

Beings, sunk in ignorance, lost in delusion, hasten from one state of suffering to another, not knowing the real cause, not knowing the escape from it. This insight into the general law of suffering is the real foundation of our compassion, not any isolated fact of suffering.

Hence our compassion will also include those who at the moment may be happy, but act with an evil and deluded mind. In their present deeds we shall foresee their future state of distress, and compassion will arise.

The compassion of the wise man does not render him a victim of suffering. His thoughts, words, and deeds are full of pity. But his heart does not waver; unchanged it remains, serene and calm. How else should he be able to help?

May such compassion arise in our hearts! Compassion that is sublime nobility of heart and intellect which knows, understands, and is ready to help.

Compassion that is strength and gives strength: this is highest compassion.

And what is the highest manifestation of compassion?

To show to the world the path leading to the end of suffering, the path pointed out, trodden, and realized to perfection by Him, the Exalted One, the Buddha.

III

Sympathetic Joy (Muditā)

Not only to compassion, but also to joy with others open your heart!

Small, indeed, is the share of happiness and joy allotted to beings! Whenever a little happiness comes to them, then you may rejoice that at least one ray of joy has pierced through the darkness of their lives, and dispelled the gray and gloomy mist that enwraps their hearts.

Your life will gain in joy by sharing the happiness of others as if it were yours. Did you never observe how in moments of happiness people's features change and become bright with joy? Did you never notice how joy rouses people to noble aspirations and deeds, exceeding their normal capacity? Did not such experience fill your own heart with joyful bliss? It is in your power to increase such experience of sympathetic joy, by producing happiness in others, by bringing them joy and solace.

Let us teach real joy to people! Many have unlearned it. Life, though full of woe, holds also sources of happiness and joy, unknown to most. Let us teach people to seek and to find real joy within themselves and to rejoice with the joy of others! Let us teach them to unfold their joy to ever sublimer heights!

Noble and sublime joy is not foreign to the Teaching of the Enlightened One. Wrongly the Buddha's Teaching is sometimes considered to be a doctrine diffusing melancholy. Far from it: the Dhamma leads step by step to an ever purer and loftier happiness.

Noble and sublime joy is a helper on the path to the extinction of suffering. Not one who is depressed by grief, but one possessed of joy finds that serene calmness leading to a contemplative state of mind. And only a mind serene and collected is able to gain the liberating wisdom.

The more sublime and noble the joy of others is, the more justified will be our own sympathetic joy. A cause for our joy with others is their noble life securing them happiness here and in lives hereafter. A still nobler cause for our joy with others is their faith in the Dhamma, their understanding of the Dhamma, their following the Dhamma. Let us give them the help of the Dhamma! Let us strive to become more and more able ourselves to render such help!

Sympathetic joy means a sublime nobility of heart and intellect which knows, understands, and is ready to help.

Sympathetic joy that is strength and gives strength: this is the highest joy.

And what is the highest manifestation of sympathetic joy?

To show to the world the path leading to the end of suffering, the path pointed out, trodden, and realized to perfection by Him, the Exalted One, the Buddha.

IV

Equanimity (Upekkhā)

Equanimity is a perfect, unshakable balance of mind, rooted in insight.

Looking at the world around us, and looking into our own heart, we see clearly how difficult it is to attain and maintain balance of mind.

Looking into life we notice how it continually moves between contrasts: rise and fall, success and failure, loss and gain, honour and blame. We feel how our heart responds to all this with happiness and sorrow, delight and despair, disappointment and satisfaction, hope and fear. These waves of emotion carry us up and fling us down; and no sooner do we find rest, than we are in the power of a new wave again. How can we expect to get a footing on the crest of the waves? How can we erect the building of our lives in the midst of this ever restless ocean of existence, if not on the Island of Equanimity.

A world where that little share of happiness allotted to beings is mostly secured after many disappointments, failures, and defeats;

a world where only the courage to start anew, again and again, promises success;

a world where scanty joy grows amidst sickness, separation, and death;

a world where beings who were a short while ago connected to us by sympathetic joy, are at the next moment in want of our compassion—such a world needs equanimity.

But the kind of equanimity required has to be based on vigilant presence of mind, not on indifferent dullness. It has to be the result of hard, deliberate training, not the casual outcome of a passing mood. But equanimity would not deserve its name if it had to be produced by exertion again and again. In such a case it would surely be weakened and finally defeated by the vicissitudes of life. True equanimity, however, should be able to meet all these severe tests and to regenerate its strength from sources within. It will possess this power of resistance and self-renewal only if it is rooted in insight.

What, now, is the nature of that insight? It is the clear understanding of how all these vicissitudes of life originate, and of our own true nature. We have to understand that the various experiences we undergo result from our *kamma*—our actions in thought, word, and deed—performed in this life and in earlier lives. *Kamma* is the womb from which we spring (*kamma-yoni*), and whether we like it or not, we are the inalienable "owners" of our deeds (*kammassaka*). But as soon as we have performed any action, our control over it is lost: it forever remains with us and inevitably returns to us as our due heritage (*kamma-dāyāda*). Nothing that happens to us comes from an "outer" hostile world foreign to ourselves; everything is the outcome of our own mind and deeds. Because this knowledge frees us from fear, it is the first basis of equanimity. When, in everything that befalls us we only meet ourselves, why should we fear?

If, however, fear or uncertainty should arise, we know the refuge where it can be allayed: our good deeds (*kamma-paṭisaraṇa*). By taking this refuge, confidence and courage will grow within us—confidence in the protecting power of our good deeds done in the past; courage to perform more good deeds right now, despite the discouraging hardships of our present life. For we know that noble and selfless deeds provide the best defence against the hard blows of destiny, that it is never too late but always the right time for good actions. If that refuge, in doing good and avoiding evil, becomes firmly established within us, one day we shall feel assured: "More and more ceases the misery and evil rooted in the past. And this present life—I try to make it spotless and pure. What else can the future bring than increase of the good?" And from that certainty our minds will become serene, and we shall gain the strength of patience and equanimity to bear with all our present adversities. Then our deeds will be our friends (*kamma-bandhu*).

Likewise, all the various events of our lives, being the result of our deeds, will also be our friends, even if they bring us sorrow and pain. Our deeds return to us in a guise that often makes them unrecognizable. Sometimes our actions return to us in the way that others treat us, sometimes as a thorough upheaval in our lives; often the results are against our expectations or contrary to our wills. Such experiences point out to us consequences of our deeds we did not foresee; they render visible half-conscious motives of our former actions which we tried to hide even from ourselves, covering them up with various pretexts. If we learn to see things from this angle, and to read the message conveyed by our own experience, then suffering, too, will be our friend. It will be a stern friend, but a truthful and well-meaning one who teaches us the most difficult subject, knowledge about ourselves, and warns us against abysses towards which we are moving blindly. By looking at suffering as our teacher and friend, we shall better succeed in enduring it with equanimity. Consequently, the teaching of *kamma* will give us a powerful impulse for freeing ourselves from *kamma*, from those deeds which again and again throw us into the suffering of repeated births. Disgust will arise at our own craving, at our own delusion, at our own propensity to create situations which try our strength, our resistance, and our equanimity.

The second insight on which equanimity should be based is the Buddha's teaching of non-self (*anattā*). This doctrine shows that in the ultimate sense deeds are not performed by any self, nor do their results affect any self. Further, it shows that if there is no self, we cannot speak of "my own." It is the delusion of a self that creates suffering and hinders or disturbs equanimity. If this or that quality of ours is blamed, one thinks: "I am blamed" and equanimity is shaken. If this or that work does not succeed, one thinks: "My work has failed" and equanimity is shaken. If wealth or loved ones are lost, one thinks: "What is mine has gone" and equanimity is shaken.

To establish equanimity as an unshakable state of mind, one has to give up all possessive thoughts of "mine," beginning with little things from which it is easy to detach oneself, and gradually working up to possessions and aims to which one's whole heart clings. One also has to give up the counterpart to such thoughts, all egoistic thoughts of "self," beginning with a small section of one's personality, with qualities of minor importance, with small weaknesses one clearly sees, and gradually working up to those emotions and aversions which one regards as the centre of one's being. Thus detachment should be practised.

To the degree we forsake thoughts of "mine" or "self," equanimity will enter our hearts. For how can anything we realize to be foreign and void of a self cause us agitation due to lust, hatred, or grief? Thus the teaching of non-self will be our guide on the path to deliverance, to perfect equanimity.

Equanimity is the crown and culmination of the four sublime states. But this should not be understood to mean that equanimity is the negation of love, compassion, and sympathetic joy, or that it leaves them behind as inferior. Far from that, equanimity includes and pervades them fully, just as they fully pervade perfect equanimity.

The Inter-Relations of the Four Sublime States

How, then, do these four sublime states pervade and suffuse each other?

Unbounded love guards compassion against turning into partiality, prevents it from making discriminations by selecting and excluding, and thus protects it from falling into partiality or aversion against the excluded side.

Love imparts to equanimity its selflessness, its boundless nature, and even its fervour. For fervour, too, transformed and controlled, is part of perfect equanimity, strengthening its power of keen penetration and wise restraint.

Compassion prevents love and sympathetic joy from forgetting that, while both are enjoying or giving temporary and limited happiness, there still exist at that time most dreadful states of suffering in the world. It reminds them that their happiness coexists with measureless misery, perhaps at the next doorstep. It is a reminder to love and sympathetic joy that there is more suffering in the world than they are able to mitigate; that, after the effect of such mitigation has vanished, sorrow and pain are sure to arise anew until suffering is uprooted entirely at the attainment of Nibbāna. Compassion does not allow love and sympathetic joy to shut themselves up against the wide world by confining themselves to a narrow sector of it. Compassion prevents love and sympathetic joy from turning into states of self-satisfied complacency within a jealously-guarded petty happiness. Compassion stirs and urges love to widen its sphere; it stirs and urges sympathetic joy to search for fresh nourishment. Thus it helps both of them to grow into truly boundless states (*appa-maññā*).

Compassion guards equanimity from falling into a cold indifference, and keeps it from indolent or selfish isolation. Until equanimity has reached perfection, compassion urges it to enter again and again the battle of the world, in order to be able to stand the test, by hardening and strengthening itself.

Sympathetic joy holds compassion back from becoming overwhelmed by the sight of the world's suffering, from being absorbed by it to the exclusion of everything else. Sympathetic joy relieves the tension of mind, soothes the painful burning of the compassionate heart. It keeps compassion away from melancholic brooding without purpose, from a futile sentimentality that merely weakens and consumes the strength of mind and heart. Sympathetic joy develops compassion into active sympathy.

Sympathetic joy gives to equanimity the mild serenity that softens its stern appearance. It is the divine smile on the face of the Enlightened One, a smile that persists in spite of his deep knowledge of the world's suffering, a smile that gives solace and hope, fearlessness and confidence: "Wide open are the doors to deliverance," thus it speaks.

Equanimity rooted in insight is the guiding and restraining power for the other three sublime states. It points out to them the direction they have to take, and sees to it that this direction is followed. Equanimity guards love and compassion from being dissipated in vain quests and from going astray in the labyrinths of uncontrolled emotion. Equanimity, being a vigilant self-control for the sake of the final goal, does not allow sympathetic joy to rest content with humble results, forgetting the real aims we have to strive for.

Equanimity, which means "even-mindedness," gives to love an even, unchanging firmness and loyalty. It endows it with the great virtue of patience. Equanimity furnishes compassion with an even, unwavering courage and fearlessness, enabling it to face the awesome abyss of misery and despair which confront boundless compassion again and again. To the active side of compassion, equanimity is the calm and firm hand led by wisdom—indispensable to those who want to practise the difficult art of helping others. And here again equanimity means patience, the patient devotion to the work of compassion.

In these and other ways equanimity may be said to be the crown and culmination of the other three sublime states. The first three, if unconnected with equanimity and insight, may dwindle away due to the lack of a stabilizing factor. Isolated virtues, if unsupported by other qualities which give them either the needed firmness or pliancy, often deteriorate into their own characteristic defects. For instance, loving-kindness, without energy and insight, may easily degenerate into a mere sentimental goodness of weak and unreliable nature. Moreover, such isolated virtues may often carry us in a direction contrary to our original aims and contrary to the welfare of others, too. It is the firm and balanced character of a person that knits isolated virtues into an organic and harmonious whole, within which the single qualities exhibit their best manifestations and avoid the pitfalls of their respective weaknesses. And this is the very function of equanimity, the way it contributes to an ideal relationship between all four sublime states.

Equanimity is a perfect, unshakable balance of mind, rooted in insight. But in its perfection and unshakable nature equanimity is not dull, heartless, and frigid. Its perfection is not due to an emotional "emptiness," but to a "fullness" of understanding, to its being complete in itself. Its unshakable nature is not the immovability of a dead, cold stone, but the manifestation of the highest strength.

In what way, now, is equanimity perfect and unshakable?

Whatever causes stagnation is here destroyed, what dams up is removed, what obstructs is destroyed. Vanished are the whirls of emotion and the meanderings of intellect. Unhindered goes the calm and majestic stream of consciousness, pure and radiant. Watchful mindfulness (*sati*) has harmonized the warmth of faith (*saddhā*) with the penetrative keenness of wisdom (*paññā*); it has balanced strength of will (*viriya*) with calmness of mind (*samādhi*); and these five inner faculties (*indriya*) have grown into inner forces (*bala*) that cannot be lost again. They cannot be lost because they do not lose themselves any more in the labyrinths of the world (*saṃsāra*), in the endless diffuseness of life (*papañca*). These inner forces emanate from the mind and act upon the world, but being guarded by mindfulness, they nowhere bind themselves, and they return unchanged. Love, compassion and sympathetic joy continue to emanate from the mind and act upon the world, but being guarded by equanimity, they cling nowhere, and return unweakened and unsullied.

Thus within the Arahat, the Liberated One, nothing is lessened by giving, and he does not become poorer by bestowing upon others the riches of his heart and mind. The Arahat is like the clear, well-cut crystal which, being without stains, fully absorbs all the rays of light and sends them out again, intensified by its concentrative power. The rays cannot stain the crystal with their various colours. They cannot pierce its hardness, nor disturb its harmonious structure. In its genuine purity and strength, the crystal remains unchanged. "Just as all the streams of the world enter the great ocean, and all the waters of the sky rain into it, but no increase or decrease of the great ocean is to be seen"—even so is the nature of holy equanimity.

Holy equanimity, or—as we may likewise express it—the Arahat endowed with holy equanimity, is the inner centre of the world. But this inner centre should be well distinguished from the numberless apparent centres of limited spheres; that is, their so-called "personalities," governing laws, and so on. All of these are only apparent centres, because they cease to be centres whenever their spheres, obeying the laws of impermanence, undergo a total change of their structure; and consequently the centre of their gravity, material or mental, will shift. But the inner centre of the Arahat's equanimity is unshakable, because it is immutable. It is immutable because it clings to nothing.

Says the Master:

"For one who clings, motion exists; but for one who clings not, there is no motion. Where no motion is, there is stillness. Where stillness is, there is no craving. Where no craving is, there is neither coming nor going. Where no coming nor going is, there is neither arising nor passing away. Where neither arising nor passing away is, there is neither this world nor a world beyond, nor a state between. This, indeed, is the end of suffering."

Udāna 8.4

The Practise of Loving-Kindness (*Mettā*)

As Taught by the Buddha in the Pali Canon

Texts compiled and translated by
Ñāṇamoli Thera

WHEEL PUBLICATION NO.07

Introduction

The word "love"—one of the most compelling in the English language—is commonly used for purposes so widely separated, so gross and so rarefied, as to render it sometimes nearly meaningless. Yet rightly understood, love is the indispensable and essential foundation no less for the growth and purification of the individual as for the construction of a peaceful, progressive, and healthy society.

Now love can be considered in two principal moods: that of lovers for each other, and that of a mother for her child. In its spiritualized form, love can draw its inspiration from either the one or the other. Spiritual love idealizing the love of lovers is often conceived as a consuming flame, and then it sometimes aspires to purification through torture and the violence of martyrdom. But spiritual love that looks for guidance to the love of a mother for her child uplifts itself to the ideal of the pure fount of all safety, welfare, and spiritual health (and a mother best serves her child if she guards her own health). It is this latter kind which the Buddha takes as the basis for his teaching of universal love.

Where Greek distinguishes between sensual *eros* and spiritual *agape*, English makes do with only the one word "love." But Pali, like Sanskrit, has many words covering many shades of meaning. The word chosen by the Buddha for this teaching is *mettā*, from *mitta*, a friend (or better "the true friend in need").

Mettā in the Buddha's teaching finds its place as the first of four kinds of contemplation designed to develop a sound pacific relationship to other living beings. The four are: *mettā*, which will be rendered here by "loving-kindness," *karuṇā*, which is "compassion" or "pity," *muditā*, which is "gladness at others' success," and *upekkhā*, which is "onlooking equanimity." These four are called "divine abodes" (*brahma-vihāra*), perhaps because whoever can maintain any one of them in being for even a moment has lived for that moment as do the *brahma-deva*, the highest gods.

In the Buddha's teaching these four divine abidings, the "greatest of all worldly merit," if practised alone, without insight into the true nature of existence, can lead to rebirth in the highest heavens. But all heavenly existence is without exception impermanent, and at the end of the heavenly lifespan—no matter how long it may last—the being dies and is reborn according to his or her past actions. This is because some craving for existence (for being or even for non-being), and some sort of view of existence that is not in conformity with truth, still remain latent in that person, to burst out again when the result of the good actions is spent. And where one will be reborn after that is unpredictable though it is certain that one will be reborn.

The Buddha's teaching of insight is—in as few words as possible—the training in knowledge and seeing of how it is that anything, whatever it may be whether objective or subjective, comes to be; how it acquires existence only in dependence on conditions, and is impermanent because none of the conditions for its existence is permanent; and how existence, always complex and impermanent, is never safe from pain, and is in need of a self—the will-o'-the-wisp idea, the rainbow mirage, which lures it on, and which it can never find; for the comforting illusion has constantly to be renewed. And that teaching also shows how there is a true way out from fear of pain. In its concise form this is expressed as the Four Noble Truths: the truth of suffering, the truth of suffering's origin (craving or need), the truth of suffering's cessation (through abandonment of craving), and the truth of the way leading to suffering's cessation. These four truths are called the teaching peculiar to Buddhas (*buddhānaṃ sāmukkaṃsika-desanā*) since the discovery of them is what distinguishes Buddhas.

The way (the fourth truth) is also called the Middle Way because it avoids the two extremes of sensual indulgence and of self-mortification. Its eight members are: right view, right intention, right speech, right action, right livelihood, right effort, right mindfulness, and right concentration. The practise of loving-kindness alone will give effect in some measure to all the members except the first: but it is only with right view (without self-deception) that Nibbāna can be reached. Right view gives insight into the real nature of existence of being and non-being, with all its mirages and deceptions, and it is only with its help that the practise of loving-kindness is perfected, lifted out of the impermanence of even the highest heavens, and directed to the true cessation of suffering.

That true cessation comes with the elimination of deception by wrong views and with the exhaustion of the stream of craving in its two forms of lust and hate. This extinction of lust, hate, and delusion, is called Nibbāna.

* * *

The discourses that follow show (in that order) the wretchedness of all anger and hate (there is no righteous anger in the Buddha's teaching); the rewards of loving-kindness; the practise of loving-kindness as a meditation and contemplation; its result in rebirth; the seeing of all things and all existence as impermanent, suffering, and non-self that is needed in order to have a vision in conformity with truth, without which the first stage of unshakable deliverance cannot be reached (for it is with this insight into how being comes to be that it is seen why the price of birth and life, even in heaven, is death); and lastly the attainment of Arahatship, by which all lust, hate, and delusion is overcome, lust for being and even for non-being cured, and rebirth ended for good.

But first, before coming to these discourses, some details from the meditation manual, the *Visuddhimagga* or "Path of Purification," will not be out of place.

Mettā (loving-kindness) is defined as follows: "Loving-kindness has the mode of friendliness for its characteristic. Its natural function is to promote friendliness. It is manifested as the disappearance of ill will. Its footing is seeing with kindness. When it succeeds it eliminates ill will. When it fails it degenerates into selfish affectionate desire."

The *Visuddhimagga* recommends going to some quiet place, where one can sit down in a comfortable position. Then, before starting the actual meditation, it is helpful to consider the dangers in hate and the benefits offered by forbearance: for it is a purpose of this meditation to displace hate by forbearance, and besides, one cannot avoid dangers one has not come to see or cultivate benefits one does not yet know.

Then there are certain types of persons towards whom loving-kindness should not be developed in the first stages. The attempt, at the outset to regard a disliked person as dear to one is fatiguing, and likewise trying to regard a dearly loved friend with neutrality, and when an enemy is recalled anger springs up. Again, it should not be directed towards members of the opposite sex to begin with, for this may arouse lust. Right at the start, the meditation of loving-kindness should be developed towards oneself repeatedly in this way: "May I be happy and free from suffering," or "May I keep myself free from hostility and trouble and live happily" (though this will never produce the full absorption of contemplation). It is by cultivating the thought "May I be happy" with oneself as example, that one begins to be interested in the welfare and happiness of other living beings, and to feel in some sense their happiness as if it were one's own: "Just as I want happiness and fear pain, just as I want to live and not to die, so do other beings." So one should first become familiar with pervading oneself as an example with loving-kindness. Only then should one choose someone who is liked and admired and much respected. The meditation can then be developed towards that person, remembering endearing words or virtues of his, and thinking such thoughts about him as "May he be happy." (In this way the full absorption of contemplation, in which the word-meditation is left behind, can be attained.)

When this has become familiar, one can begin to practise loving-kindness towards a dearly beloved companion, and then towards a neutral person as very dear, or towards an enemy as neutral. It is when dealing with an enemy that anger can arise, and all means must be tried in order to get rid of it. As soon as this has succeeded, one will be able to regard an enemy without resentment and with loving-kindness in the same way as one does the admired person, the dearly loved friend, and the neutral person. Then with repeated practise, jhāna absorption should be attained in all cases. Loving-kindness can now be effectively maintained in being towards all beings; or to certain groups of beings at a time, or in one direction at a time to all; or to certain groups in succession.

Loving-kindness ought to be brought to the point where there are no longer any barriers set between persons, and for this the following example is given: Suppose a man is with a dear, a neutral, and a hostile person, himself being the fourth; then bandits come to him and say, "We need one of you for human sacrifice." Now, if that man thinks, "Let them take this one, or that one," he has not yet broken down the barriers; and also if he thinks, "Let them take me but not these three," he has not broken down the barriers either. Why not? Because he seeks the harm of the one whom he wishes to be taken and the welfare of only the other three. It is only when he does not see a single one among the four to be chosen in preference to the other three, and directs his mind quite impartially towards himself and the other three, that he has broken down the barriers.

Loving-kindness has its "enemy within" in lust, which easily gains entry in its wake, and it must be well guarded against this. The remedy for lust is the contemplation of foulness (in the body) as in the Satipaṭṭhāna Sutta (Dīgha Nikāya Sutta No. 22 and Majjhima Nikāya Sutta No. 10). Its "enemy without" is its opposite, ill will, which finds its opportunities in the intervals when loving-kindness is not being actively practised. (Full details will be found in Chapter IX of the *Visuddhimagga.*)

In many discourses the Buddha lays emphasis on the need to balance contemplative concentration with understanding. The one supplies the deficiencies of the other. Concentration alone lacks direction; understanding alone is dry and tiring. In the discourses that follow the simile of a mother's love for her child is given. Now the incomparable value of a mother's love, which sets it above all other kinds, lies in the fact that she understands her child's welfare—her love is not blind. Not love alone, nor faith alone, can ever bring one all the way to the cessation of suffering, and that is why the Buddha, as the Supreme Physician, prescribes the development of five faculties in balanced harmony: the faculties of faith, energy, mindfulness, concentration, and understanding.

So concentration of love in its highest form—the form that only the Buddha, and no one else, has given—seen as a means to the end, becomes absolutely purified in one who has gained personal experience of the "supreme safety from bondage" (*anuttara yogakkhema*), which is Nibbāna, as the ultimate welfare of beings. For he knows from his own experience that their welfare is only assured permanently when suffering has been diagnosed, its origin abandoned, its cessation realized, and the way maintained in being.

Then he has verified the Four Noble Truths for himself and can properly evaluate beings' welfare.

"Bhikkhus, it is through not discovering, not penetrating to four truths that both you and I have been trudging and travelling through the round of rebirths for so long" (Dīgha Nikāya II 90). For the benefit of all those who have not yet done this, the way has been discovered and pointed out by the Buddha and its practicability attested by the Arahats.

The last discourse given in this collection, in fact, shows how this personal discovery and penetration to the Four Noble Truths can be achieved by using loving-kindness as the vehicle.

Note on Sources

References to the Aṅguttara Nikāya are to *nipāta* followed by the number of the sutta. The reference to Saṃyutta Nikāya is to the *saṃyutta* followed by the number of the sutta.

The Practise of Loving-Kindness

The Wretchedness of Anger

1. From the Aṅguttara Nikāya, 7:60 (spoken by the Buddha)

Bhikkhus, seven things gratifying and helpful to an enemy befall one who is angry, whether a woman or a man. What are the seven?

Here, bhikkhus, an enemy wishes thus for his enemy: "Let him be ugly." Why is that? No enemy relishes an enemy's beauty. Now when this person is angry, a prey to anger, ruled by anger, be he ever so well bathed and well anointed, with hair and beard trimmed, and clothed in white, yet he is ugly through his being a prey to anger. This is the first thing gratifying and helpful to an enemy that befalls one who is angry, whether a woman or a man.

Also an enemy wishes thus for his enemy: "Let him lie in pain." Why is that? No enemy relishes an enemy's lying in comfort. Now when this person is angry, a prey to anger, ruled by anger, for all he may lie on a couch spread with rugs, blankets, and counterpanes with a deerskin cover, a canopy, and red cushions for the head and feet, yet he lies only in pain through his being a prey to anger. This is the second thing gratifying to an enemy that befalls one who is angry, whether a woman or a man.

Also an enemy wishes thus for his enemy: "Let him have no prosperity." Why is that? No enemy relishes an enemy's prosperity. Now when this person is angry, a prey to anger, ruled by anger, he mistakes bad for good and he mistakes good for bad, and each being taken wrongly in the other's sense, these things for long conduce to his harm and suffering, through his being a prey to anger. This is the third thing gratifying and helpful to an enemy that befalls one who is angry, whether a woman or a man.

Also an enemy wishes thus for his enemy: "Let him not be rich." Why is that? No enemy relishes an enemy's having riches. Now when a person is angry, a prey to anger, should he have riches gained by endeavour, built up by the strength of his arm, earned by sweat, lawful and lawfully acquired, yet the king's treasury gathers (in fines) through his being a prey to anger. This is the fourth thing gratifying and helpful to an enemy that befalls one who is a prey to anger, whether a woman or a man.

Also an enemy wishes thus for his enemy: "Let him not be famous." Why is that? No enemy relishes an enemy's having fame. Now when a person is angry, a prey to anger, ruled by anger, what fame he may have acquired by diligence he loses through his being a prey to anger. This is the fifth thing gratifying and helpful to an enemy that befalls one who is a prey to anger, whether a woman or a man.

Also an enemy wishes thus for his enemy: "Let him have no friends." Why is that? No enemy relishes an enemy's having friends. Now when this person is angry, a prey to anger, ruled by anger, the friends he may have, his companions, relatives, and kin, will keep away from him through his being a prey to anger. This is the sixth thing gratifying and helpful to an enemy that befalls one who is a prey to anger, whether a woman or a man.

Also an enemy wishes thus for his enemy: "Let him, on the dissolution of the body, after death, reappear in a state of deprivation, in a bad destination, in perdition, even in hell." Why is that? No enemy relishes an enemy's going to a good destination. Now when this person is angry, a prey to anger, ruled by anger, he misconducts himself in body, speech, and mind, and by his misconduct in body, speech, and mind, on the dissolution of the body, after death, he reappears in a state of deprivation, in a bad destination, in perdition, even in hell, through his being a prey to anger. This is the seventh thing gratifying and helpful to an enemy that befalls one who is angry, whether a woman or a man.

When anger does possess a man,
He looks ugly; he lies in pain;
What benefit he may come by
He misconstrues as a mischance;
He loses property (through fines)
Because he has been working harm
Through acts of body and speech
By angry passion overwhelmed;
The wrath and rage that madden him
Gain him a name of ill-repute;
His fellows, relatives and kin,
Will seek to shun him from afar;
And anger fathers misery:
This fury does so cloud the mind
Of man that he cannot discern
This fearful inner danger.

An angry man no meaning knows,
No angry man sees the Dhamma,
So wrapped in darkness, as if blind,
Is he whom anger dogs.

Someone a man in anger hurts;
But, when his anger is later spent
With difficulty or with ease,
He suffers as if seared by fire.
His look betrays the sulkiness
Of some dim smoky smoldering glow.
Whence may flare up an anger-blaze
That sets the world of men aflame.
He has no shame or conscience curb,
No kindly words come forth from him,
There is no island refuge for
The man whom anger dogs.

Such acts as will ensure remorse,
Such as are far from the true Dhamma:
It is of these that I would tell,
So harken to my words.

Anger makes man a parricide,
Anger makes him a matricide,
Anger can make him slay the saint
As he would kill the common man.
Nursed and reared by a mother's care,
He comes to look upon the world,
Yet the common man in anger kills
The being who gave him life.

No being but seeks his own self's good,
None dearer to him than himself,
Yet men in anger kill themselves,
Distraught for reasons manifold:
For crazed they stab themselves with daggers,
In desperation swallow poison,
Perish hanged by ropes, or fling
Themselves over a precipice.
Yet how their life-destroying acts
Bring death unto themselves as well,
That they cannot discern, and that
Is the ruin anger breeds.

This secret place, with anger's aid,
Is where mortality sets the snare.
To blot it out with discipline,
With vision, strength, and understanding,
To blot each fault out one by one,
The wise man should apply himself,
Training likewise in the true Dhamma;
"Let smoldering be far from us."
Then rid of wrath and free from anger,
And rid of lust and free from envy,
Tamed, and with anger left behind,
Taintless, they reach Nibbāna.

How to Get Rid of Anger

2. From the Dhammapada, vv. 3–5, and Majjhima Nikāya, Sutta 128 (spoken by the Buddha)

"He abused me, he beat me,
He worsted me, he robbed me."
Hate never is allayed in those
Who cherish suchlike enmity.

"He abused me, he beat me,
He worsted me, he robbed me."
Hate surely is allayed in those
Who cherish no such enmity.

For enmity by enmity
Is never in this world allayed;
It is allayed by amity—
That is an ancient principle.

3. From the Aṅguttara Nikāya, 5:161 (spoken by the Buddha)

Bhikkhus, there are these five ways of removing annoyance, by which annoyance can be entirely removed by a bhikkhu when it arises in him. What are the five?

Loving-kindness can be maintained in being towards a person with whom you are annoyed: this is how annoyance with him can be removed. Compassion can be maintained in being towards a person with whom you are annoyed; this too is how annoyance with him can be removed. Equanimity can be maintained in being towards a person with whom you are annoyed; this too is how annoyance with him can be removed. The forgetting and ignoring of a person with whom you are annoyed can be practised; this too is how annoyance with him can be removed. Ownership of deeds in a person with whom you are annoyed can be concentrated upon thus: "This good person is owner of his deeds, heir to his deeds, his deeds are the womb from which he is born, his deeds are his kin for whom he is responsible, his deeds are his refuge, he is heir to his deeds, be they good or bad." This too is how annoyance with him can be removed. These are the five ways of removing annoyance, by which annoyance can be entirely removed in a bhikkhu when it arises in him.

Loving-Kindness and Its Rewards

4. From the Majjhima Nikāya, Sutta 21 (spoken by the Buddha)

Bhikkhus, there are five modes of speech that others may use when they address you. Their speech may be timely or untimely, true or untrue, gentle or harsh, for good or harm, and may be accompanied by thoughts of loving-kindness or by inner hate.

Suppose a man came with a hoe and a basket, and he said, "I shall make this great earth to be without earth"; and he dug here and there and strewed here and there, and spat here and there, and relieved himself here and there, saying, "Be without earth, be without earth." What do you think, bhikkhus, would that man make this great earth to be without earth?—No, venerable sir. Why is that? Because this great earth is deep and measureless; it cannot possibly be made to be without earth. So the man would reap only weariness and disappointment.

Suppose a man came with lac or gamboge or indigo or carmine, and he said, "I shall draw pictures, I shall make pictures appear, on this empty space." What do you think, bhikkhus, would that man draw pictures, would he make pictures appear, on that empty space?—No, venerable sir. Why is that? Because that empty space is formless and invisible; he cannot possibly draw pictures, make pictures appear there. So the man would reap weariness and disappointment.

So too, bhikkhus, there are these five modes of speech that others may use when they address you. Their speech may be timely or untimely, true or untrue, gentle or harsh, for good or for harm, and may be accompanied by thoughts of loving-kindness or by inner hate. Now this is how you should train yourselves here: "Our minds will remain unaffected, we shall utter no bad words, we shall abide friendly and compassionate, with thoughts of loving-kindness and no inner hate. We shall abide with loving-kindness in our hearts extending to that person, and we shall dwell extending it to the entire world as our object, with our hearts abundant, exalted, measureless in loving-kindness, without hostility or ill will." That is how you should train yourselves.

Even were bandits savagely to sever you limb from limb with a two-handled saw, he who on that account entertained hate in his heart would not be one who carried out my teaching.

Bhikkhus, you should keep this instruction on the Simile of the Saw constantly in mind.

5. From the Itivuttaka, Sutta 27 (spoken by the Buddha)

Bhikkhus, whatever kinds of worldly merit there are, all are not worth one sixteenth part of the heart-deliverance of loving-kindness; in shining and beaming and radiance the heart-deliverance of loving-kindness far excels them.

Just as whatever light there is of stars, all is not worth one sixteenth part of the moon's; in shining and beaming and radiance the moon's light far excels it; and just as in the last month of the rains, in the autumn when the heavens are clear, the sun as it climbs the heavens drives all darkness from the sky with its shining and beaming and radiance; and just as, when night is turning to dawn, the morning star is shining and beaming and radiating; so too, whatever kinds of worldly merit there are, all are not worth one sixteenth part of the heart-deliverance of loving-kindness; in shining and beaming and radiance the heart-deliverance of loving-kindness far excels them.

6. From the Aṅguttara Nikāya, 11:16 (spoken by the Buddha)

Bhikkhus, when the heart-deliverance of loving-kindness is maintained in being, made much of, used as one's vehicle, used as one's foundation, established, consolidated, and properly managed, then eleven blessings can be expected. What are the eleven?

One sleeps in comfort; one wakes in comfort; one dreams no evil dreams; one is dear to human beings; one is dear to non-human beings; the gods guard one; no fire or poison or weapon harms one; one's mind can be quickly concentrated; the expression of one's face is serene; one dies without falling into confusion; and, even if one fails to penetrate any further, one will pass on to the world of High Divinity, to the Brahma world.

7. From the Saṃyutta Nikāya, 20:3 (spoken by the Buddha)

Bhikkhus, just as clans with many women and few men are readily ruined by robbers and bandits, so too any bhikkhu who has not maintained in being and made much of the heart-deliverance of loving-kindness is readily ruined by non-human beings. And just as clans with few women and many men are not readily ruined by robbers and bandits; so too any bhikkhu who maintains in being and makes much of the heart-deliverance of loving-kindness is not readily ruined by non-human beings.

So, bhikkhus, you should train in this way: "The heart-deliverance of loving-kindness will be maintained in being and made much of by us, used as our vehicle, used as our foundation, established, consolidated, and properly managed." That is how you should train.

8. From the Aṅguttara Nikāya, 1:53–55, 386 (spoken by the Buddha)

Bhikkhus, if a bhikkhu cultivates loving-kindness for as long as a fingersnap, he is called a bhikkhu. He is not destitute of *jhāna* meditation, he carries out the Master's teaching, he responds to advice, and he does not eat the country's almsfood in vain. So what should be said of those who make much of it?

9. From the Dīgha Nikāya, Sutta 33 (spoken by the Arahat Sāriputta)

Here, friends, a bhikkhu might say: "When the heart-deliverance of loving-kindness is maintained in being and made much of by me, used as my vehicle, used as my foundation, established, consolidated, and properly managed, ill will nevertheless still invades my heart and remains." He should be told: "Not so! Let the worthy one not say so. Let him not misrepresent the Blessed One. It is not good to misrepresent the Blessed One. The Blessed One would not express it thus." Friends, it is impossible, it cannot happen, that when the heart-deliverance of loving-kindness is maintained in being and made much of, used as one's vehicle, used as one's foundation, established, consolidated, and properly managed, ill will can invade the heart and remain; for this, that is to say, the heart-deliverance of loving-kindness, is the escape from ill will.

Loving-Kindness as a Contemplation

10. Metta Sutta From the Suttanipāta, vv. 143 –152 (spoken by the Buddha)

What should be done by one skillful in good
So as to gain the State of Peace is this:

Let him be able, and upright and straight,
Easy to speak to, gentle, and not proud,
Contented too, supported easily,
With few tasks, and living very lightly;
His faculties serene, prudent, and modest,
Unswayed by the emotions of the clans;
And let him never do the slightest thing
That other wise men might hold blameable.

(And let him think:) "In safety and in bliss
May creatures all be of a blissful heart!
Whatever breathing beings there may be,
No matter whether they are frail or firm,
With none excepted, be they long or big
Or middle-sized, or be they short or small
Or thick, as well as those seen or unseen,
Or whether they are dwelling far or near,
Existing or yet seeking to exist.
May creatures all be of a blissful heart!

Let no one work another one's undoing
Or even slight him at all anywhere.
And never let them wish each other ill
Through provocation or resentful thought."

And just as might a mother with her life
Protect the son that was her only child,

So let him then for every living thing
Maintain unbounded consciousness in being.
And let him too with love for all the world
Maintain unbounded consciousness in being
Above, below, and all round in between,
Untroubled, with no enemy or foe.
And while he stands or walks or while he sits
Or while he lies down, free from drowsiness,
Let him resolve upon this mindfulness:
This is Divine Abiding here, they say.

But when he has no trafficking with views,
Is virtuous, and has perfected seeing,
And purges greed for sensual desires,
He surely comes no more to any womb.

11. Methodical Practise, from the Paṭisambhidāmagga (traditionally ascribed to the Arahat Sāriputta)

The heart-deliverance of loving-kindness is practised with unspecified extension, with specified extension, and with directional extension.

That with unspecified extension is practised in five ways as follows: May all beings be freed from enmity, distress, and anxiety, and may they guide themselves to bliss.

May all breathing things ... all creatures ... all persons ... May all those who are embodied be freed from enmity, distress, and anxiety, and may they guide themselves to bliss.

That with specified extension is practised in seven ways as follows: May all women be freed from enmity, distress, and anxiety, and may they guide themselves to bliss. May all men ... all noble ones ... all who are not noble ones ... all deities ... all human beings ... May all those in the states of deprivation be freed from enmity, distress, and anxiety, and may they guide themselves to bliss.

That with directional extension is practised in ten ways as follows: May all beings in the eastern direction be freed from enmity, distress, and anxiety, and may they guide themselves to bliss. May all beings in the western direction ... in the northern direction ... in the southern direction ... in the eastern intermediate direction ... in the western intermediate direction ... in the northern intermediate direction ... in the southern intermediate direction ... in the downward direction ... May all those in the upward direction be freed from enmity, distress, and anxiety, and may they guide themselves to bliss.

May all breathing things ... May all creatures ... May all persons ... May all who are embodied ... May all women ... May all men ... May all noble ones ... May all who are not noble ones ... May all deities ... May all human beings ...

May all those in the states of deprivation in the eastern direction be freed from enmity, distress, and anxiety, and may they guide themselves to bliss ... May all those in states of deprivation in the upward direction be freed from enmity, distress, and anxiety, and may they guide themselves to bliss.

12. From the Abhidhamma Piṭaka, Appamaññavibhaṅga (traditionally ascribed to the Buddha)

And how does a bhikkhu abide with his heart imbued with loving-kindness extending over one direction? Just as he would feel friendliness on seeing a dearly beloved person, so he extends loving-kindness to all creatures.

As practised *without* Insight into the Four Noble Truths.

13. From the Majjhima Nikāya, Sutta 99 (spoken by the Buddha)

"Master Gotama, I have heard it said that the Monk Gotama teaches the path to the retinue of the High Divinity. It would be good if Master Gotama would teach me that."

"Then listen and attend carefully to what I shall say."

"Even so, sir," the student Subha Todeyyaputta replied. The Blessed One said this:

"And what is the path to the retinue of the High Divinity? Here a bhikkhu abides with his heart imbued with loving-kindness extending over one quarter, likewise the second quarter, likewise the third quarter, likewise the fourth quarter, and so above, below, around, and everywhere and to all as to himself; he abides with his heart abundant, exalted, measureless in loving-kindness, without hostility or ill will, extending over the all-encompassing world. While this heart-deliverance of loving-kindness is maintained in being in this way, no action restricted by limited measurement is found there, none persists there. Just as a vigorous trumpeter could easily make himself heard in the four directions, so too when the heart-deliverance of loving-kindness is maintained in being in this way no action restricted by limited measurement is found there, none persists there. This is the path to the retinue of the High Divinity."

As practised *with* Insight into the Four Noble Truths.

14. From the Aṅguttara Nikāya, 4:125 (spoken by the Buddha)

Here, bhikkhus, a certain person abides with his heart imbued with loving-kindness extending over one quarter, likewise the second quarter, likewise the third quarter, likewise the fourth quarter, and so above, below, around, and everywhere, and to all as to himself; he abides with his heart abundant, exalted, measureless in loving-kindness, without hostility or ill will, extending over the all-encompassing world.

He finds gratification in that, finds it desirable and looks to it for his well-being; steady and resolute thereon, he abides much in it, and if he dies without losing it, he reappears among the gods of a High Divinity's retinue.

Now the gods of a High Divinity's retinue have a lifespan of one aeon. An ordinary person (who has not attained the Noble Eightfold Path) stays there for his lifespan; but after he has used up the whole lifespan enjoyed by those gods, he leaves it all, and (according to what his past deeds may have been) he may go down even to hell, or to an animal womb, or to the ghost realm. But a disciple of the Perfect One stays there (in that heaven) for his lifespan, and after that he has used up the whole life span enjoyed by those gods, he eventually attains complete extinction of lust, hate, and delusion in that same kind of heavenly existence.

It is this that distinguishes, that differentiates, the wise disciple who is ennobled (by attainment of the noble path) from the unwise ordinary man, when, that is to say, there is a destination for reappearance (after death, but an Arahat has made an end of birth).

15. From the Aṅguttara Nikāya, 4:126 (spoken by the Buddha)

Here, bhikkhus, a certain person abides with his heart imbued with loving-kindness extending ... over the all-encompassing world.

Now whatever therein (during that state of contemplation) exists classifiable as form, classifiable as a feeling (of pleasure, pain, or neutrality), classifiable as perception, classifiable as determinative acts, or classifiable as consciousness, such things he sees as impermanent, as liable to suffering, as a disease, as a cancer, as a barb, as a calamity, as an affliction, as alien, as being worn away, as void, as not-self. On the dissolution of the body, after death, he reappears (as a non-returner) in the retinue of the Gods of the Pure Abodes (where there are only those who have reached the noble path and where extinction of greed, hate, and delusion is reached in less than seven lives without return to this world). And this kind of reappearance is not shared by ordinary men (who have not reached the Noble Eightfold Path).

The Arahat

16. From the Aṅguttara Nikāya, 3:66 (spoken by the Arahat Nandaka)

Thus I heard. On one occasion the Venerable Nandaka was living at Sāvatthī in the Eastern Monastery, Migāra's Mother's Palace. Then Migāra's grandson, Sāḷha, and Pekhuniya's grandson, Rohana, went to the Venerable Nandaka, and after salutation they sat down at one side. When they had done so the Venerable Nandaka said to Migāra's grandson Sāḷha:

"Come, Sāḷha, do not be satisfied with hearsay or with tradition or with legendary lore or with what has come down in scriptures or with conjecture or with logical inference or with weighing evidence or with a liking for a view after pondering it or with someone else's ability or with the thought, 'The monk is our teacher.' When you know in yourself, 'These things are unprofitable, liable to censure, condemned by the wise, being adopted and put into effect, they lead to harm and suffering,' then you should abandon them. What do you think? Is there greed?"—"Yes, venerable sir."—"Covetousness is the meaning of that, I say. Through greed a covetous man kills breathing things, takes what is not given, commits adultery, and utters falsehood, and he gets another to do likewise. Will that be long for his harm and suffering?"—"Yes, venerable sir."—"What do you think, is there hate?"—"Yes, venerable sir."—"Ill-will is the meaning of that, I say. Through hate a malevolent man kills breathing things ... Will that be long for his harm and suffering?"—"Yes, venerable sir."—"What do you think? Is there delusion?" —"Yes, venerable sir."—"Ignorance is the meaning of that, I say. Through ignorance a deluded man kills breathing things ... Will that be long for his harm and suffering?"—"Yes, venerable sir."

"What do you think? Are these things profitable or unprofitable?"—"Unprofitable, venerable sir."—"Reprehensible or blameless?"—"Reprehensible, venerable sir."—"Condemned or commended by the wise?"—"Condemned by the wise, venerable sir."—"Being adopted and put into effect, do they lead to harm and suffering, or do they not, or how does it appear to you in this case?"—"Being adopted and put into effect, venerable sir, they lead to harm and suffering. So it appears in this case."—"Now that was the reason why I told you 'Come, Sāḷha, do not be satisfied with hearsay ... When you know in yourself, "These things are unprofitable," then you should abandon them.'

"Come, Sāḷha, do not be satisfied with hearsay ... or with the thought, 'The monk is our teacher.' When you know in yourself, 'These things are profitable, blameless, commended by the wise, being adopted and put into effect they lead to welfare and happiness,' then you should practise them and abide in them. What do you think? Is there non-greed?"—"Yes, venerable sir."—"Uncovetousness is the meaning of that, I say. Through non-greed an uncovetous man does not kill breathing things or take what is not given or commit adultery or utter falsehood, and he gets another to do likewise. Will that be long for his welfare and happiness?"—"Yes, venerable sir."—"What do you think? Is there non-hate?"—"Yes, venerable sir."—"Non ill will is the meaning of that, I say. Through non ill will an unmalevolent man does not kill breathing things ... Will that be long for his welfare and happiness?”—“Yes, venerable sir.”—“What do you think? Is there non-delusion?”—“Yes, venerable sir.”—“True knowledge is the meaning of that, I say. Through non-delusion a man with true knowledge does not kill breathing things ... Will that be long for his welfare and happiness?”—“Yes, venerable sir.”

“What do you think? Are these things profitable or unprofitable?”—“Profitable, venerable sir.”—“Reprehensible or blameless?”—“Blameless, venerable sir.” —“Condemned or commended by the wise?”— “Commended by the wise, venerable sir.”—“Being adopted and put into effect, do they lead to welfare and happiness, or do they not, or how does it appear to you in this case?”—“Being adopted and put into effect, venerable sir, they lead to welfare and happiness. So it appears to us in this case.”—“Now that was the reason why I told you, ‘Come Sāḷha, do not be satisfied with hearsay ... when you know in yourself, “These things are profitable ...” then you should practise them and abide in them.’

“Now a disciple who is ennobled (by reaching the noble path), who has rid himself in this way of covetousness and ill will and is undeluded, abides with his heart imbued with loving-kindness extending over one quarter, likewise the second quarter, likewise the third quarter, likewise the fourth quarter, and so above, below, around, and everywhere, and to all as to himself; he abides with his heart abundant, exalted, measureless in loving-kindness, without hostility or ill will, extending over the all-encompassing world. He abides with his heart imbued with compassion ... gladness ... equanimity ... extending over the all-encompassing world. Now he understands this state of contemplation in this way: ‘There is this (state of divine abiding in me who have entered the stream). There is what has been abandoned (which is the amount of greed, hate, and delusion exhausted by the stream-entry path). There is a superior goal (which is Arahatship). And there is an ultimate escape from this whole field of perception.’

“When he knows and sees in this way, his heart is liberated from the taint of sensual desire, from the taint of being, and from the taint of ignorance. When liberated (by reaching the Arahat path), there comes thereafter the knowledge that it is liberated. He knows that birth is ended, that the divine life has been lived out, that what had to be done is done, and that there is no more of this to come. He understands thus: 'Formerly there was greed which was bad, and now there is none, which is good. Formerly there was hate, which was bad, and now there is none, which is good. Formerly there was delusion, which was bad, and now there is none, which is good.' So here and now in this very life he is parched no more (by the fever of craving's thirst, his fires of greed, hate and delusion are) extinguished and cooled out; experiencing bliss, he abides (for the remainder of his last lifespan) divinely pure in himself."

Kālāma Sutta

The Buddha's Charter of Free Inquiry

Translated from the Pali by

Soma Thera

WHEEL PUBLICATION NO. 08

Preface

The instruction to the Kālāmas (Kālāma Sutta) is justly famous for its encouragement of free inquiry; the spirit of the sutta signifies a teaching that is exempt from fanaticism, bigotry, dogmatism, and intolerance.

The reasonableness of the Dhamma, the Buddha's teaching, is chiefly evident in its welcoming careful examination at all stages of the path to enlightenment. Indeed the whole course of training for wisdom culminating in the purity of the consummate one (the arhat) is intimately bound up with examination and analysis of things internal: the eye and visible objects, the ear and sounds, the nose and smells, the tongue and tastes, the body and tactile impressions, the mind and ideas.

Thus since all phenomena have to be correctly understood in the field of the Dhamma, insight is operative throughout. In this sutta it is active in rejecting the bad and adopting the good way; in the extracts given below in clarifying the basis of knowledge of conditionality and arhatship. Here it may be mentioned that the methods of examination found in the Kālāma Sutta and in the extracts cited here, have sprung from the knowledge of things as they are and that the tenor of these methods are implied in all straight thinking. Further, as penetration and comprehension, the constituents of wisdom are the result of such thinking, the place of critical examination and analysis in the development of right vision is obvious. Where is the wisdom or vision that can descend, all of a sudden, untouched and uninfluenced by critical thought?

The Kālāma Sutta, which sets forth the principles that should be followed by a seeker of truth, and which contains a standard things are judged by, belongs to a framework of the Dhamma; the four solaces taught in the sutta point out the extent to which the Buddha permits suspense of judgment in matters beyond normal cognition. The solaces show that the reason for a virtuous life does not necessarily depend on belief in rebirth or retribution, but on mental well-being acquired through the overcoming of greed, hate, and delusion.

More than fifty years ago, Moncure D. Conway, the author of *My Pilgrimage to the Wise Men of the East*, visited Colombo.

He was a friend of Ponnambalam Ramanathan (then Solicitor General of Ceylon), and together with him Conway went to the Vidyodaya Pirivena to learn something of the Buddha's teaching from Hikkaduve Siri Sumangala Nāyaka Thera, the founder of the institution. The Nāyaka Thera explained to them the principles contained in the Kālāma Sutta and at the end of the conversation Ramanathan whispered to Conway: "Is it not strange that you and I, who come from far different religions and regions, should together listen to a sermon from the Buddha in favour of that free thought, that independence of traditional and fashionable doctrines, which is still the vital principle of human development?"—Conway: "Yes, and we with the (Kālāma) princes pronounce his doctrines good."

Supplementary Texts

"Friend Saviṭṭha, apart from faith, apart from liking, apart from what has been acquired by repeated hearing, apart from specious reasoning, and from a bias towards a notion that has been pondered over, I know this, I see this: 'Decay and death are due to birth.'" (SN 12:68)

"Here a bhikkhu, having seen an object with the eye, knows when greed, hate, and delusion are within, 'Greed, hate, and delusion are in me'; he knows when greed, hate, and delusion are not within, 'Greed, hate, and delusion are not in me.' Bhikkhus, have these things to be experienced through faith, liking, what has been acquired by repeated hearing, specious reasoning, or a bias towards a notion that has been pondered over?"—"No, venerable sir."—"Bhikkhus, this even is the way by which a bhikkhu, apart from faith, liking, what has been acquired by repeated hearing, specious reasoning, or a bias towards a notion that has been pondered over, declares realisation of knowledge thus: I know that birth has been exhausted, the celibate life has been lived, what must be done has been done and there is no more of this to come." (SN 35:152)

The Instruction to the Kālāmas

The Kālāmas of Kesaputta go to see the Buddha

1. I heard thus. Once the Blessed One[1], while wandering in the Kosala country with a large community of bhikkhus, entered a town of the Kālāma people called Kesaputta. The Kālāmas who were inhabitants of Kesaputta heard: "Reverend Gotama, the monk, the son of the Sakyans, has, while wandering in the Kosala country, entered Kesaputta. The good repute of the Reverend Gotama has been spread in this way: Indeed, the Blessed One is thus consummate, fully enlightened, endowed with knowledge and practice, sublime, knower of the worlds, peerless, guide of tameable men, teacher of divine and human beings, enlightened, blessed. He makes known this world with its beings, its māras and its brahmas, and the group of creatures, with its monks and brahmins, and its divine and human beings, which he by himself has through direct knowledge understood clearly. He sets forth the Dhamma, good in the beginning, good in the middle, good in the end, possessed of meaning and the letter, and complete in everything; and he proclaims the holy life that is perfectly pure. Seeing such consummate ones is good indeed."

2. Then the Kālāmas who were inhabitants of Kesaputta went to where the Blessed One was. On arriving there some paid homage to him and sat down on one side; some exchanged greetings with him and after the ending of cordial memorable talk, sat down on one side; some saluted him raising their joined palms and sat down on one side; some announced their name and family and sat down on one side; some, without speaking, sat down on one side.

The Kālāmas of Kesaputta ask for guidance from Buddha

3. The Kālāmas who were inhabitants of Kesaputta sitting on one side said to the Blessed One: "There are some monks and brahmins, venerable sir, who visit Kesaputta. They expound and explain only their own doctrines; the doctrines of others they despise,

---

1. Aṅguttara Nikāya, Tika Nipāta, Mahāvagga, Sutta No. 65.

revile, and pull to pieces. Some other monks and brahmins too, venerable sir, come to Kesaputta. They also expound and explain only their own doctrines; the doctrines of others they despise, revile, and pull to pieces. Venerable sir, there is doubt, there is uncertainty in us concerning them. Which of these reverend monks and brahmins spoke the truth and which falsehood?"

The criterion for rejection

4. "It is proper for you, Kālāmas, to doubt, to be uncertain; uncertainty has arisen in you about what is doubtful. Come, Kālāmas. Do not go upon what has been acquired by repeated hearing; nor upon tradition; nor upon rumour; nor upon what is in a scripture; nor upon surmise; nor upon an axiom; nor upon specious reasoning; nor upon a bias towards a notion that has been pondered over; nor upon another's seeming ability; nor upon the consideration, 'The monk is our teacher.' Kālāmas, when you yourselves know: 'These things are bad; these things are blameable; these things are censured by the wise; undertaken and observed, these things lead to harm and ill,' abandon them."

Greed, hate, and delusion

5. "What do you think, Kālāmas? Does greed appear in a man for his benefit or harm?"—"For his harm, venerable sir."—"Kālāmas, being given to greed, and being overwhelmed and vanquished mentally by greed, this man takes life, steals, commits adultery, and tells lies; he prompts another too, to do likewise. Will that be conducive for his harm and ill for a long time?"—"Yes, venerable sir."

6. "What do you think, Kālāmas? Does hate appear in a man for his benefit or harm?"—"For his harm, venerable sir."—"Kālāmas, being given to hate, and being overwhelmed and vanquished mentally by hate, this man takes life, steals, commits adultery, and tells lies; he prompts another too, to do likewise. Will that be conducive for his harm and ill for a long time?"—"Yes, venerable sir."

7. "What do you think, Kālāmas? Does delusion appear in a man for his benefit or harm?"—"For his harm, venerable sir."—"Kālāmas, being given to delusion, and being overwhelmed

and vanquished mentally by delusion, this man takes life, steals, commits adultery, and tells lies; he prompts another too, to do likewise. Will that be conducive for his harm and ill for a long time?"—"Yes, venerable sir."

8. "What do you think, Kālāmas? Are these things good or bad?"—"Bad, venerable sir"—"Blameable or not blameable?"—"Blameable, venerable sir."—"Censured or praised by the wise?"—"Censured, venerable sir."—"Undertaken and observed, do these things lead to harm and ill, or not? Or how does it strike you?"—"Undertaken and observed, these things lead to harm and ill. Thus it strikes us here."

9. "Therefore, did we say, Kālāmas, what was said thus, 'Come Kālāmas. Do not go upon what has been acquired by repeated hearing; nor upon tradition; nor upon rumour; nor upon what is in a scripture; nor upon surmise; nor upon an axiom; nor upon specious reasoning; nor upon a bias towards a notion that has been pondered over; nor upon another's seeming ability; nor upon the consideration, 'The monk is our teacher.' Kālāmas, when you yourselves know: 'These things are bad; these things are blameable; these things are censured by the wise; undertaken and observed, these things lead to harm and ill,' abandon them."

The criterion for acceptance

10. "Come, Kālāmas. Do not go upon what has been acquired by repeated hearing; nor upon tradition; nor upon rumour; nor upon what is in a scripture; nor upon surmise; nor upon an axiom; nor upon specious reasoning; nor upon a bias towards a notion that has been pondered over; nor upon another's seeming ability; nor upon the consideration, 'The monk is our teacher.' Kālāmas, when you yourselves know: 'These things are good; these things are not blameable; these things are praised by the wise; undertaken and observed, these things lead to benefit and happiness,' enter on and abide in them."

Absence of greed, hate, and delusion

11. "What do you think, Kālāmas? Does absence of greed appear in a man for his benefit or harm?"—"For his benefit, venerable sir."—"Kālāmas, being not given to greed, and being not overwhelmed

and not vanquished mentally by greed, this man does not take life, does not steal, does not commit adultery, and does not tell lies; he prompts another too, to do likewise. Will that be conducive for his benefit and happiness for a long time?"—"Yes, venerable sir."

12. "What do you think, Kālāmas? Does absence of hate appear in a man for his benefit or harm?"—"For his benefit, venerable sir."—"Kālāmas, being not given to hate, and being not overwhelmed and not vanquished mentally by hate, this man does not take life, does not steal, does not commit adultery, and does not tell lies; he prompts another too, to do likewise. Will that be conducive for his benefit and happiness for a long time?"—"Yes, venerable sir."

13. "What do you think, Kālāmas? Does absence of delusion appear in a man for his benefit or harm?"—"For his benefit, venerable sir."—"Kālāmas, being not given to delusion, and being not overwhelmed and not vanquished mentally by delusion, this man does not take life, does not steal, does not commit adultery, and does not tell lies; he prompts another too, to do likewise. Will that be conducive for his benefit and happiness for a long time?"—"Yes, venerable sir."

14. "What do you think, Kālāmas? Are these things good or bad?"—"Good, venerable sir."—"Blameable or not blameable?"—"Not blameable, venerable sir."—"Censured or praised by the wise?"—"Praised, venerable sir."—"Undertaken and observed, do these things lead to benefit and happiness, or not? Or how does it strike you?"—"Undertaken and observed, these things lead to benefit and happiness. Thus it strikes us here."

15. "Therefore, indeed, did we say, Kālāmas, what was said thus, 'Come Kālāmas. Do not go upon what has been acquired by repeated hearing; nor upon tradition; nor upon rumour; nor upon what is in a scripture; nor upon surmise; nor upon an axiom; nor upon specious reasoning; nor upon a bias towards a notion that has been pondered over; nor upon another's seeming ability; nor upon the consideration, 'The monk is our teacher.' Kālāmas, when you yourselves know: 'These things are good; these things are not blameable; these things are praised by the wise; undertaken and observed, these things lead to benefit and happiness,' enter on and abide in them."

The four exalted dwellings

16. "The disciple of the Noble Ones, Kālāmas, who in this way is devoid of coveting, devoid of ill will, undeluded, clearly comprehending and mindful, dwells having pervaded with the thought of amity one quarter; likewise the second; likewise the third; likewise the fourth; so above, below, and across; he dwells, having pervaded because of the existence in it of all living beings, everywhere, the entire world, with the great, exalted, boundless thought of amity that is free of hate or malice.

"He lives, having pervaded with the thought of compassion one quarter; likewise the second; likewise the third; likewise the fourth; so above, below, and across; he dwells, having pervaded because of the existence in it of all living beings, everywhere, the entire world, with the great, exalted, boundless thought of compassion that is free of hate or malice.

"He lives, having pervaded with the thought of gladness one quarter; likewise the second; likewise the third; likewise the fourth; so above, below, and across; he dwells, having pervaded because of the existence in it of all living beings, everywhere, the entire world, with the great, exalted, boundless thought of gladness that is free of hate or malice.

"He lives, having pervaded with the thought of equanimity one quarter; likewise the second; likewise the third; likewise the fourth; so above, below, and across; he dwells, having pervaded because of the existence in it of all living beings, everywhere, the entire world, with the great, exalted, boundless thought of equanimity that is free of hate or malice."

The four solaces

17. "The disciple of the Noble Ones, Kālāmas, who has such a hate-free mind, such a malice-free mind, such an undefiled mind, and such a purified mind, is one by whom four solaces are found here and now.

"'Suppose there is a hereafter and there is a fruit, result, of deeds done well or ill. Then it is possible that at the dissolution of the body after death, I shall arise in the heavenly world, which is possessed of the state of bliss.' This is the first solace found by him.

"'Suppose there is no hereafter and there is no fruit, no result, of deeds done well or ill. Yet in this world, here and now, free from hatred, free from malice, safe and sound, and happy, I keep myself.' This is the second solace found by him.

"'Suppose evil (results) befall an evil-doer. I, however, think of doing evil to none. Then, how can ill (results) affect me who do no evil deed?' This is the third solace found by him.

"'Suppose evil (results) do not befall an evil-doer. Then I see myself purified in any case.' This is the fourth solace found by him.

"The disciple of the Noble Ones, Kālāmas, who has such a hate-free mind, such a malice-free mind, such an undefiled mind, and such a purified mind, is one by whom, here and now, these four solaces are found."

"So it is, Blessed One. So it is, Sublime One. The disciple of the Noble Ones, venerable sir, who has such a hate-free mind, such a malice-free mind, such an undefiled mind, and such a purified mind, is one by whom, here and now, four solaces are found.

"'Suppose there is a hereafter and there is a fruit, result, of deeds done well or ill. Then it is possible that at the dissolution of the body after death, I shall arise in the heavenly world, which is possessed of the state of bliss.' This is the first solace found by him.

"'Suppose there is no hereafter and there is no fruit, no result, of deeds done well or ill. Yet in this world, here and now, free from hatred, free from malice, safe and sound, and happy, I keep myself.' This is the second solace found by him.

"'Suppose evil (results) befall an evil-doer. I, however, think of doing evil to none. Then, how can ill (results) affect me who do no evil deed?' This is the third solace found by him.

"'Suppose evil (results) do not befall an evil-doer. Then I see myself purified in any case.' This is the fourth solace found by him.

"The disciple of the Noble Ones, venerable sir, who has such a hate-free mind, such a malice-free mind, such an undefiled mind, and such a purified mind, is one by whom, here and now, these four solaces are found.

"Marvellous, venerable sir! Marvellous, venerable sir! As if, venerable sir, a person were to turn face upwards what is upside down, or to uncover the concealed, or to point the way to one who is lost or to carry a lamp in the darkness, thinking, 'Those who have eyes will see visible objects,' so has the Dhamma been set forth in many ways by the Blessed One. We, venerable sir, go to the Blessed One for refuge, to the Dhamma for refuge, and to the Community of Bhikkhus for refuge. Venerable sir, may the Blessed One regard us as followers who have gone for refuge for life, from today." (AN 3:65)

Sakka's Quest

Sakkapañhā Sutta

Introduction, Translation and Comments by

Sister Vajirā

WHEEL PUBLICATION NO. 10

Introduction

The Buddhist text (sutta or discourse) discussed here belongs to a group of Buddhist scriptures called Dīgha-Nikāya, the collection of long discourses, and is the twenty-first discourse in it. It tells the story of a deity descending from his heavenly realm to our earth for meeting and questioning the Buddha, the Enlightened One. So, at first glance, it may appear that it is quite a miraculous story, and some even may regard it as a 'fairy tale'; but it has a very realistic and quite topical background because that deity's visit to the Buddha had a purpose that concerns all humans in the very same way as it concerned that deity, Sakka, two thousand and five hundred years ago.

Before presenting to the reader the translation of the text, it seems desirable to give first some general information about it. The questions and answers themselves which form the core of the text, will be explained at the places where they occur. It is, however, not the purpose of what was originally a lecture to deal with them in full, which would require a separate treatment. Here will chiefly be stressed those characteristic qualities of Sakka which mark him an individual ripe for the first stage of sainthood, stream-entry (*sotāpatti*). Such an individual, a *sotāpanna*, breaks the lowest and most vital bonds that chain us to the sorrow-laden cycle of repeated births and deaths—to which also a deity is subject—and enters the stream towards final deliverance.

The spot in India where our text is located and where the visit of the deity, Sakka, took place became famous throughout the Buddhist world and is remembered up to the present day as the Indasālaguhā, the Grotto of the Indasāla. Indasāla is the name of a tree which must have stood near that grotto. The village near the Grotto of the Indasāla was at that time called Ambasaṇḍa, and was inhabited by Brahmins. Today its name is Giriyek, situated about six miles east of modern Rājgīr or Rājagaha; it is a lovely spot, surrounded by hills, with ancient ruins.

In later times, the scene described in our text—the heavenly visitors appearing before the Buddha—has been represented quite frequently in the sculptural art of India and Ceylon (now Sri

Lanka), and some of these works of considerable artistic merit are still preserved.

Reproduced from Foucher's L'Art Greco-boudhique du Gandhāra (Paris 1905). Note at the Buddha's left the figure of Sakka, with a parasol being held over him; and on his right Pañchasikha with his lyre (fragmentary). The sculpture is in Gandhāri style (Greek influence) and originates from Loriyān Thangai, being preserved in the museum of Calcutta.

We shall now introduce briefly the heavenly personages appearing in our text. Sakka is chief of Tāvatiṃsā, the heaven of the thirty-three gods, which still belongs to the world of sensual desire (*kāma-loka*), and ranges next but one to our own terrestrial sphere. Sakka and his gods of the thirty-three are thus comparatively low deities.

As the Bhagavā, the Exalted One, himself says in our sutta, it was indeed surprising that Sakka, king of gods, found the time and, what is more, actually thought of seeing the Buddha. According to the texts, the deities of the thirty-three have a lifetime of thirty-six millions of years. What is with them a day and a night are here on earth a hundred years. That means those gods do not even spend a day-night while a man spends a full life. Since the texts tell us of several visits paid by Sakka to the Exalted One, we have to understand that he has visited the Buddha several times during only a single of his heavenly days, for the Master lived on earth as a Buddha, an Enlightened One, for less than half a century—which to Sakka is less than a day. And this frequency of Sakka's visits to the Bhagavā is indeed striking if we compare his attitude with our own attitude towards spiritual things—though our pleasures and activities are surely much less engaging than the pleasures and activities of such a powerful god.

Between Sakka's realm and ours, range the Cātumahārājika Devā, the Four Great Kings or Guardians of the Four Quarters. They are closely connected with Sakka and the thirty-three gods. One of these Four Great Kings is Vessavana or Kuvera, lord over the northern direction and the treasures of the Himalayan regions. He is mild and benevolent, and his is the ideal land of perfect beauty, harmony and abundance—the utopia dreamt of by many a poet. One fairy of his suite occurs in the sutta. Her name is Bhuñjatī.

The Gandhabbas, subjects of the Four Great Kings, are the heavenly musicians attending on Sakka and the thirty-three gods. The King of the Gandhabbas is Timbaru, famed for his excellence in music, and his lovely daughter is Baddhā Sūriya-vaccasā, engaged to the son of Sakka's charioteer, Mātali.

Of the Gandhabbas one is repeatedly mentioned in the suttas. It is Pañcasikha, the young Gandhabba, possessor of the miraculous *panduvīnā* which is said to have belonged once to Māra, the Evil One. This famous *panduvīnā*, some say, is a yellow lute of bael wood; others say it is a lyre of the same wood. In our sutta, where the young Gandhabba, Pañcasikha, also plays his role, it is described as a lyre of red bael wood.

The deities mentioned so far are all voluntary subjects of Sakka and the thirty-three, and are higher beings than men. Sakka, however, has also some powerful and ferocious foes—the Asuras, ranging lower than men. They are said to be a kind of giant, living in the ocean. Further it is said of them that they once were Sakka's brothers; for reasons unknown they were banished by Sakka into the ocean with the help of Sakka's thunderbolt. The hostility between Tāvatiṃsa Devas and Asuras becomes acute from time to time, and battles take place between them.

What now about the spiritual standard of all these beings? Early Buddhist tradition reveals that in general the Buddha and his great disciples show little regard for these pleasure-loving deities of inferior intellect and superficial understanding of the Dhamma. The Buddha and his early disciples call them the '*puthukāya*,' the common folk, as we shall see. Only later, when actual knowledge of these beings disappeared, were intellectual abilities, superior to those of men, falsely attributed to them. A good proof of their inadequacy is given in our sutta. The young Gandhabba, Pañcasikha, with his lyre of red bael-wood, being requested by Sakka first to 'win over' the Bhagavā before he himself would come into presence of the Buddha, foolishly produces a song which is nothing more than a love poem—though Pañcasikha tries much to give some spiritual airs to it. It may well be a beautiful song, but a man of tact and some understanding would hardly expect a personality like the Buddha even to listen to it much less to be pleased with it. But Sakka as well as Pañcasikha both firmly believed this. That is why the Bhagavā makes a somewhat ironical remark about it, as we shall see later. But polite as the Bhagavā is, he carries on a conversation with them and never fails to address Sakka as 'king of gods,' sometimes addressing him '*āyasmā*,' 'Venerable One.' Two further names of Sakka occur—Kosiya, being the name of his father, and Vasavā.

It is true that a great many of these deities are fond of the Bhagavā; not, however, for the Bhagavā's profound wisdom and pure virtue, which they are hardly able to appreciate, but rather because they know that the appearance of a Buddha increases their power and weakens their opponents, the Asuras and other lower beings. They know that a Buddha makes many follow the good path and discourages them from following the evil path; and so he uplifts many to heaven and prevents many from downfall.

Sakka, however, is an exception altogether. He, as already indicated by the frequency of his visits to the Bhagavā, is sincerely devoted to the Buddha as the teacher of deliverance and aspires after the goal proclaimed by him.

One event that took place in his own realm evidently impressed him deeply and became the immediate cause of his present visit to the Bhagavā. He had seen two gods lower than himself, who formerly had been monks (bhikkhus) of the Bhagavā, suddenly, and before his very sight, transcend even him and pass into the Brahma-world, which is far higher then the realm of the thirty-three. This happened after another god, who likewise was a former disciple of the Bhagavā, reminded them of the Buddha *sāsana*, the dispensation of the Buddha, and of their former aspirations which, in the enjoyment of heavenly pleasures, they had almost forgotten.

Sakka evidently had lived up to the principles of the Dhamma and had succeeded in purifying his mind from grosser defilements. His questions are put with great thoughtfulness and skill, and the profound answers were received with the joy that arises from understanding.

It is by the understanding of the Bhagavā's replies that Sakka, king of the thirty-three gods, attains *sotāpatti*, the first stage of sainthood, and joyfully proclaims his achievement. He sees now his possible future lives (which, for a *sotāpanna*, cannot exceed seven in number) reduced to two at the most: one as a man, where he possibly will achieve sainthood, or, failing that, he will become an *anāgāmī*, once-returner, spending his last life among the deities of the Pure Abodes (*suddhāvāsā*).

Sakka's attainment of *sotāpatti* during this discourse gives deep significance to this sutta, and it forms a striking contrast to the elaborate framework of our text that depicts, in a sometimes humorous way, a world of ease and superficiality.

Sakka's Quest

1. Thus I heard. Once the Bhagavā[1] dwelt in Magadha, to the east of Rājagaha, in the Indasāla Grotto, on the Vediya mountain, to the north of the Brahmin village, Ambasaṇḍa. At that time there arose in Sakka, the king of gods, a desire to see the Bhagavā and he thought to himself, "Where may the Bhagavā at present abide, the Arahant, Sammā Sambuddha, the Holy One, fully enlightened?" And he beheld the Bhagavā staying in Magadha, to the east of Rājagaha, in the Indasāla Grotto, on the Vediya mountain, to the north of the Brahmin village, Ambasaṇḍa.

2. And Sakka, the king of gods, addressed the gods of the thirty-three and Pañcasikha, the young Gandhabba, "Sirs, the Bhagavā dwells in Magadha, to the east of Rājagaha. What, sirs, if we were to go and see the Bhagavā, the Arahant, Sammā-Sambuddha?"

"So be it! And good luck unto you!" said the gods of the thirty-three and Pañcasikha, the young Gandhabba, in assent to Sakka, the king of gods; and Pañcasikha, the young Gandhabba, took his lyre of red bael-wood and followed in attendance on Sakka, the king of gods.

And Sakka, the king of gods, surrounded by the gods of the thirty-three and attended by Pañcasikha, the young Gandhabba, had, as quickly as a strong man might stretch out the bent arm or draw in the arm stretched out, vanished from the heaven of the thirty-three and appeared in Magadha, to the east of Rājagaha, on the Vediya mountain, to the north of the Brahmin village, Ambasanda.

3. And, verily, at that time the Vediya mountain together with the Brahmin village, Ambasanda, was bathed in a splendid radiance, as if through the heavenly power of the gods. And the people round about in the village said, "As if set on fire, the Vediya mountain shines today! As if burning and blazing! What may have happened today to the Vediya mountain that it is bathed in a splendid radiance, together with the Brahmin village, Ambasaṇḍa,—as if through the heavenly power of the gods?" And they were amazed, with hair standing on end.

---

1. *Bhagavā*, "the Exalted One" is a frequent appellation of the Buddha.

4. Now Sakka, the king of gods, addressed Pañcasikha, the young Gandhabba, "Hard of access, my dear Pañcasikha, are Tathāgatas (Perfect Ones) to folks like us; mostly are they in retreat, absorbed in meditation, delighted therein. What, my dear Pañcasikha, if you first were to gain over the Bhagavā? Gained over by you, my dear, we afterwards shall draw near to see the Bhagavā, the Arahant, Sammā-Sambuddha."

"So be it! And good luck unto you," said Pañcasikha, the young Gandhabba, in assent to Sakka, the king of gods, and took his lyre of red bael-wood and approached the Indasāla Grotto.

5. Having drawn near, he thought to himself, "From here it will be neither too far nor too near for the Bhagavā to hear the song," and he stood aside. Standing aside, Pañcasikha, the young Gandhabba, let his lyre of red vilva wood be heard and a song alluding to the Buddha, the Dhamma, to Arahants, and to love.

6. The song being over, the Bhagavā addressed Pañcasikha, the young Gandhabba, "The sound of your strings, Pañcasikha, harmonizes with that of your song, and the sound of your song with that of your strings; but, verily, Pañcasikha, your strings neither go beyond your song, nor does your song go beyond your strings. But when, Pañcasikha, did you compose these stanzas alluding to the Buddha, the Dhamma, Arahants, and to love?"

"There was a time, Lord, when the Bhagavā dwelt at Uruvelā, on the bank of the Nerañjanā river, at the foot of the goatherds' banyan tree, soon after his supreme enlightenment. At that very time, Lord, was I enamoured of Baddhā Sūriya-vaccasā, the daughter of Timbaru, King of the Gandhabbas. This girl, however, Lord, was in love with another, with Sikkhaddhī, the son of the charioteer Mātali, for whom she longed. Since I could not win that girl by any means whatsoever, I took my lyre of red bael-wood, approached the abode of Timbaru, king of the Gandhabbas, and, having drawn near, let my lyre of red bael-wood be heard and the song alluding to the Buddha, the Dhamma, Arahants, and to love.

7. "The song being over, Baddhā Sūriya-vaccasā addressed me: 'I did not see yet, Sir, that Bhagavā face to face. However, I have heard of the Bhagavā when I went to dance at the pleasure hall of the thirty-three gods. Since you, Sir, spoke in praise of that Bhagavā, let there be a meeting between us today.' And so, Lord,

there was a meeting between that girl and me; but don't let me speak on this any further."

8. Now, Sakka, the king of gods, thought to himself: "Pañcasikha, the young Gandhabba, is in pleasant conversation with the Bhagavā and the Bhagavā with him." And he addressed Pañcasikha, the young Gandhabba: "My dear Pañcasikha, you now pay my respects to the Bhagavā and say, 'Sakka, Lord, the king of gods, with his ministers and suite pays homage at the feet of the Bhagavā.'"

"So be it! And good luck unto you!" said Pañcasikha, the young Gandhabba, in assent to Sakka, the king of gods, and did as requested.

"Happiness be unto Sakka, the king of gods, and his ministers and suite! For desirous of happiness are gods and men, Asuras, Nāgas, Gandhabbas, and other common folks." This is the way Tathāgatas greet these hosts of great power.

So greeted, Sakka, the king of gods, entered the Bhagavā's Grotto of the Indasāla, saluted the Bhagavā and stood aside, and so did the gods of the thirty-three and Pañcasikha, the young Gandhabba.

9. But verily, at that time those uneven spots of the Indasāla Grotto had become even, the narrow spaces widened, the darkness vanished, and light had arisen, as if through the heavenly power of the gods.

Thereupon the Bhagavā addressed Sakka, the king of gods, "Wonderful is this, quite wonderful, that the Venerable Kosiya, with so much work to do, despite his many obligations, yet has come here!"

"For a long time, Lord, was I desirous of seeing the Bhagavā; but engaged in many activities on behalf of the thirty-three gods, I was not able to come. However, Lord, on one occasion when the Bhagavā was dwelling in Sāvatthī, in the Bower of the Salala creeper, I went to see the Bhagavā.

10. "But at that very time, Lord, the Bhagavā was seated in a state of absorption, and Bhuñjatī of Vessavana's suite, with clasped hands saluting the Bhagavā stood near. Then I, addressing Bhuñjatī, said: 'Sister, you pay my respects to the Bhagavā and say, 'Sakka, Lord, the king of gods, with his ministers and suite pays homage at the feet of the Bhagavā.' To my request Bhuñjatī

replied, 'Sir, it is not the proper time now to see the Bhagavā; the Bhagavā is in seclusion.' 'Well, sister, you then may salute the Bhagavā in my name after the Bhagavā has arisen from that absorption.' Did, Lord, that sister salute the Bhagavā, and does the Bhagavā remember her words?"

"That sister, king of gods, did salute me, and I do remember her words. I had arisen from that absorption through the sound of the Venerable's chariot wheels."

11. "From those gods, Lord, who were born before us in the realm of the thirty-three, I have heard that whenever Tathāgatas arise in the world, Arahants, Sammā-Sambuddhas, the heavenly hosts grow in number and the Asura hosts decrease. And that is true, Lord, I myself have realized it, for since the Tathāgata, the Arahant, Sammā-Sambuddha, has appeared in the world, the heavenly hosts grew in number and Asura hosts decreased.

"Take this instance, Lord. There was, Lord, a daughter of the Sākyan clan in Kapilavatthu. Her name was Gopikā. She was devoted to the Buddha, the Dhamma and Sangha and was of accomplished virtue. Disgusted with the womanly nature, she cultivated the nature of a man, and at the breaking up of the body, after death, she rose to a happy state, to the heavenly world, to community with the gods of the thirty-three, and obtained 'sonship' by us. And there they know him as 'Gopaka, son of the gods.'

"But, Lord, three bhikkhus who had led the holy life under the Bhagavā were born in the lower rank of Gandhabbas. They enjoy the five sense pleasures surrounding them, and they come to wait upon and minister to us. This being so, Gopaka, the son of gods, admonished them: 'Where were your ears I wonder, Sirs, when you listened to the doctrine of the Bhagavā? I, having been only a female lay disciple, am now a god, son of Sakka, the king of gods. You, however, Sirs, who led the holy life under the Bhagavā have risen but to the lower rank of Gandhabbas. A sad sight indeed is this to us that we should see the followers of the higher life appearing in the lower rank of Gandhabbas!'

"Of those, Lord, admonished by Gopaka, the son of the gods, two gods regained mindfulness at once, and passed into the world of *Brahma Purohita*, and only one god remained in sensual pleasures."

12. (Gopaka's[2] Song)

"Gopikā, the Seer's devotee[3] was I.
Faithful to the Buddha and the Law,
To the Community I happily ministered,
Untiringly conforming to the Buddha's Norm.

To Tāvatiṃsa's realm I rose, am Sakka's son,
Of power great and splendour great,
As 'Gopaka' they know me here,
But, among Gandhabba-folks,
The monks of Gotama I saw
To whom we formerly, at home,
Seated at the bhikkhus' feet,
Had offered food and drink.

Why did you, sirs, not grasp
The Buddha's Law, well-propounded,
Evident, and recognized
By them who have eyes to see?

From you it was I too have learnt
This teaching fair: Am Sakka's son,
Of power great and splendour great,
To Tāvatiṃsa's realm I rose.

But you, though choosing what is best,
The unsurpassed Life of Purity,
Have now appeared in lower rank:
Inappropriate your rebirth seems!

A sad sight indeed is this to us—
The followers of the Higher Life
Appearing but in lower rank:
As Gandhabba-folks, O sirs,
You come to wait upon us gods!

I stayed at home, yet behold the difference:
A woman then, today I am a man, a god,
And heavenly delights are mine!"

---

2. 'Gopaka' is the masculine and 'Gopikā' the feminine form of the name.
3. *Upāsikā*: a female lay disciple of a Buddha

Gopaka, stalwart of the Norm,
Thus incited awe in them;
Falling in with him, they spoke:
"Well then,
An effort let us make, let's strive on!
Lest the servants we would be of others here!"

And two of them put forth their energy,
The Norm of Gotama they called to mind;
They cleansed their thoughts without delay,
And realized the wretchedness of carnal joys.

As an elephant might break his chains,
So they cast off the bounds of fleshly lusts,
The yokes of Māra, hard to overcome,
And left behind the realm of thirty-three.

Putting an end to passion,
The stainless heroes transcended all:
The gods who were assembled
In Tāvatiṃsa's pleasure-hall,
Together with their chief and queens,

Thrilled with this sight, Vāsavā,
Lord over gods, amid celestial hosts,
Spoke this:
"Alas! These, born in lower rank,
They leave behind the thirty-three!"

Beholding him, the deeply agitated,
Gopaka spoke this to Vāsavā:
"The Buddha verily is god among men,
Conqueror over sense-desire,
The Wise of Sākyans' clan!

These sons of His, on passing thence,
Their insight lost, but got it back through me.
Of those who stayed with us,
One still remains among Gandhabba-folks.
But two trace out the path to Perfect Knowledge,
Their minds set firm, and they now pity us!
For in whatever disciple

The Law should manifest itself:
Doubts do not beset his course.

We hail the Buddha who has crossed the flood
And cut off doubts, the Victor, Chief of Men.
Here from You they learnt the Norm—
A blessing verily it was to them:
Two to Brahma-Purohita's excellence attained!
We too have come, O Lord,

This Law, it is our quest!
See us appearing here!
Would, O Lord, that we
A question from the Bhagavā may ask!"

13. Thereupon the Bhagavā thought to himself, "Long indeed has this Sakka been pure in mind; whatever question he will ask me it will be to good purpose, not vain; and the answer I shall give, he will quickly understand." And so the Bhagavā addressed Sakka, the king of gods, by this stanza:

"Free are you O Vāsavā,
To ask at will thy questions;
And all thy problems I shall solve for you."

II

1. Received into audience, Sakka, the king of gods, put the first question to the Bhagavā: "What bond, O Lord, holds gods and men, Asuras, Nāgas, Gandhabbas, and other common folks who aspire for living in amity, in harmlessness, in clemency, in benevolence, without hostility, but yet who live in hostility, in violence, in cruelty, in malevolence, not in friendliness?" This was the question Sakka, the king of gods, put to the Bhagavā. The Bhagavā made answer:

"The bond, O king of gods, is envy and selfishness; bound by the bond of envy and selfishness, gods and men, Asuras, Nāgas, Gandhabbas, and other common folks live in hostility, in violence, in cruelty, in malevolence; not in friendliness—even though they aspire for living in amity, in harmlessness, in benevolence, without hostility." In this manner the Bhagavā answered the question put by Sakka, the king of gods. Edified, Sakka, the king of gods, approved of the Bhagavā's saying and took delight in it: "Thus it is, O Blessed One. Conquered are my doubts, gone my uncertainty, having heard the Bhagavā's answer to this question."

* * *

Comment. Sakka obviously is concerned about the hostility as it exists between a great many beings of the sensual sphere (*kāma-loka*); between gods, men, Asuras, Nāgas, Gandhabbas and other common folk. But also something else did he observe. Animosity of any kind, be it open warfare or a single malicious thought, is unpleasant to anyone afflicted with it, and so beings resolve not to surrender to it; but for the most part they fail utterly even as a habitual drunkard cannot by a mere resolution possibly abstain from intoxicants. And here, in the disparity between a mental resolution and the inability to follow it up, Sakka saw the problem; and the Buddha reveals to him that this is due not to something outward, but to conditions inherent in beings themselves—to envy and selfishness.

Of mental defilements, envy and selfishness (*issā-macchariya*) are the most vital, existing in almost all beings of the sensual sphere in some degree or other. These defilements, however hidden they may be, by their very nature trespass on the domain of others, and so introduce ill-feeling which, at any occasion, may result in open hostility.

Sakka at once comprehends the importance of the Bhagavā's answer. He is jubilant to find the remedy to what so sorely aggrieved him, namely, to purify one's mind from envy and selfishness. Here too his lofty spirit is revealed. It must be remembered that Sakka, as a deity, extremely seldom, perhaps once in millions of years, personally experiences the harmful result of envy and selfishness, namely animosity. His life for the most part is full of harmony because of the comparative weakness of these defilements within him. But Sakka, having once fully understood that envy and selfishness are evil, is no longer interested in more or less of them; he wants to see nothing but the final destruction of envy and selfishness.

So deeply concerned is he with the matter that he now begins a radical inquiry into the conditions which bring on envy and selfishness and the conditions necessary for the eradication of these defilements. He does this with the admirable skill that was already evident from his first question.

* * *

2. And Sakka, the king of gods, approving of the Bhagavā's saying and delighting in it, put a further question: "But what, O Lord, brings on envy and selfishness? What is their origin? From what do they spring? What gives rise to them? What being present, envy and selfishness appear? What not being present, envy and selfishness do not appear?"

"What brings on envy and selfishness, O king of gods, are likes and dislikes. Likes and dislikes are their origin. From likes and dislikes do they spring. Likes and dislikes give rise to them. Likes and dislikes being present, envy and selfishness appear. Likes and dislikes not being present, envy and selfishness do not appear."

"But what, O Lord, brings on likes and dislikes? What is their origin? From what do they spring? What gives rise to them? What being present, likes and dislikes appear? What not being present, likes and dislikes do not appear?"

"What brings on likes and dislikes, O king of gods, is desire. Desire is their origin. From desire do they spring. Desire gives rise to them. Desire being present, likes and dislikes appear. Desire not being present, likes and dislikes do not appear."

"But what, O Lord, brings on desire? What is its origin? From what does it spring? What gives rise to it? What being present, desire appears? What not being present, desire does not appear?"

"What brings on desire, O king of gods, is (wrong) reflection.[4] Reflection is its origin. From reflection does it spring. Reflection gives rise to it. Reflection being present, desire appears. Reflection not being present, desire does not appear."

"But what, O Lord, makes for (wrong) reflection? What is its origin? From what does it spring? What gives rise to it?

4. By reflection is meant here a thought influenced by *āsavas* (taints).

What being present, reflection appears? What not being present, reflection does not appear?"

"What makes for (wrong) reflection, O king of gods, is multiplicity of perception. Multiplicity of perception is its origin. From multiplicity of perception does it spring. Multiplicity of perception gives rise to it. Multiplicity of perception being present, reflection appears. Multiplicity of perception not being present, reflection does not appear."

* * *

Comment. In this set of questions and answers the core of the Buddha's teaching is represented, the idea of conditionality (*paṭiccasamuppāda*), in a new formula. The condition of envy and selfishness (*issāmacchariya*) is likes and dislikes (*piyappiyā*); the condition of likes and dislikes is desire (*chanda*); the condition of desire is (wrong) reflection (*vitakka*); and the condition of reflection is multiplicity of perception (*papañca-saññā-saṅkha*). By the cessation of multifarious perception reflection ceases; by the cessation of reflection desire ceases; by the cessation of desire likes and dislikes cease; and by the cessation of likes and dislikes envy and selfishness are uprooted, and so all animosity.

The idea of conditionality (*paṭiccasamuppāda*) is known to Sakka; that is evident from the way he questions. And it is indeed the profundity of Sakka's quest that has led to such philosophical heights. For now it has to be understood that envy and selfishness, and the hostility they imply, are so deep-rooted that their destruction ultimately becomes possible only when diversified perception ceases; in other words, envy and selfishness and hostility are inevitable facts of existence.

Multiplicity of perception is a simplified translation of *papañcā-sañña-saṅkhā*, a Pali term difficult to translate. *Papañca-saññā-saṅkhā* includes any perception that enters individual experience, anything perceived by mind or sense-faculties. *Papañca-saññā-saṅkhā* is the continual influx of multifarious perceptions which is evoked by, or finds response in, craving.[5] It is the inner and outer

5. Dhammapada v. 254: '*Papañcabhiratā pajā, nippapañcā Tathāgatā*

world of an individual, dependent on former action (kamma), and the cause of fresh one.

The cessation of diversified perception thus really means the cessation of existence itself (= cessation of kamma), the ultimate goal, Nibbāna. And this is evident to Sakka at once. He has found the comprehensive outlook that appeals to him; now he wants to know how this can be brought about.

* * *

3. "And how, O Lord, must a bhikkhu conduct himself to be endowed with the path fit for leading to the dissolution of the continual influx of multifarious perceptions?"

"Happiness, O king of gods, I declare to be twofold, as to be followed after and not to be followed after. Sorrow too, O king of gods, I declare to be twofold, as to be followed after and not to be followed after. And also indifference, O king of gods, I declare to be twofold, as to be followed after and not to be followed after.

"Happiness, O king of gods, I declare to be twofold, as to be followed after and not to be followed after. And why? If one knows of a happiness: 'This happiness when followed after by me makes evil states (*akusalā dhammā*) grow and good states (*kusalā dhammā*) vanish,' then that happiness, the happiness connected with worldliness, should not be followed after.[6] And again, if one knows of a happiness: 'This happiness when followed after by me makes evil states vanish and goods states grow,' then that happiness, [the happiness that arises from truly understanding the evanescent nature of all phenomena, and the detachment connected with such an understanding],[7] should be followed after. This may be done with reflection and discursive thinking (*savitakka-savicāra*)[8]

'Mankind delights in diversity, but not Tathāgatas'; i.e., variety of experience is the very thing commonly wanted. Further references: Majjhima Nikāya Sutta 18; Suttanipāta vv. 530, 874, 916.

6. See Majjhima Nikāya 137 (pleasant, etc., feelings connected with worldliness and with renunciation).

7. Explanatory addition by the translator.

8. This refers to beneficial (*kusala*) reflection on the normal level of consciousness and to the tranquillized and reduced reflection existing in the

or without reflection and discursive thinking (*avitakka-avicāra*). Of the two, that without reflection and discursive thinking is the better.[9] Happiness, O king of gods, I declare to be twofold as to be followed after and not to be followed after. If this was said, it was said for that reason.

"Sorrow too, O king of gods, I declare to be twofold, as to be followed after and not to be followed after. And why? If one knows of a sorrow: 'This sorrow when followed after by me makes evil states grow and good states vanish,' then that sorrow [the frustration that sensual indulgence inevitably results in] should not be followed after. And again, if one knows of a sorrow: 'This sorrow when followed after by me makes evil states vanish and good states grow,' then that sorrow [the sorrow of a holy disciple who craves for accomplishment but has not yet achieved the destruction of the taints (*āsavā*)] should be followed after. This may be done with reflection and discursive thinking or without reflection and discursive thinking. Of the two, that without reflection and discursive thinking is the better. Sorrow too, O king of gods, I declare to be twofold, as to be followed after and not to be followed after. If this was said, it was said for that reason.

"And also indifference, O king of gods, I declare to be twofold: as to be followed after and not to be followed after. And why? If one knows of an indifference: 'This indifference when followed after by me makes evil states grow and good states vanish,' then that indifference [the stupidity and dullness of an ordinary man who remains indifferent, intoxicated by delusion] should not be followed after. And again, if one knows of an indifference: 'This indifference when followed after by me makes evil states vanish and good states grow,' then that indifference [the true equanimity of a holy disciple, arising from insight and detachment] should be followed after. This may be done with reflection and discursive thinking or without reflection and discursive thinking.[10] Of the two, that without reflection is the better. Indifference too, O king

first absorption (*jhāna*).

9. This refers to the second and third state of absorption where reflection and discursive thinking are absent.

10. The latter alternative refers to the fourth absorption.

of gods, I declare to be twofold, as to be followed after and not to be followed after. If this was said, it was said for that reason.

"It is thus, O king of gods, that a bhikkhu must conduct himself to become fit for the path leading to the dissolution of the continual influx of multifarious perceptions."

In this manner it was that the Bhagavā answered the question put by Sakka, the king of gods. Edified, Sakka, the king of gods, approved of the Bhagavā's saying and took delight in it: "Thus it is, O Bhagavā! Thus it is, O Sugata! Conquered are my doubts, gone is my uncertainty, having heard the Bhagavā's answer to this question."

* * *

Comment. A task such as the dissolution of diversified perception rooted in diversifying of craving is but one of the many courses of training towards the same ultimate goal of Nibbāna. It can be attempted only by a bhikkhu. That much is quite clear to Sakka. That is, he does not hope for its accomplishment in his present life as a deity, but dedicates himself to the life of a bhikkhu in a birth to come which will be in the human world, as he himself later announces.

It was said earlier that multiplicity of perception (*papañca-saññā-saṅkhā*) comprises the whole of possible experience, for every single perception, be it a form, a sound, an odour, a taste, a touch or an idea, is connected with one of the three feelings, either with happiness (*somanassa*), or with sorrow (*domanassa*), or with indifference (*upekhā*). An untrained mind neither comprehends this fact nor, and still less so, attempts to control the immensity of impressions, but indiscriminately follows after whatever feeling begets. But the Buddha declares that not any type of happiness, not any type of sorrow, and not any type of indifference should be pursued, whilst, on the other hand, a certain happiness, a certain unhappiness, and a certain indifference should be cultivated, as indicated in the context above. This is the standard that a trained mind applies to feelings, whether their pursuit is conducive to Nibbāna or not.

And so the path which the Buddha shows to Sakka is a radical re-evaluation of all experience, taking place in a strenuous course of individual application. And this is *bhāvanā,* a 'making become'; bringing into being; an actualization of the Dhamma which has to be pursued until what is now dimly perceived, or not at all, becomes a dominant mental force through which one acts effortlessly, in perfect accordance with reality, freed from taints (*āsava*).

And Sakka has understood this too. There remain to be clarified for him the moral conduct obligatory on a bhikkhu and the restraint of sense faculties.

* * *

4. And Sakka, the king of gods, approving of the Bhagavā's saying and delighting in it, put a further question: "And how, O Lord, must a bhikkhu conduct himself to be endowed with the restraint of the Code of Discipline (*pātimokkha*)."

"Bodily conduct, O king of gods, I declare to be twofold, as to be followed after and not to be followed after. Conduct by speech too, O king of gods, I declare to be twofold, as to be followed after and not to be followed after. And also pursuit (*pariyesanā*), O king of gods, I declare to be twofold, as to be followed after and not to be followed after.

"Bodily conduct, O king of gods, I declare to be twofold as to be followed after and not to be followed after. And why? If one knows of a bodily conduct: 'This bodily conduct when followed after by me makes evil states grow and good states vanish, then that bodily conduct [killing, stealing and sexual acts] should not be followed after. And again, if one knows of a bodily conduct: 'This bodily conduct when followed after by me makes evil states vanish and good states grow,' then that bodily conduct [abstaining from killing, stealing and sexual acts] should be followed after. Bodily conduct, O king of gods, I declare to be twofold, as to be followed after and not to be followed after. If this was said, it was said for that reason.

"Conduct by speech too, O king of gods, I declare to be twofold, as to be followed after and not to be followed after. And why? If one knows of a conduct by speech: 'This conduct by speech when followed after by me makes evil states grow and good states vanish,' then that conduct by speech [lying, slander, harsh words and frivolous talk] should not be followed after. And again, if one knows of a conduct by speech, 'This conduct by speech when followed after by me makes evil states vanish and good states grow,' then that conduct by speech [abstaining from lying, slander, harsh words and frivolous talk] should be followed after. Conduct by speech too, O king of gods, I declare to be twofold, as to be followed after and not to be followed after. If this was said, it was said for that reason.

"And also pursuit, O king of gods, I declare to be twofold, as to be followed after and not to be followed after. And why? If one knows of a pursuit: 'This pursuit when followed after by me makes evil states grow and good states vanish,' then that pursuit [worldly pursuit, *āmisa pariyesanā*] should not be followed after. And again, if one knows of a pursuit: 'This pursuit when followed after by me makes evil states vanish and good states grow,' then that pursuit [pursuit of the truth, *dhamma pariyesanā*] should be followed after. And also pursuit, O king of gods, I declare to be twofold, as to be followed after and not to be followed after. If this was said, it was said for that reason.

"It is thus, O king of gods, that a bhikkhu must conduct himself to be endowed with the moral restraint obligatory on him."

In this manner the Bhagavā answered the question put by Sakka, the king of gods. Edified, Sakka, the king of gods, approved of the Bhagavā's saying and took delight in it. "Thus it is, O Bhagavā! Thus it is, O Sugata! Conquered are my doubts, gone is my uncertainty, having heard the Bhagavā's answer to this question."

5. And Sakka, the king of gods, approving of the Bhagavā's saying and delighting in it, put a further question: "And how, O Lord, must a bhikkhu conduct himself to be endowed with restraint of his sense faculties?"

"Form, O king of gods, perceptible by the eye, I declare to be twofold, as to be followed after and not to be followed after. Sound, O king of gods, perceptible by the ear, I declare to be twofold, as to be followed after and not to be followed after. Odour, O king of gods, perceptible by the nose, I declare to be twofold, as to be followed after and not to be followed after. Taste, O king of gods, perceptible by the tongue, I declare to be twofold, as to be followed after and not to be followed after. Touch, O king of gods, perceptible by the body, I declare to be twofold, as to be followed after and not to be followed after. Mind-object, O king of gods, perceptible by the mind, I declare to be twofold, as to be followed after and not to be followed after."

When this was said, Sakka, the king of gods, spoke thus to the Bhagavā: "The meaning of what was said in brief by the Bhagavā, O Lord, I understand in full thus: A form, O Lord, perceptible by the eye, which makes evil states grow and good states vanish, should not be followed after; and again, O Lord, a form perceptible by the eye, which makes evil states vanish and good states grow, should be followed after. A sound, O Lord, perceptible by the ear, which makes evil states grow and good states vanish should not be followed after; and again, O Lord, a sound perceptible by the ear, which makes evil states vanish and good states grow, should be followed after. An odour, O Lord, perceptible by the nose, which makes evil states grow and good states vanish, should not be followed after; and again, O Lord, an odour perceptible by the nose, which makes evil states vanish and good states grow, should be followed after. A taste, O Lord, perceptible by the tongue, which makes evil states grow and good states vanish, should not be followed after; and again, O Lord, a taste, perceptible by the tongue, which makes evil states vanish and good states grow, should be followed after. A touch, O Lord, perceptible by the body, which makes evil states grow and good states vanish, should not be followed after; and again, O Lord, a touch perceptible by the body, which makes evil states vanish and good states grow, should be followed after. A mind-object, O Lord, perceptible by the mind, which makes evil states grow and good states vanish, should not be followed after; and again, O Lord, a mind-object perceptible by the mind, which makes evil states vanish and good states grow, should be followed after.

Thus do I understand the meaning in full, O Lord, of what was said in brief by the Bhagavā. Conquered are my doubts, gone is my uncertainty, having heard the Bhagavā's answer to this question."

6. And Sakka, the king of gods, approving of the Bhagavā's saying and delighting in it, put a further question: "Have, O Lord, all Samaṇas and Brāhmaṇas the same doctrine, the same moral code, the same aspiration, the same aim?"

"They have not, O king of gods."

"But why, O Lord, have they not?"

"Many are the conditions of mind, O king of gods, various are the conditions of mind existing in this world. To whatever condition, out of these, the beings adhere, to that only they obstinately and tenaciously cling, maintaining, 'Only this is truth, anything else is folly!' Therefore do not all Samaṇas and Brāhmaṇas have the same doctrine, the same moral code, the same aspiration, the same aim."

"But, O Lord, are all Samaṇas and Brāhmaṇas absolutely perfect, absolutely secure, absolutely purified, of absolutely highest achievements?"

"They are not, O king of gods."

"But why, O Lord, are they not?"

"Those Samaṇas and Brāhmaṇas, O king of gods, who have achieved deliverance through the destruction of craving, they only are absolutely perfect, absolutely secure, absolutely purified, of absolutely highest achievement. Therefore are not all Samaṇas and Brāhmaṇas absolutely perfect, absolutely secure, absolutely purified, of absolutely highest achievement."

In this manner it was that the Bhagavā answered the question put by Sakka, the king of gods. Edified, Sakka, the king of gods, approved of the Bhagavā's saying and took delight in it: "Thus it is, O Bhagavā! Thus it is, O Sugata! Conquered are my doubts, gone is my uncertainty, having heard the Bhagavā's answer to this question."

7. And Sakka, the king of gods, approving of the Bhagavā's saying and delighting in it, addressed the Bhagavā and spoke: "Passion,[11] O Lord, is disease, passion is a cancer, passion is a dart. Passion drags a man about from one existence to another, so that he finds himself now up above, then down below. These problems, O Lord, which were rankling in me for a long time, and to which other Samaṇas and Brāhmaṇas have lent no ear, these the Bhagavā has solved for me, and has removed the dart of doubt and uncertainty."

"Then, O king of gods, do you remember to have asked these questions from other Samaṇas and Brāhmaṇas?"

"I do remember, O Lord, to have done so."

"And in which way did they explain them to you, O king of

11. *Ejā* (drive, urge) is a synonym of *taṇhā* 'craving.'

gods? If this is not inconvenient to you, you may speak."

"Not, O Lord, is it inconvenient to me when the Bhagavā is present or others like him."

"Then, O king of gods, you may speak."

"Whom I deemed to be Samaṇas and Brāhmaṇas, O Lord, were hermits, living solitary in the forest. Them I approached and put these questions. But they made no answer, but rather asked of me a counter question, 'What is the name of the venerable one?' Thus asked, I made answer, 'I am, Sirs, Sakka, the king of gods.' And they went on questioning me, 'Pray, by what deed did the venerable king of gods rise to that state?' And I expounded to them the Dhamma, as it was heard and understood by me, and they were satisfied, even with that little: 'Verily, we have seen Sakka, the king of gods! And what we asked of him, that he has answered!' And they actually became my disciples, rather than *I* the follower of them.

"But I, O Lord, am the follower of the Bhagavā. A stream-enterer[12] am I, delivered from downfall, assured, bound for enlightenment."

"Do you remember, O king of gods, ever before to have experienced such a feeling of satisfaction and happiness?"

"I do remember it, O Lord."

"And in which way, O king of gods, do you remember it?"

"Once, O Lord, there took place a fight between gods and Asuras. In this fight, O Lord, the gods were victorious, and the Asuras were defeated. The fight being over, the battle being won, I thought to myself, 'What there is of heavenly power and what there is of Asura power, both will now be enjoyed by the gods!' And so, O Lord, that feeling of satisfaction and happiness was mixed up with thoughts of war and battle, not leading to disenchantment, not leading to dispassion, not leading to cessation, not leading to higher knowledge, not leading to enlightenment, not leading to Nibbāna.

"But this feeling of satisfaction and happiness, O Lord, I experience, having heard the Dhamma from the Bhagavā, is not mixed up with thoughts of war and battle. This solely leads to disenchantment, to dispassion, to cessation, to inner calm, to higher knowledge, to enlightenment and to Nibbāna."

---

12. *Sotāpanna*—the first of the four stages of sainthood.

8. "But, O king of gods, what reasons do you perceive to announce the experience of such a feeling of satisfaction and happiness?"

"Six reasons do I perceive, O Lord:

> While living here itself,
> Born a god as I am—
> Fresh potency of life I win.
> This I announce to you, O Lord.

This is, O Lord, the first reason.

> Departed from the realm of gods,
> Heavenly potency being spent,
> Mindfully I choose the womb
> In which to be reborn my mind delights.

This is, O Lord, the second reason.

> Unconfused in understanding,
> Delighted in the Buddha's Law,
> Wisely shall I dwell,
> Clearly comprehending, mindful.

This is, O Lord, the third reason.

> And if, while faring along wisely,
> Enlightenment should be my part,
> I then would dwell in perfect knowledge,
> And thus achieve the end.

This is, O Lord, the fourth reason.

> Or if, departed from the realm of men,
> Human potency being spent,
> Again I should become a god:
> Chiefest I would be of all the worlds divine.

This is, O Lord, the fifth reason.

> Among the deities most sublime,
> Among Akaniṭṭha so glorious,
> I then would spend the last turn of life;
> That abode too awaits me.

This is, Lord, the sixth reason.

These are, O Lord, the six reasons I perceive to announce the experience of such a feeling of satisfaction and happiness."

9. Sakka's Song

"Seeking the Tathāgata, I wandered long,
My mind in doubt, steeped in perplexity,
With problems none could solve.

The Samaṇas of lonely dwellings,
Their company I sought, sat near;
Buddhas I imagined them to be.

'What makes men reach accomplishment,
What makes them fail?' This I asked of them;
But neither way nor method did they know.

And when they came to understand
That Sakka of the gods it was
Who had appeared to them,
They even asked of me
What skill brought me the fair result.

I taught them what I knew,
The lore preserved among the folk,
And they rejoiced and said,
'Vāsava it was we saw!'

But the Buddha I beheld today!
Conqueror over Doubts:
Freed am I from fear,
In finding him who truly knows!

Remover of the dart of craving,
Enlightened, Man without Compare:
Him the hero great I worship,
Him, the Kinsman of the Sun!

The worship once I offered Brahmā,
Together with the mighty gods,
We offer now to you, O Lord.

The Enlightened One you are indeed,
Teacher beyond compare:

Throughout the world of gods and men
Your equal none can find!"

10. And Sakka, the king of gods, addressed Pañcasikha, the young Gandhabba: "Of great service have you been to me, my dear Pañcasikha, in so far as you first gained over the Bhagavā; gained over by you, my dear, we afterwards drew near to see the Bhagavā, the Arahant, Sammā-Sambuddha. I appoint you to your paternal heritage. You shall be king over the Gandhabbas; and Baddha Sūriya-vaccasā, the sun maiden longed for by you, I give her to you."

And Sakka, the king of gods, having touched the earth with his hand, made three times this solemn utterance:

Namo tassa Bhagavāto, Arahato, Sammā-Sambuddhassa!
Namo tassa Bhagavāto, Arahato, Sammā-Sambuddhassa!
Namo tassa Bhagavāto, Arahato, Sammā-Sambuddhassa

Honour to Him, the Exalted One, the Worthy, the Fully Enlightened!
Honour to Him, the Exalted One, the Worthy, the Fully Enlightened!
Honour to Him, the Exalted One, the Worthy, the Fully Enlightened!"

And while this discourse had taken place, there arose in Sakka, the king of gods, and also in another eighty thousand deities, the pure, spotless eye of the Dhamma:

Yaṃ kiñci samudaya-dhammaṃ sabbaṃ taṃ nirodha-dhamman'ti

Every phenomenon-of-origin is a phenomenon-of-dissolution.

Such were the questions which Sakka, the king of gods was invited to ask and were answered by the Bhagavā. Therefore is this exposition called "The Questions of Sakka."

Anattā and Nibbāna

Egolessness and Deliverance

by

Nyanaponika Thera

WHEEL PUBLICATION NO. 11

A slightly differing German version of this essay appeared in 1951 in the magazine *Die Einsicht.* The English version was first published in the quarterly *The Light of the Dhamma,* Vol. IV, No. 3 (Rangoon 1957) under the title "Nibbāna in the Light of the Middle Doctrine."

Introduction

> This world, Kaccāna, usually leans upon a duality: upon (the belief in) existence or non-existence.... Avoiding these two extremes, the Perfect One shows the doctrine in the middle: Dependent on ignorance are the kamma-formations.... By the cessation of ignorance, kamma-formations cease.... (SN 12:15)

The above saying of the Buddha speaks of the duality of existence (*atthitā*) and non-existence (*natthitā*). These two terms refer to the theories of eternalism (*sassata-diṭṭhi*) and annihilationism (*uccheda-diṭṭhi*), the basic misconceptions of actuality that in various forms repeatedly reappear in the history of human thought.

Eternalism is the belief in a permanent substance or entity, whether conceived as a multitude of individual souls or selves, created or not, as a monistic world-soul, a deity of any description, or a combination of any of these notions. *Annihilationism*, on the other hand, asserts the temporary existence of separate selves or personalities, which are entirely destroyed or dissolved after death. Accordingly, the two key words of the text quoted above refer (1) to the absolute, i.e., eternal, existence of any assumed substance or entity, and (2) to the ultimate, absolute annihilation of separate entities conceived as impermanent, i.e., their non-existence after the end of their life-span. These two extreme views stand and fall with the assumption of something static of either permanent or impermanent nature. They will lose their basis entirely if life is seen in its true nature, as a continuous flux of material and mental processes arising from their appropriate conditions—a process which will cease only when these conditions are removed. This will explain why our text introduces here the formula of dependent origination (*paṭicca-samuppāda*), and its reversal, dependent cessation.

Dependent *origination*, being an unbroken process, excludes the assumption of an absolute non-existence, or naught, terminating individual existence; the qualifying term *dependent* indicates that there is also no absolute, independent existence, no static being *per se*, but only an evanescent arising of phenomena dependent on likewise evanescent conditions.

Dependent *cessation* excludes the belief in absolute and permanent existence. It shows, as well, that there is no automatic lapse into non-existence, for the cessation of relative existence too is a conditioned occurrence.

Thus these teachings of dependent origination and dependent cessation are a true doctrine in the middle, transcending the extremes of existence and non-existence.

Thinking by way of such conceptual contrasts as existence and non-existence has, however, a powerful hold on man. The hold is so powerful because this way of thinking is perpetually nourished by several strong roots deeply embedded in the human mind. The strongest of them is the practical and theoretical assumption of an ego or self. It is the powerful wish for a preservation and perpetuation of the personality, or a refined version of it, that lies behind all the numerous varieties of eternalistic belief. But even with people who have discarded eternalistic creeds or theories, the instinctive belief in the uniqueness and importance of their particular personalities is still so strong that they take death, the end of the personality, to mean complete annihilation or non-existence. Thus the belief in a self is responsible not only for eternalism, but also for the annihilationist view, either in its popular unphilosophical form which regards death as the utter end or in materialistic theories elaborating the same position.

There are other contributory roots of these notions of existence and non-existence closely connected with the main root of ego-belief. There is, for instance, a *linguistic* root, consisting in the basic structure of language (subject and predicate, noun and adjective) and its tendency to simplify affirmative and negative statements for the sake of easy communication and orientation. The structural features of language and linguistic habits of simplified statements have exercised a subtle but strong influence on our way of thinking, making us inclined to assume that "there must be a thing if there is a word for it."

These one-sided views may also spring from *emotional* reasons, expressive of basic attitudes to life. They may reflect the moods of optimism and pessimism, hope and despair, the wish to feel secure through metaphysical support, or the desire to live without inhibitions in a materialistically conceived universe. The theoretical views of eternalism or annihilationism held by an individual may well change during his lifetime, together with the corresponding moods or emotional needs.

There is also an *intellectual* root: the speculative and theorizing propensity of the mind. Certain thinkers, people of the theorizing type (*diṭṭhicarita*) in Buddhist psychology, are prone to create various elaborate philosophical systems in which, with great ingenuity, they play off against each other the pairs of conceptual opposites. The great satisfaction this gives to those engaged in such thought-constructions further reinforces the adherence to them.

From these brief remarks, one will be able to appreciate the strength and variety of the forces which induce man to think, feel and speak in the way of these opposites: absolute existence or absolute non-existence. Thus the Buddha had good reason for saying, in our introductory passage, that people *usually* lean upon a duality. We need not be surprised that even Nibbāna, the Buddhist goal of deliverance, has been wrongly interpreted in the sense of these extremes. But rigid concepts of existence and non-existence cannot do justice to the dynamic nature of actuality. Still less do they apply to Nibbāna, which the Buddha declared to be supramundane (*lokuttara*) and beyond conceptual thinking (*atakkāvacara*).

In the early days, when knowledge of Buddhist teachings had just reached the West, most writers and scholars (with a few exceptions like Schopenhauer and Max Müller) took Nibbāna to be pure and simple *non-existence*. Consequently, Western writers too readily described Buddhism as a nihilistic doctrine teaching annihilation as its highest goal, a view these writers condemned as philosophically absurd and ethically reprehensible. Similar statements still sometimes appear in prejudiced non-Buddhist literature. The pendular reaction to that view was the conception of Nibbāna as *existence*. It was now interpreted in the light of already familiar religious and philosophical notions as pure being, pure consciousness, pure self or some other metaphysical concept.

But even Buddhist thought could not always keep clear of a lopsided interpretation of Nibbāna. This happened even in early times: the sect of the Sautrāntikas had a rather negativistic view of Nibbāna, while the Mahāyānistic conceptions of Buddha-fields (*Buddhakṣtra*), Primordial Buddha (*Ādibuddha*), Tathāgatagarbha, etc., favoured a positive-metaphysical interpretation.

It is, therefore, not surprising that modern Buddhist writers also sometimes advocate these extremes. In Buddhist countries of the East, however, there is now not a single Buddhist school or sect known to the writer that favours a nihilistic interpretation of Nibbāna. Contrary to erroneous opinions, voiced mainly by uninformed or prejudiced Western authors, Theravada Buddhism is definitely averse to the view that Nibbāna is mere extinction. This statement will be substantiated in the first main section of this essay.

For reasons mentioned earlier, it is not always easy to steer clear of those two opposite views of existence and non-existence, and to keep closely to the middle path shown by the Buddha, the teaching of dependent origination and dependent cessation. Until that way of thinking in terms of conditionality has been fully absorbed into the mind, constant watchfulness will be required to avoid slipping unaware into either eternalism or annihilationism, or coming too close to them. When discussing these questions, there is the danger one will be carried away by one's own arguments and counter one extreme by endorsing its opposite. Therefore, in the treatment of that problem, great caution and self-criticism is required lest one lose sight of the middle path.

The primary purpose of this treatise is to offer material for clearly demarcating the Buddha's doctrine of Nibbāna from both misinterpretations. Its intention is not to encourage speculations on the nature of Nibbāna, which are bound to be futile and may even be detrimental to the endeavour to attain it. The canonical texts elucidating the Four Noble Truths say that Nibbāna, the third truth, is to be realized (*sacchikātabbaṃ*); it is not to be understood (like the first truth), nor to be developed (like the fourth truth). We must also emphasize that the material presented here should not be used in a one-sided manner as an argument in favour of either extreme against the other. Each of the two main sections of this treatise requires the other for its qualification and completion. It is hoped that the material from canonical and commentarial sources collected in these pages, by clarifying the position of Theravada, will at least reduce the points of conflict between the opposing interpretations.

I. The Nihilistic-Negative Extreme

Section 1

We shall first consider the basic work of post-canonical Theravada literature, *The Path of Purification* (*Visuddhimagga*), compiled in the 5th century AC by the great commentator, Bhadantācariya Buddhaghosa. This monumental work furnishes a comprehensive and systematic exposition of the principal Buddhist doctrines. It is derived from the Pali Canon and the ancient commentarial literature which partly incorporates material that may well go back to the earliest times of the teaching.

In this work, in Chapter XVI on the Faculties and Truths, in the section dealing with the third noble truth, we find a lengthy disquisition on Nibbāna. It is striking that the polemic part of it is exclusively directed against what we have called the "nihilistic-negative extreme" in the interpretation of Nibbāna. We cannot be sure about the reason for that limitation, since no explicit statement is given. It is, however, possible that the Venerable Buddhaghosa (or perhaps the traditional material he used) was keen that the Theravada teachings on that subject should be well distinguished from those of a prominent contemporary sect, the Sautrāntikas, which in other respects was close to the general standpoint of Theravada. The Sautrāntikas belonged to that group of schools which we suggest should be called *Sāvakayāna*, following the *early* Mahāyānist nomenclature, instead of the derogatory "Hīnayāna." The Theravādins obviously did not want to be included in the accusation of nihilism which the Mahāyānists raised against the Sautrāntikas. This might have been the external reason for the *Visuddhimagga*'s emphasis on the rejection of the nihilistic conception of Nibbāna.

As to the positive-metaphysical view, the Venerable Buddhaghosa perhaps thought it sufficiently covered by the numerous passages in the *Visuddhimagga* dealing with the rejection of the eternity-view and of a transcendental self. However that may be, even nowadays Buddhism, and Theravada in particular, is quite often wrongly accused of nihilism. It is therefore apposite to summarize here the arguments found in the *Visuddhimagga*, followed (in Section 2) by additions from the commentary to that work.[1] Many passages from the suttas relevant to a rejection of nihilism are quoted in both these extracts, making it unnecessary to deal with them separately.

In the aforementioned chapter of the *Visuddhimagga*, the argument proper is preceded by a definition of Nibbāna. The definition uses three categories usually employed in commentarial literature for the purpose of elucidation:

Nibbāna has peace as its *characteristic.* Its *function* is not to die; or its function is to comfort. It is *manifested* as the signless [without the "signs," or marks, of greed, hatred and delusion]; or it is manifested as non-diversification.

In the argument proper, the Venerable Buddhaghosa first rejects the view that Nibbāna is non-existent, holding it must exist as it can be realized by practising the path. The adversary, however, while admitting that Nibbāna is not non-existent, still insists on a negative understanding of the nature of Nibbāna. He argues first that Nibbāna should be understood simply as the absence of all the factors of existence, i.e., the five aggregates. Buddhaghosa counters this by replying that Nibbāna can be attained during an individual's lifetime, while his aggregates are still present. The adversary then proposes that Nibbāna consists solely in the destruction of all defilements, quoting in support of his contention the sutta passage: "That, friend, which is the destruction of greed, hate and delusion that is Nibbāna" (SN 38:1). Buddhaghosa rejects this view too, pointing out that it leads to certain undesirable consequences: it would make Nibbāna temporal, since the destruction of the defilements is an event that occurs in time; and it makes Nibbāna conditioned, since the actual destruction of the defilements occurs through conditions. He points out that Nibbāna is called the destruction of greed, hate and delusion in a metaphorical sense: because the unconditioned

1. The extracts from both works have mainly been taken, with a few alterations, from Bhikkhu Ñāṇamoli's translation (see Note on Sources). Explanatory additions by this writer are in brackets, those by Bhikkhu Ñāṇamoli in parentheses.

reality, Nibbāna, is the basis or support for the complete destruction of those defilements.

Venerable Buddhaghosa next deals with the negative terminology the Buddha uses to describe Nibbāna. He explains that such terminology is used because of Nibbāna's extreme subtlety. The opponent argues that since Nibbāna is attained by following the path, it cannot be uncreated. Buddhaghosa answers that Nibbāna is only reached by the path, but not produced by it; thus it is uncreated, without beginning, and free from aging and death. He then goes on to discuss the nature of Nibbāna more explicitly:

> ... The Buddha's goal is one and has no plurality. But this (single goal, Nibbāna) is firstly called "with result of past clinging left" (*sa-upādisesa*) since it is made known together with the (aggregates resulting from past) clinging still remaining (during the Arahat's life), being thus made known in terms of the stilling of defilements and the remaining (result of past) clinging that are present in one who has reached it by means of development. But secondly, it is called "without result of past clinging left" (*anupādisesa*) since after the last consciousness of the Arahat, who has abandoned arousing (future aggregates) and so prevented kamma from giving result in a future (existence), there is no further arising of aggregates of existence, and those already arisen have disappeared. So the (result of past) clinging that remained is non-existent, and it is in terms of this non-existence, in the sense that "there is no (result of past) clinging here" that that (same goal) is called "without result of past clinging left." (See It 44.)

Because it can be arrived at by distinction of knowledge that succeeds through untiring perseverance,[2] and because it is the word of the Omniscient One,[3] Nibbāna is not non-existent as regards its nature in the ultimate sense (*paramatthena nāvijjamānaṃ*

2. Comy.: This is to show that, for Arahants, Nibbāna is established by their own experience.

3. Comy.: For others it is established by inference based on the words of the Master.

sabhāvato nibbānaṃ); for this is said: "Bhikkhus, there is an unborn, an unbecome, an unmade, an unformed". (Ud 73; It 45)

Section 2

Taking up the last quotation, the commentary to the *Visuddhimagga* (*Paramatthamañjūsā*),[4] written by Ācariya Dhammapāla (6th century), says:

> By these words the Master proclaimed the actual existence of Nibbāna in the ultimate sense.* But he did not proclaim it as a mere injunction of his [i.e., as a creedal dogma], saying "I am the Lord and Master of the Dhamma"; but, in his compassion for those to whom intellectual understanding is the highest that is attainable, he also stated it as a reasoned conclusion in the continuation of the passage quoted above (Udāna 73): "If, bhikkhus, there were not the unborn, etc., an escape from what is born, etc., could not be perceived. But because, bhikkhus, there is an unborn, etc., an escape from what is born, etc., can be perceived."
>
> This is the meaning: if the unformed element (Nibbāna), having the nature of being unborn, etc., did not exist, no escape from the formed or conditioned, i.e., the five aggregates, could be perceived in this world; their final coming-to-rest (i.e., cessation) could not be perceived, could not be found or apprehended, would not be possible. But if right understanding and the other path factors, each performing its own function, take Nibbāna as object, then they will completely destroy the defilements. Therefore one can perceive here a getting-away, an escape from the suffering of existence in its entirety.
>
> Now, in the ultimate sense the existingness of the Nibbāna-element has been demonstrated by the Fully Enlightened One, compassionate for the whole world, by many sutta passages, such as "Dhammas without condition," "Unformed dhammas" (see *Dhammasaṅgaṇī*, Abhidhamma

4. The paragraphs beginning with * are translated by the author of this essay; those without, by Bhikkhu Ñāṇamoli (taken from the notes to his translation of the *Visuddhimagga*).

Piṭaka); "Bhikkhus, there is that sphere (*āyatana*) where neither earth..." (Udāna 71); "This state is very hard to see, that is to say, the stilling of all formations, the relinquishing of all substance of becoming" (DN 14; MN 26); "Bhikkhus, I shall teach you the unformed and the way leading to the unformed" (SN 43:12) and so on; and in this sutta, "Bhikkhus, there, is an unborn..." (Udāna 73)...

The words "Bhikkhus, there is an unborn, an unmade, an unformed" and so on, which demonstrate the existingness of Nibbāna in the ultimate sense, are not misleading because they are spoken by the Omniscient One, like the words "All formations are impermanent, all formations are painful, all *dhammas* (states) are not self" (Dhp vv. 277–79; AN 3:134, etc.).

*If Nibbāna were mere non-existence, it could not be described by terms such as "profound [deep, hard to see, hard to comprehend, peaceful, lofty, inaccessible to ratiocination, subtle, to be known by the wise]," etc.; or as "the unformed, [the cankerless, the true, the other shore]," etc.[5]; or as "kammically neutral, without condition, unincluded [within the three realms of existence]," etc.[6]

Section 3

The references to sutta-texts, quoted in the extracts from the *Visuddhimagga* and its commentary, make it quite clear that the Buddha declared Nibbāna to be an attainable entity and did not conceive it as the mere fact of extinction or cessation. All negatively formulated statements on Nibbāna should be understood in the light of the sutta passages quoted here, and do not admit an interpretation contradictory to these texts. Any forced or far-fetched interpretation of them will be contrary to the whole straightforward way of the Buddha's exposition.

If we have spoken above of Nibbāna as an "entity," it should be taken just as a word-label meant to exclude "non-existence." It

5. These are some of the altogether 33 designations of Nibbāna in SN 43:12-44.

6. This refers to Abhidhammic classifications in which Nibbāna is included, occurring, for instance, in the *Dhammasaṅgaṇī*.

is used in the same restricted sense of a linguistic convention as the emphatic words in the Udāna: "There *is* an unborn..."; "There *is* that sphere where neither earth...." It is not meant to convey the meaning of "existence" in the usual sense, which should be kept limited to "the five aggregates or any one of them." Nibbāna is indescribable in the strictest sense (*avacanīya*).

Our extracts from such an authoritative work as the *Visuddhimagga* show how emphatically the Theravada tradition rejects a nihilistic conception of its highest ideal, Nibbāna. This fact may perhaps help to remove one of the points of controversy among modern writers and Buddhist schools: the prejudice that Theravada, or even the Pali Canon, advocates "annihilation" as its highest goal.

There is, however, another principal point of difference in the interpretation of Buddhism, and of the Pali Canon in particular, which is likewise closely connected with the conception of Nibbāna. It is the question of the range of validity, or application, of the Anattā doctrine, i.e., the doctrine of impersonality. This doctrine, we maintain, applies not only to the world of conditioned phenomena, but also to Nibbāna. As far as the denial of its application to the latter falls under the heading of the "positive-metaphysical extreme," it will be treated in the following sections.

II. The Positive-Metaphysical Extreme

Section 4

In India, a country so deeply religious and philosophically so creative, the far greater danger to the preservation of the Dhamma's character as a "middle way" came from the other extreme. It consisted in identifying, or connecting, the concept of Nibbāna with any of the numerous theistic, pantheistic or other speculative ideas of a positive-metaphysical type, chiefly with various conceptions of an abiding self.

According to the penetrative analysis in the Brahmajāla Sutta (DN 1), all the diverse metaphysical and theological views concerning the nature of the self, the world and a divine ground from which they might come, arise from either of two sources: (1) from a limited and misinterpreted meditative experience (in which we may also include supposed revelations, prophetic inspirations, etc.), and (2) from bare reasoning (speculative philosophy and theology). But behind all these metaphysical and theological notions, there looms, as the driving force, the powerful urge in man to preserve, in some way, his belief in an abiding personality which he can invest with all his longings for permanence, security and eternal happiness. It is therefore not surprising that a number of present-day interpreters of Buddhism perhaps through the force of that powerful, instinctive urge for self-preservation and the influence of long-cherished and widely-held views, advocate a positive-metaphysical interpretation of Nibbāna and Anattā. Some of these sincerely believe themselves to be genuine Buddhists, and possess a genuine devotion towards the Buddha and a fair appreciation of other aspects of his teaching. We shall now look at these views.

In the spirit of the middle way, the following refutation of the positive-metaphysical extreme is also meant to guard against any metaphysical conclusions which may be wrongly derived from our rejection of nihilism in the first part of this essay. In the reverse, that first section may serve to counter an excessive "defence-reaction" against the metaphysical views to be treated now.

The positive-metaphysical extreme in the interpretation of Nibbāna consists in the identification, or metaphysical association, of a refined or purified self (*attā*) with what, in the context of the respective view, is held to be Nibbāna. Two main types of the metaphysical view can be distinguished, as the preceding paragraph already implies.

(1) The assumption of a universal and unitary (non-dual and non-pluristic) principle with which a purified self, one thought to be liberated from the empirical personality, either merges, or is assumed to be basically one. These views might differ in details, according to their being influenced either by Theosophy, Vedānta or Mahāyāna (the latter, with varying degrees of justification).[7]

(2) The assumption that the transcendental "selves" of the Arahats, freed from the aggregates, enter Nibbāna, which is regarded as their "eternal home" and as "the only state adequate to them." Nibbāna itself is admitted to be non-self (*anattā*), while the Holy Ones (Arahats) are supposed to retain "in Nibbāna" some kind of individuality, in a way unexplained and unexplainable. This view is, to our knowledge, advocated in such a way only by the German author Georg Grimm and his followers.

---

7. The *theosophical* variant, is, e.g., represented by neo-Buddhist groups in Britain and elsewhere which otherwise have done good work in introducing Westerners to Buddhism or to their conception of it. The Vedāntic influence is conspicuous, e.g., in the utterances of well-meaning Indians, among them men of eminence, maintaining the basic identiey or similarity, of the Vedāntic and Buddhist position concerning Ātman. This is, by the way, quite in contrast to opinion on that subject, expressed by the great classical exponents of Vedānta. See *Vedānta and Buddhism* by H. v. Glasenapp (*Wheel Publication* No. 2).

Māhāyanistic influence may be noticeable in some representatives of the former two variants. But also in the Mahāyāna literature itself, the positive-metaphysical extreme is met with in varying degrees. Ranging from the Madhyamika scriptures where it is comparatively negligible, up to the Yogāvacara school where Asaṅga uses even the terms *mahātma* and *paramātma* in an approving sense (see *Mahāyāna-sūtrālaṅkāra-śāstra* and Asaṅga's own commentary).

Section 5

(a) Common to both views is the assumption of an eternal self supposed to exist beyond the five aggregates that make up personality and existence in its entirety. The supposition that the Buddha should have taught anything like that is clearly and sufficiently refuted by the following saying alone:

> Any ascetics or brāhmans who regard manifold (things or ideas) as the self, all regard the five aggregates (as the self) or any one of them. (SN 22:47)

This textual passage also excludes any misinterpretation of the standard formulation of the Anattā doctrine: "This does not belong to me, this I am not, this is not my self." Some writers believe that this formula permits the conclusion that the Buddha supposed a self to exist outside, or beyond, the five aggregates to which the formula usually refers. This wrong deduction is disposed of by the statement of the Buddha quoted above which clearly says that all the manifold conceptions of a self can have reference only to the five aggregates either collectively or selectively. How else could any idea of a self or a personality be formed, if not from the material of the five aggregates and from a misconception about them? On what else could notions about a self be based? This fact about the only possible way whereby ideas of a self can be formed was expressed by the Buddha himself in the continuation of the text quoted above:

> There is, bhikkhus, an uninstructed worldling... He regards corporeality as self, or the self as possessing corporeality, or the corporeality as being within the self, or the self within corporeality (similarly with the four mental aggregates).[8] In this way he arrives at that very conception "I am."

Further it was said: "If there are corporeality, feeling, perception, formations and consciousness, on account of them and dependent on them arises the belief in individuality... and speculations about a self." (SN 22:154, 155)

(b) If the words "I," "ego," "personality" and "self" should have meaning at all, any form of an ego-conception, even the

8. These are the twenty kinds of individuality-belief (*sakkāya-diṭṭhi*).

most abstract and diluted one, must necessarily be connected with the idea of particularity or separateness with a differentiation from what is regarded as *not* "ego." But from what would that particularity or differentiation be derived if not from the only available data of experience, the physical and mental phenomena comprised by the five aggregates?

In the Majjhima Nikāya Sutta called "The Simile of the Snake" (MN 22), it is said: "If, monks, there is a self, will there also be what belongs to self?" — "Yes, Lord." — "If there is what belongs to self, will there also be 'My self'?" — "Yes, Lord." — "But since a self and self's belongings cannot truly be found, is this not a perfectly foolish doctrine: 'This is the world, this the self. Permanent, abiding, eternal, immutable shall I be after death, persisting in eternal identity'?" — "It is, Lord, a perfectly foolish doctrine."[9]

The first sentence of that text expresses, in a manner as simple as it is emphatic, the fact pointed out before: that the assumption of a self requires also something belonging to a self (*attaniya*), i.e., properties by which that self receives its distinguishing characteristics. To speak of a self devoid of such differentiating attributes, having therefore nothing to characterize it and to give meaningful contents to the word, will be entirely senseless and in contradiction to the accepted usage of these terms "self," "ego," etc. But this very thing is done by those who advocate the first of the two main-types of the "positive-metaphysical extreme": that is, the assumption of a "great universal self or over-self" (*mahātman*) supposed to merge with, or be basically identical with, a universal and undifferentiated (*nirguṇa*) metaphysical principle which is sometimes equated with Nibbāna. Those who hold these views are sometimes found to make the bold claim that the Buddha wanted to deny only a separate self and that in none of his utterances did he reject the existence of a transcendental self. What has been said before in this section may serve as an answer to these beliefs.

Those views which we have assigned to the second category take an opposite view. They insist on the separate existence of liberated, transcendental selves within the Nibbāna-element. However, their advocates leave quite a number of issues unexplained. They do

9. See *The Discourse on the Snake Simile*, tr. by Nyanaponika Thera (Wheel No. 48/49).

not indicate how they arrive at the idea of separateness without reference to the world of experience; and they fail to show what that separateness actually consists in and how it can be said to persist in the Nibbāna-element, which, by definition, is undifferentiated (*nippapañca*), the very reverse of separateness.

Both varieties of individuality-belief wish to combine various conceptions of self with the Buddhist teaching of Nibbāna. They are, at the very outset, refuted by the philosophically very significant statement in the discourse on the "Simile of the Snake," implying that "I" and "mine," owner and property, substance and attribute, subject and predication are inseparable and correlative terms, which, however, lack reality in the ultimate sense.

Section 6

The two main-types of a positive-metaphysical interpretation of Nibbāna can be easily included in a considerable number of false views mentioned, classified and rejected by the Buddha. A selection of applicable classifications will be presented in what follows. This material, additional to the fundamental remarks in the preceding section, will furnish an abundance of documentation for the fact that not a single eternalistic conception of self and Nibbāna, of any conceivable form, is reconcilable with the teachings of the Buddha as found in their oldest available presentation in the Pali Canon.

(a) In the Saṃyutta Nikāya (SN 22:86) we read: "Do you think, Anurādha, that the Perfect One (*tathāgata*) is apart from corporeality (*aññatra rūpā*)...apart from consciousness?"[10]—"Certainly not, O Lord." — "Do you think that the Perfect One is someone without corporeality (*arūpī*)...someone without consciousness?"[11]— "Certainly not, O Lord." — "Since the Perfect One, Anurādha, cannot, truly and really, be found by you even during lifetime, is it befitting to declare: 'He who is the Perfect One, the highest being...that Perfect One can be made known outside of these four possibilities: The Perfect One exists after death...does not exist... exists in some way and in another way not...can neither be said to exist nor not to exist'?" — "Certainly not, O Lord."

10. I.e., outside the aggregates taken singly.
11. I.e., outside the aggregates as a whole.

This text applies to both main-types of view which assume a self beyond the aggregates. It should be mentioned here that the commentary paraphrases the words "the Perfect One" (*tathāgata*) by "living being" (*satta*). That is probably meant to show that the statements in the text are valid not only for the conventional term "the Perfect One" but also for any other terms designating an individuality.

(b) Since the concept of a self is necessarily linked with that of an ownership of qualities and possessions (see 5b), both main-types come under the following heading of the twenty kinds of individuality-belief (*sakkāya-diṭṭhi;* see 5a).

He regards the self as possessing corporeality...as possessing feeling...perception...formations...consciousness.

This applies, in particular, to the second main-type advocated by Georg Grimm, who expressly speaks of the five aggregates as "attributions" ("Beilegungen") of the self. It does not make any difference here that these "attributions" are regarded by Grimm as "incommensurate" to the self and as capable of being discarded. What matters is the fact that such a relationship between the self and the aggregates is assumed, and this justifies the inclusion of that view in the aforementioned type of individuality belief.

(c) From the "Discourse on the Root Cause" (Mūlapariyāya Sutta; MN 1) the following categories apply to both types: "He thinks (himself) different from (or beyond) the four material elements, the heavenly worlds, the uncorporeal spheres; from anything seen, heard, (differently) sensed and cognized; from the whole universe (*sabbato*)." To the second type are applicable the views: "He thinks (himself) in Nibbāna (*nibbānasmiṃ maññati*) or as different from Nibbāna (*nibbānato maññati*)." That is, he believes the liberated self which is supposed to enter the Nibbāna-element to be different from it.

(d) In the sutta "All Cankers" (Sabbāsava Sutta; MN 2) the following instances of unwise and superficial thinking (*ayoniso manasikāra*) are mentioned and rejected:

Six theories about the self from which the following are applicable here: "I have a self" and "By the self I know the self."[12]

---

12. Pali: *attanā'va attānaṃ sañjānāmi.* This refers to Vedāntic conceptions. Quite similar formulations are found already in the Saṃhitās, the pre-

Sixteen kinds of doubt about the existence and nature of the self, with reference to the past, present and future, e.g., "Am I or am I not?", "What am I?", "Shall I be or not?", "What shall I be?"

Hereby any type of speculation about an alleged self is rejected.

(e) In the Brahmajāla Sutta (DN 1) the theories about a self are specified as to their details. Those, however, who advocate the two main-types of the positive-metaphysical extreme, with which we are here concerned, generally avoid or reject detailed statements on the nature of Nibbāna and the self. But if they assume an eternal and transcendental self, it must be conceived as being passive, motionless and immutable. For any active relationship to the world would involve an abandonment of the transcendental state assumed. Therefore both main-types fall under the eternalist view, characterized and rejected in the Brahmajāla Sutta as follows: "Eternal are self and world, barren, motionless like a mountain peak, steadfast like a pillar."

(f) The rejection of any belief in a self (as abiding or temporarily identical), and of the extremes of existence and not-existence, cannot be better concluded than by quoting the continuation of the saying that forms the motto of this treatise:

> For him, Kaccāna, who considers, according to reality and with true wisdom, the origination of (and in) the world, there is not what in the world (is called) "non-existence" (*natthitā*). For him, Kaccāna, who considers, according to reality and with true wisdom, the cessation of (and in) the world, there is not what in the world (is called) "existence" (*atthitā*). This world, Kaccāna, is generally fettered by propensities, clingings, and biases. But concerning these propensities, clingings, fixed mental attitudes, biases and deep-rooted inclinations, he (the man of right understanding) does not come near, does not cling, does not have the mental attitude: "I have a self" (*n'adhiṭṭhāti attā me'ti*). He has no doubt or uncertainty that it is suffering, indeed, that arises, and suffering that ceases. Herein his knowledge does not rely on others. In so far, Kaccāna, is one a man of right understanding. (SN 12:15)

Buddhist Upanishads, and later in the *Bhagavadgītā*.

III. Transcending the Extremes

If we examine the utterances on Nibbāna in the Pali Canon, we find that it is described (or better: paraphrased) in both positive and negative terms. Statements of a positive nature include designations like "the profound, the true, the pure, the permanent, the marvellous," etc. (SN 43); and such texts as those quoted above (see Section 2), "There is that sphere...", "There is an unborn...", etc. Statements in the form of negative terms include such definitions of Nibbāna as "the destruction of greed, hate and delusion" and as "cessation of existence" (*bhava-nirodha*). If the Buddhist conception of Nibbāna is to be understood correctly, one will have to give full weight to the significance of both types of utterance. If one were to quote only one type as a vindication of one's own one-sided opinion, the result would be a lopsided view.

To the utterances of positive character we may ascribe the following purposes: (1) to exclude the nihilistic extreme; (2) to allay the fears of those who are still without an adequate grasp of the truths of suffering and *anattā*, and thus shrink back from the final cessation of suffering, i.e., of rebirth, as if recoiling from a fall into a bottomless abyss; (3) to show Nibbāna as a goal capable of attainment and truly desirable.

The emphatic "There is" that opens the two well-known texts on Nibbāna in the Udāna, leaves no doubt that Nibbāna is not conceived as bare extinction or as a camouflage for an absolute zero. But, on the other hand, as a precaution against a metaphysical misinterpretation of that solemn enunciation "There is...(*atthi*)," we have that likewise emphatic rejection of the extremes of existence (*atthitā*) and non-existence (*natthitā*).

But even those utterances on Nibbāna which are phrased positively, include mostly negative terms too:

> "There is that sphere where there is neither earth...neither this world nor the next, neither coming nor going."
>
> "There is an *un*born, an *un*become...."
>
> "I shall teach you the unformed...the profound...and the way to it. What now is the unformed...the profound? It is

the destruction of greed, the destruction of hatred, the destruction of delusion."

These texts, combining positive and negative statements, illustrate our earlier remark that both the positive and the negative utterances on Nibbāna require mutual qualification, as a precaution against sliding into an extremist position.

Negative utterances are meant to emphasize the supramundane and ineffable nature of Nibbāna, which eludes adequate description in positive terms. Our language is basically unsuited for such description, since it is necessarily related to the world of our experience from which its structure and terms are derived. Therefore the positive statements in the suttas cannot be more than allusions or metaphors (*pariyāya desanā*). They make use of emotional values intelligible to us to characterize experiences and reactions known to those who have trodden the path to the Pathless. Though for the reasons mentioned above they have great practical value, they are evocative rather than truly descriptive. Negative statements, however, are quite sound and legitimate in themselves. They relate Nibbāna to the world of experience only by negations. The negating method of approach consists in a process of eliminating what is inapplicable to Nibbāna and incommensurate with it. It enables us to make much more definite and useful statements about the supramundane state of Nibbāna than by the use of abstract terms, the positive character of which can be only metaphorical. Negative statements are also the most appropriate and reverential way to speak of that which has been called "the marvellous" (*acchariya*) and "the extraordinary" (*abbhuta*).

Negative ways of expression have another important advantage. Statements like those defining Nibbāna as "the destruction of greed, hatred and delusion" indicate the direction to be taken, and the work to be done to actually *reach* Nibbāna. And it is this which matters most. These words on the overcoming of greed, hatred and delusion set a clear and convincing task which can be taken up here and now. Further, they not only point to a way that is practicable and worthwhile for its own sake, but they also speak of the lofty goal itself which likewise can be experienced here and now, and not only in an unknown beyond. For it has been said:

> If greed, hatred and delusion have been completely destroyed, insofar is Nibbāna visible here and now, not delayed, inviting inspection, and directly experienceable by the wise. (AN 3:55)

That visible Nibbāna has been lauded by those who attained to it as an unalloyed and inalienable happiness, as the highest solace, as the unspeakable relief of being freed from burden and bondage. A faint foretaste of it may be experienced in each act of joyful renunciation and in moments of serene detachment. To know oneself, if but temporarily and partially, to be free from the slavery of passions and the blindness of self-deception; to be master of oneself and to live and think in the light of knowledge, if but for a time and to a limited extent—these are truly not "mere negative facts," but the most positive and elevating experiences for those who know more than the fleeting and deceptive happiness of the senses.

> There are two kinds of happiness, O monks: the happiness of sense-pleasures and the happiness of renunciation. But the greater of them is the happiness of renunciation. (AN 2:64)

Thus these seemingly negative words of the destruction of greed, hatred and delusion will convey to the thoughtful and energetic a stirring positive message of a way that can here be trodden, of a goal that can here be reached, of a happiness that can here be experienced.

That aspect of a lofty happiness attainable here and now should, however, not be allowed to cover for us the fact that the attainment of Nibbāna is the end of rebirth, the cessation of becoming. But this end or cessation in no way involves the destruction or annihilation of anything substantial. What actually takes place is the ending of new origination owing to the stopping of its root-causes: ignorance and craving.

He who sees deeply and thoroughly the truth of suffering is "no longer carried away by the unreal, and no longer shrinks back from the real." He knows: "It is suffering, indeed, that arises, it is suffering that ceases." With a mind unswerving he strives after the deathless, the final cessation of suffering—Nibbāna.

The Holy Ones know it as bliss:
the personality's cessation;
Repugnant to the worldly folk,
but not to those who clearly see.

What others count as highest bliss,
the Holy Ones regard as pain;
What those regard as only pain
is for the Holy Ones sheer bliss.

(Sn vv. 761–62)

The Case for Rebirth

by

Francis Story
The Anāgārika Sugatānanda

WHEEL PUBLICATION NO. 12/13

Foreword to the Second Edition

The first edition of this book was published in 1959. Since then, thanks to valuable assistance given by a Parapsychology Foundation in the United States, which is here gratefully acknowledged, I have been enabled to extend my researches over a wider field of cases of the recollection of previous lives in Ceylon, Thailand, and India. I am particularly indebted to the Society for Psychical Research of Thailand; under the patronage of His Holiness Somdej Phra Mahā-virawongsa, and its members, including Dr. Chien Siriyananda, psychiatrist in charge of the Medical Division, Central Juvenile Court, Bangkok, for the help they have freely given to my researches in Thailand.

The cases I have personally studied, together with reports of others received from various parts of the world, are now being evaluated and classified, and the results will be published in due course. Until the work on them is completed it is not possible to publish the cases in detail, but I have added at the end of the book, in the form of notes, some tentative conclusions which at the time of writing seem to be indicated. It must be understood that these represent my own interpretations based upon my reading of the case histories as a Buddhist, and in the light of Buddhist doctrine as I understand it. I may find cause to modify them later on, and if that be the case I shall not hesitate to do so.

The body of evidence for the truth of rebirth has increased substantially since the book was first written. One highly interesting fact which has emerged is that despite the wide range of experiences, the cases presented, which is to be expected in view of the diverse religious, cultural, and racial backgrounds of the persons claiming to have these memories, show many striking features in common.

The similarities are especially noticeable in the accounts given of experiences in the intermediate state between one human life and another. These seem definitely to point to a universal type of post-mortem experience—one which may be coloured by the individual's preconceived ideas and his customary background of living, but is erected upon a psychological groundwork common to all peoples in all ages. One man may travel by jet airliner, another on horseback, but different though their means of transportation may be, they have one thing in common, the fact of travel. So it is with the state between one life on earth and another; the post-mortem experiences vary according to the individual *kamma* (Skt. *karma*) and the details of the preconceived ideational worlds of those who undergo them, but fundamentally they follow the same pattern for all.

This being so, it may be possible in time to extract from these cases some fundamental principles which will enable us to formulate a psychology of rebirth and perhaps even to bring the process under some measure of control. The ethico-psychology of Buddhism already offers the means of doing this, but until the fact of rebirth is more widely accepted and its principles more generally understood, the greater portion of mankind will still continue to blunder along from birth to birth in ignorance of the moral laws that govern human destiny.

As individuals, each with his own particular *kamma*, we cannot know precisely "what dreams may come when we have shuffled off this mortal coil," but by an extension of knowledge, man may ultimately learn how to control them for his own well-being, and in learning how to die, discover the way to live.

Francis Story
December 1963

The Case for Rebirth

I

The doctrine of reincarnation, the ceaseless round of rebirths, is not, as many people imagine, confined to Buddhism and Hinduism. It is found in some form or another in many ancient religious and philosophical systems and in many parts of the world.

In the oldest records of man's religious thinking we find traces of a belief in the 'transmigration of souls.' Some of the forms it took were naturally primitive and crudely animistic. There is for instance a theory that the ancient Egyptians embalmed their dead to prevent the Ka, or soul, from taking another body. If the idea existed in Egypt it almost certainly must have been familiar also to the Babylonians and Assyrians, who shared many of the most important religious beliefs of the Egyptians.

Coming to later times we find reincarnation prominent in the Orphic cult of Greece in the 6th century BCE, when it formed part of the teaching of Pherecydes of Syros. In the Orphic view of life, man is dualism: part evil and part divine. Through a succession of incarnations the individual has to purge himself of the evil in his nature by religious rites and moral purity. When this is accomplished he becomes liberated from the 'circle of becoming' and is wholly divine.

This corresponds very closely to the Buddhist, Hindu, and Jain teaching, and there may have been a connection between them; but it is not possible to establish one on historical evidence. Although by the 6th century BCE, doctrine had already been developed in the Brāhmaṇas and Upanishads, and may have travelled west along the trade routes, there is still a possibility that it arose spontaneously in Greece. The emphasis on ritualism differentiates it from the Buddhist view, but it is significant that it was at about the same time in both Greece and India that the idea of reincarnation first became linked with a scheme of moral values and spiritual evolution. The connection of Orphism with the mysteries of ceremonial magic must not be allowed to blind us to the fact that it represented a great advance in religious thinking.

Hitherto, reincarnation had been regarded in primitive cults as a merely mechanical process, to be controlled, if at all, by spells, incantations, and physical devices. This is the idea still prevalent in certain parts of Africa, Polynesia, and elsewhere, where, far removed from Indian influences, the idea of metempsychosis must have sprung up spontaneously.

Through Orphism reincarnation came to be taught by, among others, Empedocles and Pythagoras. In the hands of the latter the Orphic mysticism was converted into a philosophy. This philosophical aspect of the teaching was inherited by the Platonists, while its mystical character was preserved in the traditions of Gnosticism.

In many respects Greek Gnosticism resembled Hinduism; it was syncretic and eclectic, capable of absorbing into itself ideas from outside sources while at the same time it impregnated with its own thought the beliefs peculiar to other systems. Its influence was felt over many centuries, persisting into the Middle Ages of Europe. In the early centuries of the Christian era we find it in the teaching of men as dissimilar in the general character of their outlook as Plotinus, Cerinthus, and Marcion.

Clement of Alexandria, about the second century CE, wrote very largely from the Gnostic standpoint. He combined reincarnation with the necessity of striving for an enlightened moral elevation: a result that could be achieved only through a development taking place not merely in the present life but in past and future incarnations as well. This belief was shared by the *Pre existiani*, a sect that numbered among its adherents some of the most advanced thinkers of the period, including Justin Martyr and the great theologian Origen. They represented a very powerful intellectual movement, one in which the natural freedom of Greek intellectualism was struggling for survival in a world that was sliding towards the Dark Ages. Many of their ideas survived in Neoplatonism; but for the most part they were driven underground, to find an insecure refuge in the suppressed teachings of the so-called heretical sects that came to be known collectively as the Cathars, or 'illuminati.'

A not dissimilar doctrine of transmigration is found in the Kabbalah, where it goes under the Hebrew name Gilgul. It forms an integral part of the kabbalistic system and is one of the features that distinguish kabbalism from primitive Judaic thought. The Hekhāloth, a kabbalistic work of the Gaonic era, gives Gnostic and Pythagorean ideas along with the orthodox stream of Talmudic teaching. The result may be regarded as Hellenised Judaism, but modern research on the Kabbalah tends to suggest that its original sources may be much older than has hitherto been granted. It may in fact preserve a very ancient rabbinical tradition which was not intended for the masses. Much of its philosophical content is of a high order and reveals a creative expansion of Jewish thought in which reincarnation occupies a significant place.[1]

The idea of a transmigrating soul is the central theme of the Bhagavadgīta:

"As the soul in this body passes through childhood, youth, and old age, even so does it pass to another body. As a person casts off worn-out garments and puts on others that are new, so does

1. Since this was written, confirmation of the view that reincarnation beliefs in Kabbalistic Judaism are of considerable antiquity has been found in an article, "Seelenwanderung und Sympathie der Seelen in der Jüdischen Mystik" ("Transmigration and the Sympathy of Souls in Jewish Mysticism"), by Prof. Gershom Scholem, in the *Eranos Jahrbuch* Vol XXV, 1955 (Rhein Verlag, Basel 1956).

Prof. Scholem finds the first mention of reincarnation in the book *Bahir*, edited ca. 1180 in Southern France, but notes that it is there spoken of as a matter of course, without apology or explanatory comments. Official Jewish theology emphatically opposed the doctrine, yet Kirkisani, a 10th century writer, in his *Book of the Lights* affirms that the Karaic teacher "Anan accepted the doctrine in the 8th century." Anan wrote a book on it, and his followers preserved the doctrine.

Prof. Scholem considers it open to question whether the Kabbalists developed the theory of transmigration of souls independently as a psychological assumption, or whether they adopted it from older traditions. But he draws attention to the fact that the *Bahir* contains fragments of an older, undoubtedly Oriental Jewish Gnostic source, and concludes: "All things considered, I incline to the view that we are here dealing with an older Gnostic Jewish tradition which the book *Bahir* derives through channels unknown to us."

The author is indebted to the Ven. Nyanaponika Maha Thera for the translation of Prof. Scholem's articles from the German.

the incarnate soul cast off worn-out bodies and enter into others that are new" (Gīta, Chapter II, vs. 13 and 22).

Throughout the Upanishads the idea of "soul" (*ātman*) in this sense persists; it is the totality of selfhood and personal identity which transmigrates, occupying successive bodies, becoming now a man, now a god or an animal, yet in some way preserving its uniqueness as the personal ego throughout. Because of certain difficulties attaching to this concept, however, it was somewhat modified in Vedanta, the last phase of Upanishadic thought. In its place arose the theory that the ātman, as an unborn, unoriginated principle not in any way affected by the activities, good or bad, of the phenomenal being, was not identical with the individual at all but with the "Supreme Soul," the Paramātman or (neuter) Brahman.

Mahāvīra, the founder of Jainism (the Nigaṇṭha Nātaputta of the Buddhist texts), held unequivocally to the "individual soul" theory. Jainism teaches that there are an infinite number of individual souls transmigrating in happy or unhappy states according to their deeds. But whereas in Vedanta release, or *Mokṣa*, comes with the realization that the "I" is really identical with the Paramātman or Brahman (the idea summarized in the formula "*Tat tvam asi*"—You are That), in Jainism it is believed to come only with the complete cessation of rebirth-producing activities. Since automatic and involuntary actions are considered to bear resultants as well as those performed intentionally, the Jain ideal is complete inactivity. As will be seen later, the Buddhist doctrine concerning what it is that undergoes rebirth, and the nature of the moral law that governs *kamma* and *vipāka*, or actions and results, differs from both these theories and eliminates the teleological and ethical difficulties to which they give rise.

The faith in survival after death, which is basic to religious thought, has its natural correlative in reincarnation. If life can extend forward in time beyond the grave, it must surely be capable of having extended from the past into the present. "From the womb to the tomb" has its complement in "from the tomb to the womb," and to be born many times is no more miraculous than to have been born once, as Voltaire pointed out.

The opposite view, that a being comes into existence from non-existence, implies that it can also—and most probably will—

come to an end with the dissolution of the body. That which has a beginning in time can also cease in time and pass away altogether. The doctrine of a single life on earth therefore holds out no promise of a future life in any other state; rather does it make it improbable. But if we accept that there is a survival of some part, no matter what, of the personality after death we are accepting also a very strong argument for its existence before birth. Reincarnation is the only form that after-death survival could logically take.

So it is not surprising that wherever religion has developed beyond its simplest beginnings some idea of spiritual evolution through a series of lives is found to be a part of its message. The doctrine of reincarnation, together with that of the moral law of cause and effect, not only provides an explanation of life's inequalities and the crushing burden of suffering under which countless millions of people labour, thus disposing of the problem raised by the existence of pain and evil in the world. It also gives a rational and practical hope where none existed before. It is, moreover, the supreme justification of moral values in a universe which otherwise appears to be devoid of ethical purpose. It is evident that the Orphic and Gnostic cults recognised this fact when they introduced the concept of moral values into their theology.

II

In all these systems of thought, rebirth is seen, as it is in Buddhism, to be the only means of spiritual purgation. It is necessary for the moral and spiritual evolution of the individual that he should, through a variety of experiences, by his consciously directed efforts struggle upwards from the lower planes of sensuality and passion to a state of purity in which his latent divinity becomes manifest.

That the Cathars, the Kabbalists, and others mixed up this reasoned and enlightened doctrine with the practice of what was later to become known as ritual magic, and with theories of the immortal soul that were frankly animistic, is no argument against the essential truth of their belief. Reason has to emerge slowly and painfully from unreason. It was in like manner that the true principles of science were unfolded at the time when scientific method was growing up alongside the occult practices of the astrologers and alchemists.

We may smile at the alchemist's faith that he could find a means of transmuting base metals into gold, but in this age of nuclear physics the idea does not seem quite so crazy as it once did. The alteration of atomic patterns in the structure of metals is no longer entirely outside the range of possibility. The alchemist's methods may have been hopelessly wrong; his basic assumption was not. Similarly, the transformation of the base metal of human nature into the pure gold of divinity is still a possibility. It is only a question of finding the right key to unlock the doors of the mind.

To understand how the Buddhist doctrine of rebirth differs from all those that have been mentioned, and why the term "rebirth" is preferable to "reincarnation" or "transmigration," it is necessary to glance at the main principles of Buddhist teaching: These are summed up in the Four Noble Truths:

The Truth concerning Suffering
The Truth concerning the cause of Suffering
The Truth concerning the cessation of Suffering
The Truth concerning the Way to the cessation of Suffering.

The first proposition is nothing more than a self-evident fact—that suffering is inherent in all forms of existence. No one can go through life without experiencing physical pain, sickness, disappointment and grief; none can escape old age and death.

Suffering is even more prevalent in the life of animals than in that of human beings, and Buddhism takes into account all forms of sentient life. But aside from these obvious aspects of the universal world-suffering, there is the fact that all conditioned existence is unstable, restless, and lacking in fulfilment. It is a process *of becoming* which never reaches the point of completion in *being*. This in itself is suffering.

In brief, life even at its best is unsatisfactory. In the formula of the Three Characteristics of Being, all phenomenal existence is defined as being impermanent, fraught with suffering, and devoid of self-essence. These three characteristics derive from one another; because existence is transitory it is painful; because it is transitory and painful it can have no enduring essence of selfhood.

There is no "soul" in the sense of a total personality-entity, for what we call the self is merely a current of consciousness linked to a particular physical body. This current of consciousness is made up of thought-moments of infinitesimal duration succeeding one another in a stream of inconceivable rapidity. The psychic life of the individual is just the duration of a single moment of consciousness, no more.

We are living all the time what is in reality a series of lives. The life-stream is the rapid succession of these consciousness-moments, or momentary existences, resembling the running of a reel of film through a projector. It is this which gives the illusion of a static entity of being where nothing of the kind exists. The general characteristics of personality are maintained, but only in the same way that a river maintains the same course until something diverts it or it dries up. Thus there is no "immortal soul" that transmigrates, just as there is no river, but only the passage of particles of water flowing in the same direction. Anatta, soullessness, is therefore bound up with Anicca, impermanence, and Dukkha, suffering. The three Characteristics are three aspects of the same central fact.

Yet this state of soullessness is capable of producing rebirth. How can this be so if there is no transmigrating entity—"no-soul" to reincarnate? The answer is to be found in the Buddhist system of ethico-psychology, the Abhidhamma. There it is shown that the act of willing is a creative force, which produces effects in and through the conditions of the physical world. The thought-force of a sentient being, generated by the will-to-live, the desire to enjoy sensory experiences, produces after death another being who is the causal resultant of the preceding one.

Schopenhauer expressed the same idea when he said that in rebirth, which he called "Palingenesis," it is the *will*, not an ego-entity, which re-manifests in the new life. The being of the present is not the same as the being of the past, nor will the being of the future be the same as the being of the present. Yet neither are they different beings, because they all belong to the same current of cause and effect. Each is part of an individual current of causality in which "identity" means only "belonging to the same cause-effect continuum."

Since mind and body are alike continually undergoing change—or, more precisely, they are made up of constituent factors which are arising and passing away from moment to moment—this is the only kind of "self-identity" which connects the various stages of a single life through childhood, youth, maturity and old age. Buddhism presents a dynamic view of existence in which the life-continuum is merely the current of momentary existences, or successive units of consciousness, linked together by causal relations, both mental and physical. The process may be likened to a current of electricity, which consists of minute particles called electrons. An electron is much lighter in weight than an atom of the lightest chemical element, hydrogen, yet waves of these particles in the form of an electric current can produce many different effects in heat, light, and sound, and can produce them on a tremendous scale.

In the same way the units of consciousness constitute an energy-potential which in the Buddhist view is the basic energy of the universe, operating in conjunction with natural laws.

So we see that mental force is a kind of energy, which Buddhism has linked with moral principles by way of *kamma*, actions, and *vipāka*, moral resultants. Buddhism maintains that the physical universe itself is sustained by this mental energy derived from living beings, which is identical with their *kamma*. The energy itself is generated by craving. It operates upon the atomic constituents of the physical world in such a way as to produce bodies equipped with organs of sense by means of which the desire for sensory gratification, produced by past experiences, may be satisfied again. In this world the mind-force which produces rebirth has to operate through the genetic principles known to biology; it requires human generative cells and all the favourable physical conditions of heat, nutrition, and so forth, to produce a foetus.

When it does so, the foetus and the infant that it later becomes bear both biologically inherited characteristics and the characteristics carried by the past *kamma* of the individual whose thought-force has caused the new birth.[2]

2. The formation of personality has to be considered under three heads. There is first the kammic potentiality of the individual, which is the inheritance from his own previous lives. Secondly, there is the set of hereditary

It is not a question of a "soul" entering the embryo, but of the natural formation of the foetus being moulded by an energy from without, supplied by the causative impulse from some being that lived before. It is only necessary to conceive craving-force as an energy-potential flowing out from the mind of a being at the moment of death, and carrying with it the kammic characteristics of that being, just as the seed of a plant carries with it the botanical characteristics of its type, and a mental picture is formed that corresponds roughly to what actually takes place. Mind-force is creative, and its basis is desire. Without desire there can be no will to act; consequently the "will" of Schopenhauer is identical with the Buddhist *taṇhā*, or craving.[3]

---

characteristics which he derives from his parents. This appears to be connected with the *kamma* by way of attraction, as when the rebirth takes place in the same family or in the same sociological or ethnic group, and accounts for racial characteristics the origins of which cannot be specifically determined. Thirdly, there is environmental influence, which produces modifying effects upon the developing personality. Since causality in the Buddhist sense implies multiple-causality, the kammic character-motif which represents at once the residuum of the old personality and the matrix of the new, does not exclude the other two formative factors, nor is it excluded by them.

On the other hand, the attempt to erect a theory of the origin of personality solely upon biological heredity and environmental influences is at the outset nullified by the fact that beings with the same hereditary background and reared in the same environment show marked differences in character and abilities. Such differences are frequently to be met with even in the case of twins.

3. The will to act undergoes a complete reversal when desire is totally extinguished, as in the case of the Arahat. It is not, however, converted into what would appear to be its opposite, volitional inertia. The Arahat continues to will and to act as long as he lives, but his willing is not prompted by desire; its source is the uniform, practically automatic, functioning of the impulse of disinterestedness. For this reason it is *kiriya*, or kammically neutral and non-regenerative. The personality-pattern in which desire is totally absent bears no resemblance to the psychology of the ordinary person who is subject to rebirth. A close parallel to the Buddhist conception of will as a generative force is to be found in Bergson's theory of Creative Evolution. If the Bergsonian Idea were to be enlarged, as quite logically it could be, to include a succession of lives subject to *kamma* and its results, the parallel would be exact.

The second of the Four Noble Truths, therefore, is that the cause of suffering in the round of rebirth is craving. But one cause alone is not enough to give rise to a specific result. In this case, craving is conjoined with ignorance. The mind generates craving for sensory experience because of ignorance of the fact that these experiences are impermanent, unsatisfactory, and so themselves a source of suffering. So the circle of becoming, without discernible beginning and without end, is joined. This wheel of existences does not exist in time: time exists in it. Hence it does not require a point of beginning in what we know as time. It is the *perpetuum mobile* of cause and effect, counter-cause and counter-effect, turning round upon itself.

But although, like the revolution of the planets round the sun, it goes on perpetually simply because there is nothing to stop it, it can be brought to an end by the individual for himself, through an act of will. The act of will consists in turning craving into non-craving. When this is accomplished and Nibbāna, the state of desirelessness, is reached, there is no more rebirth. The life-asserting impulses are eliminated and there is no further arising of the bases of phenomenal personality. This is the objective set forth in the third of the Noble Truths; that concerning the cessation of suffering.

The way to that cessation, which is the Noble Eightfold Path of self-discipline and meditation leading to perfect purity and insight-wisdom, is the subject of the last of the Four Noble Truths, and gives epistemological completeness to the whole.

The Buddhist system of thought is thus presented as a reasoned progression from known facts to a conclusion which is ascertainable by the individual and is also accessible to him as a personally experienced reality.

The round of rebirths, or saṃsāra, does not come to an end automatically; neither is there any point at which all beings revolving in it gain their release by reason of its ceasing, for it has no temporal boundaries. But anyone can bring to an end his own individual current of cause and effect, and the whole purpose of the Buddha's Teaching was to demonstrate the theoretical and practical means by which this can be achieved. The painful kind of "immortality" conferred by rebirth in conditioned existences is not to be regarded as a blessing, but rather as a curse which man pronounces upon himself. Nevertheless, by understanding it we are able to gain assurance that there is in truth a moral principle governing the universe; and by learning to use its laws in the right way we become able to control and guide our individual destinies by a higher spiritual purpose and towards a more certain goal.

III

Of late years, interest in the doctrine of rebirth has been greatly stimulated by the publicity given to several cases of people who have remembered previous lives. For a long time past it has been known that under deep hypnosis events in very early infancy, outside the normal range of memory, could be recovered, and this technique has been increasingly employed for the treatment of personality disorders. It cannot be used with success on all patients because of the involuntary resistance some subjects show to hypnotic suggestion, which inhibits the cooperation necessary to obtain deep trance. But where it can be applied, it has definite advantages over the usual methods of deep psycho-analysis, one of them being the speed with which results are obtained.

The technique is to induce a state of hypnosis and then carry the subject back in time to a particular point in childhood or infancy at which it is suspected that some event of importance in the psychic life may have occurred. In this state, known as hyperamnesia, the subject becomes in effect once more the child he was, and relives experiences that have long been buried in the unconscious. Memories of earliest infancy, and in some cases pre-natal memories, have been brought to the surface in this way.

Some practitioners have carried out experiments in regression even further, and have found that they were uncovering memories that did not belong to the current life of the subject at all, but to some previous existence. In cases where nothing could be proved, the rebirth explanation has been contested, and various theories such as telepathy, fantasies of the unconscious, and even clairvoyance, have been put forward to account for the phenomena. But apart from the fact that many of the alternatives offered call for the acceptance of psychic faculties which, if what is claimed for them is true, themselves bring rebirth nearer to being a comprehensible reality, none of them alone covers all the phenomena which have been brought under observation. If, for example, xenoglossy, the ability shown by some subjects under hypnosis to speak languages unknown to them in their normal state, is to be explained by telepathy we are brought face to face with a supernormal faculty of the mind which itself contributes to our understanding of the manner in which mental energy may operate in the processes of rebirth. But although telepathy has now been acknowledged as one of the unexplained phenomena of parapsychology, along with clairvoyance, telekinesis, and psychometrics, it cannot legitimately be expanded to include all the phenomena these experiments have disclosed.

To account for all of them on these lines it would be necessary to combine every one of the known extrasensory faculties into one concept, that of a freely wandering, disembodied intelligence, independent of spatial and temporal limitations. If we are to apply here the scientific law of parsimony, the more likely alternative is the obvious one that they are simply what they purport to be—memories of previous lives.

As to the theory that the memories are products of the unconscious mind, it cannot survive the proof to the contrary which comes from the revelation of facts that could not have been known to the subject in his present life. These are objective and circumstantial, and they exist in abundance, as any reading of the literature on the subject will confirm.

The best known example of this kind is the case of Bridey Murphy in America, which raised a hurricane of controversy when it broke into the news. It was followed some time later by a similar case in England in which the subject, Mrs. Naomi Henry, remembered under hypnosis two previous existences. The experiments were carried out under test conditions by Mr. Henry Blythe, a professional consultant hypnotist. In the presence of several witnesses, tape recordings were made of the sessions, which were held under the supervision of a medical practitioner, Dr. William C. Minifie, who testified that the hypnotic trance was genuine. It has been said of these recordings that they provide "what must surely be the most thought provoking, absorbing, and controversial angle ever offered" on the subject.

What happened was this: Mrs. Naomi Henry, a thirty-two-year-old Exeter housewife, the mother of four children, was cured of the smoking habit by hypnotic treatment given by Mr. Henry Blithe, of Torquay, Devon. He found her to be "an exceptionally receptive hypnotic subject," so much so that without informing her of the purpose of his experiments he began a series of sessions in which he succeeded in taking her back beyond her present life.

Mrs. Henry remembered two previous existences. In the first she gave her name as Mary Cohan, a girl of 17 living in Cork in the year 1790. Among other circumstances she told how she was married against her wishes to a man named Charles Gaul, by whom she had two children, Pat and Will. Her husband ill-treated her, and finally caused her death by a beating which broke her leg. Whilst describing these events in the trance she was evidently reliving the intense emotional experiences of the past with the vividness of a present reality rather than of a mere memory.

Intervening time had been obliterated and she was once more the illiterate Irish girl she had been over a century and a half before. Her marriage, she said, took place in St. John's Church, in a hamlet named "Grenner." Several of the facts she related were afterwards verified on the spot, but no village of the name of "Grenner" could be traced. Eventually, however, some records dating back to the 17th century were found in the possession of a parish priest, and in them mention was made of a Church of St. John in a village named Greenhalgh. The name is pronounced locally just as Mary Cohan gave it—"Grenner."

Next she remembered a life in which she was Clarice Hellier, a nurse in charge of twenty-four children at Downham in 1902. After relating what she remembered of this life she went on to describe her last illness, her death, and her funeral, which it seems she had been able to witness. She was even able to give the number of the grave, 207, in which she had been buried.

When Mrs. Henry emerged from her trance, she had no recollection of what had taken place and it was only when she heard the recording that she learned the purpose of the experiments. The authenticity of this case has been established beyond reasonable doubt.

One of the most remarkable men of recent times, Edgar Cayce, obtained evidence of an even more striking nature. Born in Christian County, Kentucky, in 1877, he suffered as a young man from a psychosomatic constriction of the throat which deprived him of his voice. Orthodox medical treatments having failed, he was treated by hypnotic suggestion, which was not a recognised form of therapy in those days. In deep trance his voice returned to normal and he diagnosed his own condition. Not only did he describe the physiological symptoms in terms of which he knew nothing in his waking state, but he also prescribed treatment.

His self-cure was so remarkable that he was persuaded, rather against his will, to try prescribing for others whose illnesses would not respond to medical treatment.

This he did with great success, using technical terms and prescribing remedies which, as a man of only moderate education, he was quite unfamiliar with in his normal state. Sometimes the medicines he prescribed were conventional remedies in unusual combinations, sometimes they were substances not found in the standard pharmacopoeia.

Cayce himself was puzzled and somewhat dismayed by his abnormal faculty, but since it was proving of benefit to an increasing number of sufferers he continued to use it, only refusing to take any payment for the help he rendered. He soon found that a hypnotist was unnecessary; his trances were really self-induced, and he worked thereafter solely through autohypnosis.

One day, while Cayce was giving a consultation, a friend who was present asked him whether reincarnation was true. Still in the trance, Cayce immediately replied that it was. In answer to further questions he said that many of the patients who came to him for treatment were suffering from afflictions caused by bad *kamma* in previous lives. It was because of this that they resisted ordinary treatment. Asked whether he was able to see the past incarnations of his patients and describe them, he said that he could.

When he was told what he had said in the trance, Cayce was more disturbed than before. The thing was getting decidedly out of hand. He had never heard the word *karma*, and his only idea of reincarnation was that it was a belief associated with some "heathen" religions. His first reaction was to give the whole thing up, as being something supernatural and possibly inimical to his Christian faith.

It was with great difficulty that he was persuaded to continue. However, he consented to be questioned further under hypnosis, and after having given some readings and more successful treatments he became convinced that there was nothing irreligious or harmful in the strange ideas that were being revealed. From that time onwards he supplemented all his diagnoses by readings of the past *kamma* of his patients. It was then found that he was able to give valuable moral and spiritual guidance to counteract bad kammic tendencies, and his treatments became even more effective. He was now treating the minds as well as the bodies of the patients who sought his help.

When Cayce discovered that he was also able to treat people living at great distances, whom he had never seen, the scope of his work broadened until it ultimately extended all over the United States and beyond. Before he died in 1945, Cayce, with the help of friends and supporters, had established an institution, the Cayce Foundation, at Virginia Beach, Virginia. It is now operating as a research institute under the direction of his associates. Cayce left a vast number of case histories and other records accumulated over the years, and these are still being examined and correlated by the Foundation. For further information on Edgar Cayce, his work and the light it throws on rebirth, the reader is referred to *Many Mansions* by Gina Cerminara, *Edgar Cayce, Mystery Man of Miracles* by Joseph Millard, and numerous publications issued by the Cayce Foundation.

There is a great deal in the evidence to suggest that Cayce in his hypnotized state had access to lost medical knowledge, as well as the power to see the previous lives of others. In the Buddhist texts of a very early date there are references to advanced medical knowledge and techniques of surgery in some ways comparable to our own. Jīvaka, a renowned physician who was a contemporary of the Buddha, is recorded as having performed a brain operation for the removal of a living organism of some kind.

But there are still older records than these. The Edwin Smith Papyrus (ca. 3500 BC) describes the treatment of cerebral injuries, and the writings attributed to Hippocrates include directions for opening the skull. The great Egyptian physician, Imhotep, who lived about three thousand years before the Christian era and was a many-sided genius comparable to Leonardo da Vinci, had such skill in medicine that he became a legend. He was deified under the Ptolemies and identified with Asklepios, the god of healing, by the Greeks; but there is no doubt whatever that he was an actual historical personage.

Without venturing beyond what is naturally suggested by Edgar Cayce's statements concerning rebirth, and their linking up with the often unusual but brilliantly successful treatments he prescribed, it is possible to see that there might be a direct connection between the knowledge possessed by these ancient physicians and the abnormal knowledge released from Cayce's unconscious mind under hypnosis.

But even Cayce was not altogether unique. Egerton C. Baptist in *Nibbāna or the Kingdom?* quotes the following from *Life and Destiny* by Leon Denis: "In 1880 at Vera Cruz, Mexico, a seven-year-old child possessed the power to heal. Several people were healed by vegetable remedies prescribed by the child. When asked how he knew these things, he said that he was formerly a great doctor, and his name was then Jules Alpherese. This surprising faculty developed in him at the age of four years."

In Buddhism, the faculty of remembering previous lives and of discerning the previous lives of others is one that is developed in the course of meditation on selected subjects. But it is acquired only when a certain precisely defined stage of *jhāna*, or mental absorption, has been reached. The subject is dealt with in the Canonical Texts of Buddhism, and at considerable length in the *Visuddhimagga* of Buddhaghosa Thera.[4]

Those who have practised meditation to this point in previous lives without having attained complete liberation from rebirth may be reborn with the faculty in a latent form. In the case of others, hypnosis seems to provide a shortcut technique to releasing some at least of the dormant memories of former lives, just as it provides a shortcut to results ordinarily reached by deep psychoanalysis. There is much to be done in the way of more extensive and systematic investigation before definite conclusions can be tabulated. The chief difficulty is to obtain suitable subjects for the tests.[5]

---

4. Translated by Bhikkhu Ñāṇamoli: *The Path of Purification*, BPS, Kandy.

5. The chief objections to the cases of apparent memories of previous lives under hypnosis may be briefly stated here. The first is that such cases can rarely be confirmed by objective evidence, and that even when such proof is given,

IV

A question that is often asked is: if rebirth is a fact, why is it so rare for people to have any recollection of their previous lives?

There are several answers to this. The first and most obvious is that even ordinary memory is very restricted, and varies greatly in extent and vividness with different people. Death itself, the Lethe of psycho-mythology, is an obliterating agent, for it is necessary for each consciousness to begin its renewed course more or less a *tabula rasa* with the formation of a new physical brain. Another factor is the nature of the lives intermediate to one human birth

---

as in the cases mentioned in Part I. It is difficult to eliminate the possibility that the subject may have acquired the information either unconsciously by normal means, from books and other sources, or telepathically from other minds. The picture is further complicated by the possibility that the source of information is the "collective unconscious," or race memory. Nevertheless, methods are being devised whereby these possibilities may be either ruled out or confirmed. The "collective unconscious" itself, if it exists, may turn out to be a misinterpretation of what are actually memories of previous lives. Rebirth would seem in fact to imply the existence of a common stock of experiences preserved on the unconscious level in each individual.

Another possibility, in cases where no objective proof can be obtained, is that the suppressed memory of a previous life may be a 'phantasy.' Experience has shown, however, that mental phantasies under hypnosis do not arise spontaneously. They come about in response to suggestions from the hypnotiser, and can readily be distinguished from genuine memories.

In the cases of spontaneous recollection, those in which a child claims, to remember a previous existence without assistance from hypnotism, it is easier to eliminate alternative explanations of the phenomenon. These cases present a much broader basis for investigation, particularly in view of the fact that, as recent examples seem to indicate, they occur when the intermediate existence between the former human life and the present one has been relatively short. A number of such cases have recently come under investigation and the findings on them will be published in the near future. They are supported by much evidential material in the form of identifications by the subjects of persons and places known to them in their previous lives. In quite a few instances the subjects have been found to be in possession of information on matters hitherto unknown to the other persons involved, which on inquiry has been found correct.

and another. There are, as Buddhism maintains, rebirths in states that are non-human and in which the consciousness does not register impressions clearly, so that a series of such lives between one human birth and another may erase all traces of memory connection between them. A study of the earliest behaviour patterns of children, however, will furnish much evidence to suggest that they bring with them into the new life certain dim awarenesses that do not belong to their present range of experience. The aptitude certain children show for acquiring some particular skills strongly suggests remembering rather than learning. The headmistress of a kindergarten school told the author that a few years after the end of the First World War she noticed that some of her boy pupils were showing a maturity of mind and a facility in gaining knowledge which was so unlike anything in her previous experience that it roused her curiosity.

After making a study of these children she came to the conclusion that they were not learning but remembering. She became convinced of the truth of rebirth when one small boy, born after the war and exhibiting a highly-strung nature which she had formerly attributed to post-war conditions, one day became violently agitated by a sudden explosive noise close behind him. The fear he showed was out of all proportion to the cause; in fact he fell into an almost cataleptic state. When he recovered, he told her that he had a vague memory of a tremendous explosion and a brilliant flash of light, and that the loud noise had brought it back to him so vividly that he felt as though he was dying. From that time she was convinced that her extremely intelligent but often nervously unstable pupils were the reincarnations of men whose immediately previous lives had been cut short by the war, and who had been reborn almost at once into the human state to complete the interrupted kammic continuity of that particular life.[6]

6. Recent investigations carried out by the author in Ceylon and Thailand appear to indicate that such memories occur when the previous life was cut short abruptly by sickness, accident or violence. From a survey of these and a number of cases gathered from other parts of the world it would seem that rebirth in the human world tends to take place more quickly after a premature death, and that it is in such cases that vestigial memories of the previous life are retained in sufficient strength to permit their spontaneous revival.

Many children lead vivid lives of the imagination, or so it is supposed. They sometimes speak of things that bear no relation to their present experiences. Parents as a rule do not encourage this kind of imaginativeness, particularly if some of its manifestations cause them embarrassment. They then peremptorily forbid the child to tell any more untruths. But are these always untruths? May they not in fact be residual memories of past experiences? In any case, they are "driven under" by the parents' unsympathetic attitude and quickly become obliterated by new impressions. In the East, where children are allowed greater latitude to prattle of what they will, this does not happen. The difference may account for the frequently noted fact that instances of people recollecting past lives are more numerous in the East than in Western countries.

The son of a distinguished Indian doctor practising in Burma started talking of his "wife" and of events and people belonging to another realm of experience as soon as he was able to speak. The boy was living in a trilingual environment where Hindi, English, and Burmese were spoken, but his father noticed that from the start he used words to denote familiar things, such as doors, tables, and houses, which were not Hindi, English or Burmese. The doctor noted down a number of these words phonetically, with the intention of later on trying to identify them. Unfortunately, at that time the Japanese occupation of Burma took place and the records were lost, so it was never possible to establish whether the words belonged to any existing language or not.

Cases of children remembering their previous lives in considerable detail are not uncommon in Asian countries. An example which bears all the classic features of this phenomenon

---

The implication is that a premature death leaves the pattern set by the regenerative *kamma* uncompleted, with the result that it is renewed more quickly, and more of the previous personality structure survives. This, of course, is a tentative supposition which further research may establish or disprove. The accumulation of evidence has to be examined in the light of the fact that personality is a composite formation, subject to alteration, disintegration, and reconstruction, and that in rebirth it is not the total personality that is transferred from one life manifestation to another but only the kammically directed impulse of the previous existence, which may reproduce more or less of the recognisable features of the former personality.

is that of Pramod, the son of Babu Bankey Lal Sharma, M.A., Shastri, a Professor in an intermediate college at Bissuli in the district of Badan. The boy was born at Bissauli on March 15th 1944. As soon as he was able to utter any words clearly he pronounced the names "Mohan," "Moradabad," and "Saharanpur." Later he said quite distinctly, "Mohan Brothers." When he saw his relatives purchasing biscuits, he told them that he had a big biscuit factory in Moradabad, and on being taken to large shops he would frequently say that his shop in Moradabad was bigger than any other shop. As time went on he became insistent that he should be taken to Moradabad, where he had a brother, sons, a daughter, and a wife.

When he was able to give a clear account of himself, he said that he was Paramanand, the brother of one B. Mohanlal, the proprietor of a catering firm, Messrs. Mohan Bros., having branches in Saharanpur and Moradabad. As Paramanand, he said, he had died of a stomach ailment at Saharanpur on May 9th 1943. The date was just nine months and six days before his birth as Pramod.

Early in the year 1949, when the boy was five, a friend of the family, Lala Raghunandanlal of Bissauli, told one of his relatives living in Moradabad about the boy and his assertions. It was then learned that there was actually a firm of Mohan Bros. caterers, the proprietor of which was named Mohan Lal. When the story was told to him, Mr. Mohan Lal visited Bissauli with some of his relatives, and there met the boy's father. Young Pramod, as it happened, was paying a visit to some relatives in a distant village at the time (July 1949) and could not be seen. Professor Bankey Lal however consented to take him to Moradabad during the forthcoming Independence Day holidays.

They arrived in Moradabad on August 15th. On alighting from the train the boy at once recognised his brother and ran to embrace him. On the way to Mohan Lal's house Pramod recognised the Town Hall and announced that his shop was close at hand. They were riding in a tonga which, to test the boy, was being driven past the shop. Pramod recognised the building and called out for the vehicle to stop. He then alighted and led the way to the house in front of Mohan Lai Brothers' premises where the late Paramanand had lived. There he entered the room which Paramanand had kept for his religious devotions, and did reverence to it. He also recognised his wife and other relatives, and recalled incidents known to them, by which he established his identity to their complete satisfaction. The only person he failed to recognise was his eldest son, who had been thirteen years old when Paramanand died and had altered greatly in the five years' interval.

After a touching reunion with the relatives of his former life, the boy expressed a desire to go to his business premises. On entering the shop he went to the soda-water machine and explained the process of making aerated water, a thing of which he could not have acquired any knowledge in his present life. Finding that the machine would not work, he at once said that the water connection had been stopped, which was a fact; it had been done to test him. After that he said he wanted to go to the Victory Hotel, a business owned by a cousin of Paramanand's, Mr. Karam Chand. The boy led the way to the building, and entering it pointed out some rooms on the upper storey which had been added since his time.

During the two days of their stay in Moradabad the boy was taken to the Meston Park by a leading citizen of the town, Sahu Nanda Lal Saran, who asked him to point out where his civil lines branch had been. At once the boy led the company to the Gujerati Building owned by Sahu Lal Saran and indicated the shop which had once been the branch of Mohan Bros. On the Way to the Meston Park he had already recognised and correctly named the Allahabad Bank, the waterworks, and the district jail. Some of the English words, such as Town Hall, were not in use in the small town of Bissauli, and Pramod had never heard them, yet he used them accurately. He not only identified his former relatives but also people who used to visit his shop on business.

The following is the account given by Mr. J. D. Mehra of Messrs. Mohan Bros., Moradabad, a brother of the late Paramanand :

"My brother, Paramanand, aged 39, died of appendicitis on 9th May 1943 at Saharanpur about 100 miles from Moradabad. Pramod, the boy concerned, was born on 15th March 1944 at Bissauli. As the boy grew up he began to utter things of his previous life. For instance, he would say to his father when offered biscuits that he would have biscuits of his own shop and that he owned a big shop at Moradabad. He used to refer to his four sons, daughter, and wife. When his mother would prepare meals, he would say to her, 'Why should you prepare meals? I have an elderly wife, send for her.'

"As requested by us it was decided to bring this boy to Moradabad on August 15th 1948 (the day of India's Independence). Sri Karam Chand, the eldest of our brothers, went to the station to receive the boy and his father. When Mr. Bankey Lal, the father, alighted from the station with his boy, Pramod spotted out Sri Karam Chand from the crowd and clung to him, and would not go to his father. When questioned whether he knew the gentleman, he at once replied, 'Yes, he is my *Bara Bhai* (elder brother).'

"Whilst passing the Town Hall compound the boy said that it was the Town Hall, an English word with which he was not familiar in his own small city. ... When taken round the place where biscuits were manufactured, he said that it was a bakery, another English word not familiar to him in his birthplace. Entering the kitchen he said that he used to sit on a wooden cot there and pray. Before he entered the room he did Namaskar to the place where he used to sit in meditation.

"Seeing his wife without the vermilion mark on her forehead he questioned her: 'Where is your Bindu (mark) on the forehead?' This was a very significant remark for a boy of his age..."

The boy's own father, Shri Bankey Lal Sharma, wrote the following testimony:

"I have read almost all the versions of the statement regarding the rebirth of Paramanand of Moradabad. As I have been the eyewitness of all these things, I can say with emphasis that everything contained in the report is true to its minutest detail.

"Paramanand is a wonderful child with a very fine intelligence. He began to utter 'Moradabad' and 'Mohan Brothers' alone one year back. Since December last he spoke of the firm he owned during his last existence and also the articles he dealt in. A few days later he made a reference to a shop of his at Saharanpur. Biscuits and tea have been his great attraction. Although nobody attaches any importance to them in my family, he is very fond of them. It was through the association of biscuits that he spoke of his previous soda water and biscuit firm.

"When he visited Moradabad he recognised almost everybody with the exception of a few, especially his eldest son who is much changed. ... He recognised other sons, his only daughter, wife, brothers, mother and father, and several others whom he contacted during his previous life ...

"I am a middle-class man, but the boy is not satisfied with the present status. He often stresses on business and opening a big shop in Bombay or Delhi. In the latter place, he says, he had been several times on business. He wants aeroplanes, ships, mansions, radios, and all modern fashions. He has a great leaning towards his past relatives and does not want to live with me. He requests me to purchase and have a bank of our own..."

It was only with great difficulty that the boy was taken away from Moradabad after the visit. He showed such unwillingness to leave his old relatives and the shop, that his present father had to carry him away in the early hours of August 17th while he was still asleep.

On the day prior to their departure, August 16th 1949, a large public meeting was held at the Arya Samaj where Prof. Bankey Lal, Pramod's father, gave a full account of the development of the boy's memories since his early childhood. The case was investigated in the full light of local publicity by people known to all the persons concerned.

Among numerous cases from Burma, the following, given on the testimony of U Yan Pa of Rangoon, is one of the most thoroughly substantiated.

In the village of Shwe Taung Pan, situated close to Dabein on the Rangoon-Pegu trunk line, the eldest daughter of a cultivator named U Po Chon and his wife, Daw Ngwe Thin, was married to another cultivator of the same village, named Ko Ba Thin. This girl, whose name was Ma Phwa Kyin, died in childbirth some time later.

Shortly afterwards, a woman in Dabein, Daw Thay Thay Hmyin, the wife of one U Po Yin, became pregnant and in due course gave birth to a daughter whom they named Ah Nyo. When she first began to speak, this child expressed a strong wish to go to the neighbouring village, Shwe Taung Pan. She declared that she had lived and died in that village, and that her name was really not Ah Nyo but Ma Phwa Kyin. Eventually her parents took her to the village. The child at once led them to the house of the late Ma Phwa Kyin, pointing out on the way a rice field and some cattle which she said belonged to her. When the father, mother, and two brothers, Mg Ba Khin and Mg Ba Yin, of Ma Phwa Kyin appeared, she at once identified them. They confirmed that the house, field, and cattle were those that had belonged to Ma Phwa Kyin, and when the child recalled to them incidents of her former life they admitted that her memories were accurate and accepted her as being without doubt the dead girl reborn. Later she convinced her other surviving relatives in the same way. The girl Ah Nyo, now about twenty-five years of age, is everywhere in the neighbourhood accepted as the former Ma Phwa Kyin reborn.

More numerous are the cases in which specific skills are carried over from one life to another, rather than any distinct recollection of identity. Among musical prodigies we find Mozart composing minuets before he was four years old; Beethoven playing in public at eight and publishing compositions at ten; Handel giving concerts at nine; Schubert composing at eleven; Chopin playing concerts in public before he was nine and Samuel Wesley playing the organ at three and composing an oratorio at eight. The musical precocity of Brahms, Dvorak, and Richard Strauss was manifest at an equally early stage.

In a less specialised field there is the case of Christian Heinrich Heinecken, born at Lubeck in 1721. At the age of ten months he was able to speak, and by the time he was one year old he knew by heart the principal incidents of the Pentateuch. "At two years of age he is said to have mastered sacred history; at three he was intimately acquainted with history and geography, ancient and modern, sacred and profane, besides being able to speak French and Latin; and in his fourth year he began the study of religions and church history."

This amazing child created a tremendous sensation, crowds of people flocking to Lubeck to see and discourse with him. He died at the age of four, soon after he had begun to learn writing. That he was able to master so many abstruse subjects before he could even write is proof that his abnormal achievements were not the result of learning but of remembering.

Saṅgāyana, the journal of the Union of Burma Buddha Sāsana Council, reported in its issue of July 1954 the case of a six-year-old girl, Ma Hla Gyi, who showed remarkable intelligence for her age, combined with a phenomenal memory. "She can read," the report stated, "the most difficult Pali verses a few times, memorise and recite them promptly and correctly." In a test given to her she recited the final stanza of the sub-commentary on the Buddhist Compendium of Philosophy in Pali without an error, after reading it five times. She was also able to recite without a single error a page of the Pali *Paṭṭhāna* text (an abstruse Abhidhamma passage) after looking at it for one minute. This might be explained by the possession of a photographic memory, but for the fact that the child could understand what she read and was able to give its meaning.

These and many other instances of the appearance from time to time of child prodigies, although not constituting direct evidence for rebirth, present phenomena for which biology and psychology cannot account. That memory itself is something extra to the activities of the brain cells is a conclusion accepted on physiological grounds by Max Loewenthal and others.

From the cases available for examination it would seem that memories carried over from one life to another are subject to the same broad, general principle as are ordinary memories belonging to the current life: we remember what most interests us, and what we most desire to remember. Therefore a strong kammic predisposition to a particular form of study is more likely to persist from the past life than are the actual details of that life, which may be connected with personal psychological reactions and emotional responses that are in the ordinary course of nature suppressed.

V

Despite great advances in the study of genetics, there is still much that is unexplained in the biological processes that produce living organisms. While the transmission of hereditary characteristics through the genes can be traced in the operation of physical laws, there is yet no known method of accounting for the sudden mutations that occur from time to time and so give rise to variations of species. Yet these mutations, and the fact that they are possible, are a matter of the first importance, since it is by them that biological evolution takes place. For many generations the structural units of a chromosome, the genes, remain the same, and produce uniform hereditary types; but suddenly, without any intermediary stages, a new type is formed from them which may or may not continue to propagate itself. A well-known example of this is the fruit fly, *Drosophila melanogaster*, which, being normally an insect with a grey body and long wings, produces from time to time a spontaneous mutation having a black body slightly different in shape, and very short wings. Many similar cases are known of this kind of departure from a hereditary form, but precisely what different combinations or genes, chromosomes or atomic patterns cause the variation, or why they occur, is still a mystery to biologists. All that can be said is that the changes are isomeric transformations of the kind found in simple molecular structures, and that they follow the laws of chemical kinetics which also apply to nonliving substances under certain conditions.

Between "living" and "nonliving" matter there is no sharp line of distinction, for it is known that the processes by which living cells nourish themselves from their surrounding medium, assimilate material for their sustenance, and divide into other cells capable of independent existence is closely paralleled by processes observable in chemical molecules. For example, virus particles, which are the simplest form of life known at present, have to be considered as living units because they perform all the essential functions of living cells, yet at the same time they are regular chemical molecules, subject to all the laws of chemistry and physics. As living molecules comparable to the genes by which organic life is propagated, they are able to multiply, and they are also capable of producing biological mutations which result in the appearance from time to time of new types of a particular virus.

Yet a purely chemical study of them shows each type of virus to be a well-defined chemical compound similar to various complex organic compounds that are not strictly "living" matter. They thus represent a "bridge" between "living" and "nonliving," substance, and possibly the point at which the "nonliving" merges into the "living."

What has to be sought is the directive principle that prompts the transformation and guides the molecules to combine into more complex organic structures. To be able to follow the process, even right from its earliest stage, is not the same as to know its cause, and it is here that scientific method has to enlarge its scope to include the study of principles and laws underlying the phenomena of the physical universe and functioning on a different level from that to which the scientist has hitherto confined himself. Inasmuch as Buddhism locates these ultimate principles in the mental and immaterial, rather than the physical realm, the enquiry must necessarily be turned towards the interaction between mind-energy and the material substance through which it manifests itself.

If the transformations of nonliving into living matter and the developments which these transformations afterwards undergo are regarded as the physical manifestation of *kamma* and *vipāka* (*kamma*-result), it is only necessary to add these to the present stock of scientific knowledge as the unknown factors that at present elude identification, for many things still obscure to become clarified, without resorting to the supernatural for an explanation.

The embryonic human being derives its hereditary characteristics from the genes of the parents, sharing in equal measure the chromosomes of father and mother, the sex being determined by the proportion of what are distinguished as X and Y chromosomes. Female cells contain always two X-chromosomes, while the male has one X and one Y, and it is in the substitution of one Y for an X-chromosome that the basic difference in sex consists. At the time of conception the male sperm cell unites with the female and by the process of syngamy forms one complete cell, which afterwards divides into two, thus starting the process of mitosis by which the complete organism eventually comes into being. Here, what is not known is exactly why in certain cases the X and Y chromosomes combine to form a female, while in others they produce a male cell.

This may be purely fortuitous, but it is more in accordance with the scientific view of cause and effect to suspect the presence of another factor that in some way determines the combination. The Buddhist view that this unknown factor is *kamma* or energy-potential, the mental impulse projected by another being which existed in the past, is one that science by itself can neither prove nor disprove, but it provides the most likely explanation—in fact, the only one which can be offered as an alternative to the improbable theory of chance.

Kamma as cause, and *vipāka* as result, also provide an explanation of the intermediate conditions in which sex characteristics are more or less equal in one individual, or where it is possible for a complete change of sex to take place. The *kamma* which in the first place produced a male may be weak, or may become exhausted before the life-supporting *kamma* comes to an end, in which case the characteristics of the opposite sex may become so marked that they amount virtually to a sex transformation, the result of a different kind of *kamma* coming into operation.[7] Similarly, masculine thoughts and habits gradually becoming dominant in a female may bring about more and more marked male characteristics with the passage of time, and these influences may be so strong that they actually reveal themselves in physical changes.

On the other hand, they may only affect the psychic life. What is certain, as this analysis will attempt to show, is that the thought accretions do have the power to affect not only the general outlook and habits but the physical body itself. For "thought-accretions" we may substitute here the Buddhist term *saṅkhāra*, since this is one of the various associated meanings of this highly comprehensive word. Individual character is usually attributed to two factors, the first being heredity. But simple physical characteristics alone are not always traceable to this cause. Colour blindness, although it can be followed back through successive generations and shows clearly marked biological transmission, is not invariably hereditary; and in those individual features that partake of both the physical and psychological, such as the sexual deviations referred to above, the hereditary influence does not provide any satisfactory explanation. That they are not hereditary is the conclusion of most authorities.

This also applies to the many examples of infant prodigies and to the less striking, but nevertheless significant, instances of children who bear no resemblance whatever to their parents or grandparents. Where hereditary traits transmitted through the

7. The Commentary to Verse 43 of the Dhammapada relates a sudden change of sex, due to exceptionally weighty *kamma*, in the case of a youth, Soreyya, who became a woman as the result of a thought of lust directed towards an Arahant, the Thera Mahā Kaccāyana.

genes of the parents cannot account for differences in character the second factor, environmental influence, is brought in to explain the variation. But this also fails to cover all the ground because the same antecedents and the same environment together frequently produce quite dissimilar personalities, and there are numerous examples of pronounced characteristics appearing at birth, before any environmental pressure is brought to bear on the developing personality.

In Buddhist philosophy it is axiomatic that more than one cause is necessary to produce a given result, so that while character may be partly drawn from heredity, and partly modified by environment, these two factors do not in any way rule out the third factor, that of the individual *saṅkhāra*, or *kamma*-formation-tendency developed in previous lives, which may prove itself stronger than either of them.

Hereditary transmissions themselves are a part of the operation of the causal law, for it happens that owing to strong attachments the same persons may be born again and again in the same family. This accounts for the fact that a child may be totally unlike either of its parents in temperament, tastes, and abilities, yet may resemble a dead grandfather or some more distant ancestor. Physical appearance may be derived in the first place from the genes of the parents, but it undergoes modifications as the individual develops along his own lines, and it is then that distinctive characteristics, the result habitual thought-tendencies stamping themselves upon the features, become more pronounced.

That the mind, or rather the mental impressions and volitional activities, produce changes in the living structure, is a fact which science is beginning to recognise. Hypnotism affords an opportunity of studying this phenomenon under test conditions. It is only recently that hypnotic suggestion as a mode of therapeutic treatment has been officially recognised by medical associations in many parts of the world, but it is already being used with success as a form of harmless anaesthesia during operations and child-birth, and as a treatment for psychological disorders. Clinical experiments with hypnosis are helping to reveal the secrets of the mysterious action of mind on body, for it has been found possible by suggestion to produce physical reactions which under ordinary conditions could only be obtained by physical means. Doubtless many of the "faith cures" of Lourdes and other religious centres are the result of a strong mental force, comparable with that produced under hypnotism, acting upon the physical body; the force in this instance being the patient's absolute conviction that a miraculous cure will take place.

The task of the hypnotic practitioner is to induce this acquiescent and receptive state of unquestioning faith by artificial means. This, of course, requires the consent and cooperation of the subject, and it is here that the difficulty usually arises. The patient must have complete faith in the operator to enable him to surrender his own will entirely, for the time being, to another person. When full control of the subject's mind is gained, the required suggestions can be made with every confidence that the mind of the subject will carry them out, and the astonishing thing is that not only does the mind obey, but the body also responds. If, for instance, the idea of a burn is conveyed through the mind, the mark of a burn duly appears on the flesh on the spot indicated, without the use of any physical means to produce it. Many similar experiments attest to this close inter relationship of the mental and physical, and prove beyond question the truth of the Buddhist teaching that mental conditions precede and determine certain classes of phenomena which we have been wont to consider purely physical and material.

Hysteria also produces marked physiological changes in certain circumstances, among them being the well-attested phenomenon of "phantom pregnancy." The abnormal mental excitation which produces phantom pregnancy is also to be found in states of religious frenzy, when an unnatural degree of strength, insensibility to pain, and even invulnerability to injury are exhibited. These unexplained phenomena point to the existence of a mental force which can not only inhibit normal reactions to sense stimuli, but more than that, is able to affect the physical structure in a particular way.

All this has a distinct bearing on the manner in which the mental impulses generated in past lives, particularly the last mental impressions at the time of the preceding death, influence the physical make up and often predetermine the very structure of the body, in the new birth. Before going more deeply into this a specific example may be offered for consideration.

Rebirth Case History

From the records of the Burma Buddhist World-Mission.
S. T. Karen, age 20. Birthplace, Upper Burma: Examined in Rangoon, 1949.

The subject, a Karen house boy employed by a friend of the writer, while he was in all other respects physically sound, well built, and well proportioned, suffered from an unusual malformation of hands and feet. Across his right hand a fairly deep, straight indentation, roughly following the heart-line of palmistry, but much deeper and sharper than any of the normal lines of the hand, and extending right across the palm, divided the hand into two sections. Above this line the hand was not as well developed as at the base of the palm, and the fingers had something of the childish, unformed appearance that is one of the physical accompaniments of cretinism, although not to the same degree. Lower down on the hand and across the forearm there were similar marks, but not so pronounced as that at the base of the fingers.

The left hand was indented in the same unusual fashion, but to a lesser degree; and linear indentations of the same kind appeared less distinctly across both feet and on the calves, the lines being roughly parallel to one another. In addition to this, two toes of the left foot were joined together.

The boy's previous employment had been with a leading Rangoon surgeon who, after examining these marks had declared that although they had been present from birth they could not have been caused by any prenatal injury or abnormal condition in the womb. Questioned about them, the boy confirmed that they were congenital, and stated that all the indentations had been much more pronounced in childhood. Furthermore, at birth three of his toes had been joined, but his father, with the rough surgery of village folk, had separated two of the toes himself. During his infancy and boyhood these malformations had been a cause of acute suffering to him, for, at times, particularly when the attention of others was drawn to them, his right arm would swell, and severe pain would be felt in all the affected parts. At such times he experienced mental as well as physical distress, being conscious of fear and depression in connection with the malformations.

According to the boy's own narrative, as a child he had been very reluctant to talk about his physical defects, but one night, lying under the mosquito net with his mother he felt a sense of security which enabled him to speak freely. He then told her that he remembered incidents of his previous life which were the cause of his terror and distress whenever he was reminded of the marks. He had been, he said, the son of a rich man, possibly a village headman, who had died leaving him three adjoining houses and a large quantity of silver stored in large vessels of the type known as Pegu jars besides other treasure secreted in various parts of the buildings.

After his father's death he had lived alone, unmarried and without servants, in one of the three houses. One night a band of dacoits, armed with bamboo spears, broke into the house and demanded to be told where the treasure was hidden. When he refused to tell them, the robbers bound him with wire in a crouching position, with his hands firmly secured between his legs. In this position, tightly bound and unable to move, they left him huddled in a corner while they ransacked the other two houses, finally making off with the entire store of silver and jewellery.

For three days he remained in that position in acute agony, and one of the things he remembered vividly was that blood, dripping from the deep cuts made in his hands by the wire, fell onto his feet and congealed between three of his toes. Some time during the third night he suddenly became aware, in his alternating periods of consciousness and insensibility, that he was looking down at a still form, crouched in a corner, and wondering who it was. It was only later that he realised the body was his own, and that his consciousness was now located in a different and less substantial form.

The rest of his recollection was confused and obscure. It seemed to him that for a long time he wandered about the scene of his former life, conscious only of a sense of loss and profound unhappiness. In this condition he appeared to have no judgement of the passage of time, and was unable to say whether it lasted for days or centuries. His sense of personal identity, too, was very feeble, his thoughts revolving entirely around the events just prior to his death and the memory of his lost treasure, which he felt a longing to regain. He seemed, he said, to have his whole existence in a single idea which was like an obsession: the loss of his wealth and the desire to recover it.[8]

After a long time he again became aware of living beings, and felt an attraction towards a certain young woman. He attached himself to her, following her movements, and eventually another transition was effected, in a manner he was unable to describe clearly, as the result of which he was reborn as the woman's child.

These were the memories that lingered with him in connection with the strange malformations of his hands and feet, and which

---

8. Several cases have been found in which the subject remembers an intermediate life. These memories show an underlying unity of pattern, and in some respects confirm the accounts given in spiritualist communications. At first the disembodied entity is not aware that death has taken place. The sensations described resemble those of persons who have had experiences of the disembodied consciousness under anaesthesia or in what is known as astral projection. The term "disembodied" is not strictly correct; the consciousness is always located in, or associated with, a body of some kind, but the physical vehicle (*rūpa*) is of the fine-material type known to Buddhist metaphysics; that is to say, while it is unsubstantial on the plane of human consciousness, it is solid on the plane of a different vibrational frequency on which it manifests.

A feature which frequently occurs in these memories is the appearance of a guide who assists and directs the discarnate entity. In the case of a Burmese Buddhist monk whose rebirth history was investigated by the author, such a guide appeared to him shortly after his death, and directed him to his new birth. Subsequently, the same personage appeared to the monk in a dream during a critical period of his present life, and gave him valuable advice. A close parallel has been found in a case in America. A connection may be traced here with the almost universal belief in the "guardian angel" or spirit guide. It is significant, also, that such helpers do not appear to be attached to every individual. The Buddhist explanation is that the guide and protector is someone who has been closely connected by ties of friendship or relationship with the individual in a past life, and who still continues to take an interest in his welfare. The case from America, referred to above, gives support to this explanation. Here again, the postmortem experience was followed by further appearances of the guiding entity in the present life, in one of which a strong hint was given of a kammic link between the two persons concerned.

he told his mother in halting, childish words when he was able to speak. The case history bears several features in common with other instances of the recollection of previous lives that are fairly frequent in the East, and so may be profitably discussed as a typical example. One fact, however, should be noted at the outset: the child who made the claim to these recollections had nothing material to gain by doing so, neither had the parents. Another noteworthy fact is that the boy was a Karen, of a family that had been nominally Christian for two generations, and would be expected to have no belief in the doctrine of rebirth.

Certain interesting and very significant features emerge from an analysis of this particular case. In the first place, the craving motif is strongly marked throughout. The young man's choice of a solitary life in a house filled with valuables suggests a fear of employing servants and a tendency towards miserliness in his character. After death, in the *peta* state (i.e., as an unhappy ghost), his attachment to the lost treasure and to the locale of his previous life persisted as the strongest element in his consciousness, up to the time when he again became attracted to another human being.

So far, this important part played by the impulse of craving and attachment links the story with other instances of Petas haunting the spots where their former property was located; but here there is another element, that of fear, combined with the attachment. This fear was generated during the days and nights when the subject crouched, bound with wire, in the empty building, with no possibility of escape. In remote spots on the outskirts of villages and townships it is even now possible for such solitude to remain unbroken for weeks at a time.

An intensely strong mental impression of the wire cutting into the flesh must have been formed during this period, and it was probably the last image present in the consciousness at death. In accordance with the principles of Abhidhamma psychology, this last thought-moment would determine the character of the *paṭisandhi-viññāṇa* (connecting-consciousness or rebirth-consciousness), and would thus become the chief factor in determining the conditions of the new birth.

To understand how this comes about we must turn to a brief consideration of the Buddhist analysis of consciousness.

The process by which thought impressions register themselves is called *citta-vīthi*, or the course of cognition, and there is a *citta-vīthi* connected with each of the organs and fields of sense-cognition; that is, eye, ear, nose, tongue, touch (body), and mind. The passive flow of the subconscious mind-continuum (*bhavaṅga*) is disturbed whenever an external impression through one or another of these six channels impinges upon it. This disturbance is called *bhavaṅga-calana* (vibration of the subconscious mind-continuum) and it lasts for exactly one thought-moment. It is followed immediately afterwards by *bhavaṅgupaccheda*, or the cutting-off of *bhavaṅga*, which is a definite interruption in the smooth flow of the subconscious current. At this point the thought-moments begin to follow a set progression of cognitive response beginning with *pañca-dvārāvajjana*, which is the turning towards the sense-door (in this case one of the five physical organs).

This is followed by the arising of the consciousness-moment appertaining to whichever of the sense-doors, eye, ear, nose, tongue, or body, is involved. This is the involuntary act of turning the attention towards the external object, and it is followed at once by *sampaṭicchana*, which is the actual seeing, hearing, smelling, tasting, or feeling as the case may be. When this has been effected, the function of *santīraṇa*, or investigation, comes into play; at this stage associative ideas arise by which the mind is able to identify the impression that has been received, so that the next stage, that of *votthapana*, or identification, can be produced. *Votthapana* is the stage of conscious recognition, at which the object assumes a definite identity in the mental awareness. This stage is then succeeded in a full course of cognition by no less than seven *javana*[9] thought-moments, during which consciousness relating to the object arises and passes away. It is followed by *tadālambana*, which is the holding of the impression and the registering of it upon the mental stream; this stage, which lasts for two thought-moments, completes the *cittavīthi* of that particular impression, making sixteen thought-moments of the course of cognition from the first awakening of attention to the object to its fixing upon the consciousness. Each of these thought-moments is complete in

9. Lit. impulsion. It is at that phase that *kamma*, good or evil, is produced.

itself, consisting of three phases: arising (*uppāda*), enduring (*ṭhiti*), and passing away (*bhaṅga*).

The relative intensity or feebleness of impressions varies considerably. One single impression may be the subject of thousands of complete *vīthi*, each of them very distinct (*atimahanta*). If the impression is less marked it is called *mahanta* (distinct), and does not give rise to the *tadālambana* stage. Still weaker is an impression that does not even reach the *javana* stage (*paritta*; i.e., feeble); while, if it is very feeble indeed (*ati-paritta*), it passes away after the *bhavaṅga-calana* (vibration of *bhavaṅga*) without any of the subsequent thought-moments arising. An extremely vivid and clear impression reaching the mind door, accompanied by a full course of cognition, is called *vibhūta* (vivid). It is such impressions as these, repeated over and over again, which influence the mind and may be capable ultimately of influencing the body, with or without the accompaniment of a volitional impulse directed towards that end.

Normally the mind is selective, turning again and again to those impressions which are most agreeable, while ignoring the others; but under certain exceptional conditions disagreeable impressions force themselves upon the attention so strongly that they cannot be thrust aside. Very often such impressions may be rejected by the conscious mind, yet linger in the *bhavaṅga* ineradicably.

We are here dealing with states of consciousness arising in the *kāmaloka* (the world of fivefold sense-perception) and such as come into being through contact with external sense-objects. The course of ideational objects, those entering through the *mano-dvāra*, mind-door, is slightly different. In the cognitive series (*cittavīthi*) dealt with above, the *javana* thought-moment occurs up to seven times, but in loss of consciousness or at the moment of death it subsides after the fifth repetition. At that moment, representing the end of the final phase of the current life, cognitive thought (*vīthi-citta*) is experienced, and this takes the form of an idea-image which may be that of predominant *kamma*, of something associated with that *kamma* and its performance, or else a representation of the destiny to which the past *kamma* has been directed. At the expiry of the cognitive thought (*vīthi-citta*) or that of the *bhavaṅga*, there arises the *cuti-citta* (death-consciousness) which performs the function of cutting off, and immediately after that the *paṭisandhiviññāṇa*, or connecting-consciousness, arises in the next life as rebirth-consciousness. In the formula of Dependent Origination (*paṭiccasamuppāda*) this is expressed as:

"*Viññāṇapaccayā nāma-rūpa*"—"From (rebirth) consciousness arise name and form", i.e., mental and physical aggregates. This consciousness, conditioned by ignorance and actions (*kamma*) motivated by craving, carrying with it predominant impressions of the last thought-moments, functions as the *bhavaṅga* of the next existence, and so determines the key, as it were, in which that life is pitched. Thus the life-continuum flows on from one existence to another in the endless succession of *paṭisandhi*, *bhavaṅga*, *vīthi*, and *cuti*.

There is no actual thought-existence that passes across from one life to another, but only an impulse. Each moment of consciousness passes away completely, but as it passes it gives rise to a successor which tends to belong to the same pattern; and this process is the same, whether it be considered from the viewpoint of the moment-to-moment life-continuum that makes up a total life-span, or from that of the connecting link between one life and the next.

The rebirth is instantaneous and directly conditioned by the preceding thought-impulse. Since both mind and body are conditioned by it, even the distinctive pattern of the brain convolutions that accompanies a particular talent, say for music or mathematics, is the result of this powerful mental force operating from the past life and stamping its peculiar features on the physical substance, the living cell tissues of the brain. It is this which accounts for the phenomenon of genius in circumstances where heredity offers no tenable explanation. In the case of the Karen boy under discussion, the most potent rebirth force, craving, was conjoined with a strong impression of physical suffering and physical marks, and this impression had been the central pivot of consciousness for three days and nights—long enough to set up a thought-construction (or a pattern impressed on the *bhavaṅga*) sufficiently emphatic to influence the succeeding phases of consciousness and the new body that was formed under its direction. In some way not yet known to science, the thought-energy released at the time of death is able to control the combinations of male and female gametes and by means of *utu* (temperature) and the other purely physical elements of generation to produce a living organism that embodies the nature and potentialities of the past *kamma* in a new life (*anāgata-vipāka-bhava*).

Here it should be noted that strongly marked tendencies, both mental and physical, as well as actual memories belonging to past lives, are most in evidence when the rebirth is direct from one human life to another. The memories themselves are transferred by impression on the brain cells, so that the ordinary rules of memory obtain here, and it is the most recent and vivid impressions that survive. Intermediate lives in one or other of the remaining thirty planes of existence can efface altogether the memory of previous human lives, and if these intermediate existences have been in any of the lower states, where consciousness is dim, or spent in the inconceivably long lifespan of the *deva* realm, it can hardly be expected that there should be any recollection at all.

This is only one of the many reasons why most people altogether fail to remember having existed in a previous state, and yet may have a vague feeling that they have done so. In the case under review the subject spent an undefined period in the state of a *peta*, or what is popularly known as an "unhappy ghost". His own belief was that this state lasted for a long time; but in such conditions time is a purely subjective element. His existence as a *peta* may in fact not have lasted for more than a few thought-moments.

Questions put to the boy by the writer, however, seemed to indicate that the interval of *peta* existence had actually been of considerable duration, for after his rebirth he had not been able to identify any places or people from the former life. Everything had changed from his memory of it. Other attempts to draw some clue as to the period of the previous life were equally profitless. The primitive weapons of the dacoits did not necessarily indicate that it took place before the invention of firearms, for the statement that they used wire points to a more recent date. It is possible, however, that the boy's use of the word "wire" was a linguistic error, he may have meant thin strands of creeper, which would produce the same effect. The joining of his toes, corresponding to the manner in which they had stuck together with the congealed blood, is a striking instance of the enduring power of a mental impression: crouched with his head bent down to his knees, his hands and feet would be the central objects of his *cittavīthi*, and what was happening to them must have stamped itself visually on his consciousness to reproduce itself later in his new body by means of *paṭisandhiviññāṇa*.

This case is the most remarkable one known to the writer for the demonstration it gives of the mind's influence upon the physical body in a direct causal sequence from one life to another.[10]

10. Cases in which the subjects have birthmarks corresponding to injuries or physical characteristics they bore in the previous life form an important class of the rebirth case histories. They include the following examples:

Thailand: Large capillary naevus on left of cranium, corresponding to fatal knife wound received in the previous life. Also malformation of big toe, corresponding to wound present at the time of death.

Thailand: Slight malformation of left ear, reproducing similar irregularity in the previous life.

Burma: Birthmark on ankle resembling the mark of adhesive tape, corresponding to mark on the dead body of the previous life where adhesive tape had been fixed for blood transfusion.

Ceylon: Extensive malformation of right arm and right upper chest. The subject remembers having killed his wife by stabbing, and relates his deformities to the use of his right hand in the slaying. Case confirmed by a number of living witnesses.

England: Round, reddish area the size of a bullet wound, corresponding in position to fatal bullet wound in the previous life.

Brazil: Pigmented mark on back, below right scapula, with area of increased hair over left ribs in front of chest. The subject as a child said that he had been killed by a bullet in World War II.

America: Scars closely resembling bullet wounds of entry and exit, front and back of left chest. Other particulars of the case suggest death by murder in the previous life.

The case in Ceylon differs from the others in that it indicates retributive kammic effect. The others in this selection would appear to be psychokinetic effects which could be explained on the assumption that the subjects in a postmortem disincarnate state saw the marks on their own bodies. These were then reproduced on the new body, as in the cases of S.T., the Karen boy, quoted in Part V (p. 287).

Well-authenticated cases of a change of sex in rebirth at present number fifteen. These are being made the subject of special study in view of the light

That the process of mutation from one existence to the next is carried out without any "soul" or transmigrating entity is another fact that becomes apparent on examination of the case history. The only factor of identity between the headman's son, the *peta* (unhappy ghost), and S. T. the Karen houseboy, was the craving impulse that carried with it the potentiality of re-manifestation: that is, *bhava* (existence) resulting from *upādāna* (attachment). The terrors and physical affliction were the direct outcome of the *upādāna*, or attachment. In terms of Dependent Origination, *saṅkhāra* (*kamma* tendencies) conditioned by *avijjā* (ignorance) had produced *viññāṇa* (consciousness), and from that consciousness had sprung a fresh *nāma-rūpa* (mind-body) bearing the marks that had impressed themselves on the last moments of consciousness during repeated *cittavīthi* on the same object. It is thus that all living beings carry with them, throughout countless existences, the inheritance of their own thoughts and actions, sprung from past tendencies and nourished on the ever-renewed craving that comes from contact between the senses and the objects of the external world. Heredity itself is merely one factor in the multiple operations of the law of *kamma* and *vipāka* (result), and it too is greatly influenced by the direction taken by past interests, activities, and attachments.

---

they may throw on sexual deviations where the cause is not traceable in the present life. In a few of the cases so far investigated there is a decided predominance of the characteristics of the opposite sex in the present personality. In others the sexual adjustment is normal. The latter cases are valuable in that they eliminate the possibility that the rebirth memories are a 'fantasy' designed to explain away the sexual aberration. In one case, that of a girl, the previous personality was a boy who had a strong desire to be of the opposite sex. The child not only identified places, and persons still living, connected with the previous life, but also showed strong liking for certain persons and dislike of others, exactly as the previous personality had done. She remembers having wished to be a girl, and is happy now that her wish has been fulfilled. One striking feature of this case is that the girl recognised a school teacher who had been kind to her in the previous life, and now shows a strong attachment to him. The teacher testified that the dead boy whom she claims to be, had asked him whether it was true that people were reborn after death. This particular case is supported by an abundance of detailed proof and contains many features of psychological interest.

In the Buddha's Teaching it is naturally the moral aspect of *kamma* and *vipāka* that is stressed; and indeed there is a moral aspect to every major volitional impulse. The relationship of good *kamma* and good *vipāka*, bad *kamma* and bad *vipāka*, however, is not always obvious at first glance. A child born with a physical deformity, as in the present case, has not necessarily inflicted injury of a similar kind on someone else in a previous life. The physical defect may be the result of a strong mental impression produced by some other means. But as in the case of the Karen boy, the ultimate cause can invariably be traced back to some moral defect of the individual concerned to some trait of character unduly dominated by the *āsavas*, the taints or fluxes associated with the grasping tendency which in *paṭiccasamuppāda* is shown as the immediate cause of the process of "becoming" (*uppāda*, or grasping, gives rise to *bhava*, or becoming, which in its turn causes *jāti*, arising or rebirth). Thus the whole individual life process, including its physical medium, the *rūpa* (body), must be viewed as "*santati*," that is, a causal-continuum of action and result; all the actions being to some degree tainted by craving for existence, passion, self-interest, and ignorance, until the attainment of Arahatship extinguishes these energy-supplying fires.

It only remains to be noted that in the operation of mental impulses upon living cells at the time of their uniting, and during the processes of syngamy and mitosis, Buddhism offers a fully scientific explanation of the biological mutations described at the beginning of this chapter.

VI

Buddhism teaches that there are altogether thirty-one planes of existence on which rebirth is possible; the human plane is only one of them. The thirty-one "abodes" comprise the states of extreme suffering, or "hells," to which people consign themselves by reason of their bad *kamma*; the realms of the unhappy spirits, or "Petas," who on account of attachment to mundane concerns of a low order are more or less earthbound; the animal world into which people may be reborn through the manifestation of bestial characteristics; the realm of superior spirits intermediate between earth and the heavenly planes themselves, which are the abodes of *devas* enjoying sense-pleasures as the result of their past good actions; and lastly the Brahma worlds, wherein beings who on earth have attained specific spiritual goals live for aeons in pure and immaterial forms. All of these states of existence, however, are impermanent; sooner or later they come to an end, when the *kamma* that has produced them is exhausted. Rebirth then takes place once more, as the result of craving and residual *kamma* of another type from past lives which then comes into operation. So the process of saṃsāra continues until all craving is extinguished and Nibbāna is reached.

It is important to realise that Buddhism does not teach rebirth only on the human level. If it did so it would leave unexplained all the phenomena of spiritualism and a great deal more besides, which has to be accounted for in human experience. Many western spiritualists have now come to accept rebirth as a fact because it is the only valid explanation of certain data which cannot otherwise be fitted into the spiritualist concept. To give only one example, it is well known that spiritualist mediums find it impossible to "contact" certain people after death, while with others they are able to do so. This has always been a great difficulty to spiritualists, but the Buddhist answer is a simple one: it is not all who are reborn into the so-called spirit worlds, and furthermore some of these planes of existence are too remote from the human world to be accessible to any ordinary "medium."

The idea of other realms of existence is more difficult for those to accept who have become conditioned to thinking in terms of "naive realism," and it sometimes happens that through a misunderstanding of the Buddhist doctrine of *anattā* (no-self) they believe that rebirth can take place only in a physical and human body. This is an error which the Buddhist texts do not support. To deny the possibility of rebirth in the animal world, for example, is a negation of the universal applicability of the moral law of cause and effect which the Buddha consistently proclaimed. Both Theravada and Mahayana Buddhism teach unequivocally that if the *kamma* of the last thought moment before death is on a low moral level governed by any of the unwholesome factors associated with lust, hatred and delusion, the next manifestation of the causal continuum will be on precisely that level. In other words, rebirth as an animal, a *peta,* or a being in one of the hell states will result.

It must be understood that this does not correspond at all to the Pythagorean idea that the "soul" of one type of being can enter the body of another.

For the sake of a clear understanding of the processes of saṃsāra in regard to other realms of existence, the following extracts from letters from the present writer to a friend are given:

"Like yourself, when I first studied Buddhism I thought of rebirth as being only in human form. In the beginning that was satisfactory; as you say, 'a nice, clear-cut philosophy, rational'—and of course ethical as well. But further consideration revealed certain mechanical difficulties in the way of direct rebirth invariably from one human state to another. It meant, for instance, that at the moment of death some conception must be taking place somewhere which was in all respects ideally suited to be the vehicle of expression for the kammic potential released by the death.

"Of course, conception is actually taking place in millions of cases all over the world at any moment one cares to name; yet still it seems that too many coincidental factors must somehow be present to bring the thing within the realms of probability. Again, if animals are to be taken into the scheme, which is philosophically necessary in order to make the worldview comprehensive and to get away from the anthropocentric idea that ethics and spiritual meanings apply only to mankind—an idea which always seemed to me quite indefensible—it must be that the rebirth concept is somehow extensible to other modes of existence besides the human. After all, why should we assume that we are the only form of sentient and intelligent existence in the cosmos? Does the scientific outlook forbid us to envisage the possibility of other modes of life, simply because we cannot see, hear or handle them? Does not science itself tell us that most of the significant things in the universe, the things that really shape the visible world, are themselves invisible and intangible forces? We have to take many things on the authority of science which we cannot see and test for ourselves. True, somebody else has presumably tested these theories and so, science being a body of shared knowledge, as distinct from the esotericism of personal revelations, we accept the findings that the universe is of such and such a construction, that man has evolved from lower forms of life, and so forth. Even when we are led by gradual degrees to Einstein's general theory of relativity, the space-time complex, curved space, the expanding universe, and other ideas which nobody, not even the scientists themselves, can demonstrate in tangible form, we go on believing something that we cannot realise, or ever hope to realise except as perhaps a mathematical concept, simply because we have faith in the former discoveries of science and have seen that the method bears results. In other words, we believe in the method, even when we cannot check its latest results for ourselves.

"At that stage very few of us are philosophers enough to ask ourselves why we believe in a substantial physical universe when every new concept of science brings us into a more abstract world and proves that the universe is in reality something quite different from the mental picture we have formed of it from the data furnished by our senses. In a universe of energy, what has become of the solid, impenetrable substance of our world? If it is not exactly illusion, it is so different from the reality that its appearance at least may be termed illusion. Because it is a *shared* illusion and one that is necessary to our continued functioning within the framework of a world that we must regard as substantial, we are compelled to go on treating it as though it were actually the thing it appears to be as interpreted by our sensory awareness. But when we try to apply the laws of Newtonian physics to nuclear physics, and Euclidean geometry to the multiple space-time dimension, we find that these laws, while they are still valid in the limited sphere of the material world, are quite inadequate to cope with the abstract and much more complicated world of mathematical (and therefore philosophical) reality. From then on we have to suspect that the relatively simple material universe, in which certain things just cannot be because they cannot be always seen, heard or felt, is only a very partial aspect of the whole. What was simple and obvious to Charles Bradlaugh becomes not quite so certain. But still, through habit we go on asserting the validity of materialistic principles in spheres where it is far from certain that they obtain. So people say that there cannot be a heaven because they were always told that heaven existed somewhere up above the clouds, and stellar exploration (even before it becomes a fact) has disproved this.

"But on what principle do we insist that heaven or hell must have an objective, external existence? If 'heaven' is happiness and 'hell' misery, they are personal and subjective states; they exist independently of physical location. To take a concrete example, two men may be sitting side by side in a bus. One is desperately unhappy, perhaps through remorse, unsatisfied longing, anger, or any one of the myriad causes of human misery; he may be contemplating suicide, even. The other is blissfully happy; he has perhaps got promotion in his job, just had his first book published and the reviewers have been enthusiastic, or he has married the girl he loves. Each of these two men is inhabiting his own personal world, which has nothing to do with the world of the other; yet physically they are sitting side by side in this familiar world shared by us all. They may both get off at Sloane Square, but for one of them Sloane Square is a bus stop in heaven, while for the other it is located nowhere but in hell. So these states of being—really the only true states, since the external world has no part in making them what they are, but itself takes on whatever aspect they give to it—are internal, subjective, and purely mental states. As such they have no connection with location in time or space, or the events of the world going on about them. Each of us lives and has his own peculiar experience in a separate world, to which the external world presents only points of contact and general reference.

"So, if this can be the case in regard to two living men in a bus, whose physical bodies are touching one another but whose minds—and therefore real being—are living in different realms, why do we insist that if heaven exists as a reality it must be accessible by space travel or anything of that kind? In doing so we are naively applying laws that are relevant to physical space and time to other modes of conscious being where they are not relevant at all.

"What I am trying to express is a different vision of the world of reality. To me it seems that the real world is an intangible world of mental events and concepts, to which the external is only incidental. This may of course take the appearance of Berkeleyan idealism or, worse still, mysticism. But in reality it differs fundamentally from both: it is not Berkeleyan idealism because it does not attempt to brush aside the physical world as being nonexistent. It accepts that world as a reality, but not the whole or the final reality. It differs from mysticism in that it does not lose touch with the conditions in which we function as living, material organisms, and does not postulate any invasion of the laws governing extra-physical phenomena into the realm of the physical to the disorganisation of the latter. The worlds exist side by side, interpenetrating one another and affecting one another in various ways, but only within the limits imposed by the laws peculiar to each, and in conformity with those laws. Each world stands in relation to the others as a teleological necessity."

It may be objected that of the two men in the bus, the happiness of the one and the wretchedness of the other have certainly been caused by external events; something has happened to them to put them into their respective heaven and hell. That is true, but it is retrospective to the cause, while we are dealing with the effect as it now is. Their present conditions, whatever may have induced them, have no reference to one another nor to the objective world they share. They are living in discrete worlds that have been created for them by their reaction to some previous events.

Now had they been indifferent to those events they could not have been plunged into hell or exalted to heaven by them. So finally their condition can be traced back to their own minds and the degree of their susceptibility to external occasions for joy or sorrow. A certain thing happening to one man may cause him a mild and fleeting unhappiness; the same thing happening to another may reduce him to suicidal despair. The same kind of event objectively, but vastly different in its results—that is, in the kind of world it creates internally. If that is the cause, which is the more significant—the event in itself or the respective mental conditions of the two men, which have invested it with such different degrees of importance? If we say, as it seems to me we are bound to say, that the mental condition is the more significant, it must follow that it is the mental state, not the event, that represents the true reality in any situation. The illustration of the two men in the bus may be a trite and obvious one, but from it we are entitled to draw certain inferences concerning the nature of state of being in terms of isolated experiences. One of them is that the mind has its own habitat and a limitless capacity for creating its own worlds out of the raw materials of any situation. That these worlds of subjectivity have their counterparts in planes of existence other than our own is borne out by the testimony of Swedenborg, William Blake, and a host of others whose independent experience has given them glimpses of their reality. The part science plays in life is only on the fringe of mankind's collective experience.

In any case, when we bring science into the problem of being we ought to begin by defining just what we mean by the word. The most we can say is that science is a body of knowledge concerning accepted facts, gained by the pursuit of a certain method which has been found to give results in the past and so is presumed to be valid for all investigations. Scientific theories are constantly subject to alteration as knowledge increases, but scientific method remains the same. Therefore at any given point it is the method that is more important than any particular stage it has brought us to in the never-ending pursuit. But there can be no assurance that the method will eventually succeed in revealing everything. In fact, its progress suggests that the more it reveals the more there remains to be explored. It continually opens up new vistas, each of which demands that it be explored with new compasses. The 'expanding universe' may be just a natural allegory of man's expanding knowledge of the universe, something to which there can be no final limit. It becomes increasingly difficult to apply any sort of scientific knowledge to ontological questions, even when it seems to have some bearing on what we desire to know. Science may destroy religious myths but it has not made any important change in the terms of philosophical thought. It has given us a wider range of symbols and a more exact terminology, but that is all. We are no longer obliged to talk of the elements of earth, air, fire, and water, but the philosophical concepts they stood for remain fairly constant. Everything we know is merely a subjective experience based upon data presented by our senses, and these data come to us in the form of impressions which are in most cases far removed from the nature of the object as it really is. All that physics tells us is that the objects of the external world would appear to us quite differently if we possessed a different kind of cognitive apparatus. But even this was known long ago. Things that we see, hear, smell, taste, and touch have no intrinsic properties, only the characteristics we invest them with in the course of cognising and appraising. Thus the world of aesthetic values lies only in ourselves, and is in some respects different for each of us. In this mental world, made up of highly individualised impressions combined with the concepts that have gathered about them from prior association and, in the field of abstract concepts, the biases, predilections, and prejudices that are personal to the individual concerned, the range of variations becomes limitless. No two people think exactly alike, which means that no two people inhabit precisely the same world. Two persons may agree on all factual points, yet the interpretation they give to the totality may produce two quite different pictures.

So the world we live in is largely, if not wholly, a mental construct. Science gives us information about the external world which we know to be true so far as it goes. It is true because it is seen to work; if we apply the knowledge practically we get the expected results. Constructing a machine in accordance with certain proved laws of physics we get something that flies, defying another law of physics, gravitation. Something which one law seems to make impossible thus becomes practicable by the understanding and use of other laws. It is this form of progression from the impossible to the possible that has made our world what it is. The laws governing the propagation of sound make it possible for the of voice of someone talking in London to be heard in New York, and three hundred years ago the "natural philosopher" would have been content to leave it at that and would have had a hearty laugh at the notion of radio. But Newton would probably not have dismissed it as impossible because the genius of a really great scientist is like all other forms of genius—it includes a large amount of imagination. Had it not been for the old alchemists with their absurd theory that somehow the elements of one metal could be rearranged to form another, we should never have had modern chemistry. Even those who went further than the elixir of life and the transmutation of metals, and tried to produce the 'homunculus,' an artificial man, were only in a crude way trying to anticipate something which biochemistry may one day make possible.

And here it may be noted in passing that even if science should ultimately succeed in generating life from nonliving matter, the achievement will make no difference to the Buddhist doctrine of rebirth according to karma. The kammic causal current may manifest through vital elements brought together artificially in the same way as it does through the natural biological processes. The artificial production of living organisms may deal the final blow to the theory of divine creation, but it will not in any way affect the Buddhist explanation of life.

The laws that work in science are continually having to give way before the discovery of fresh laws which either cancel them out or modify them, or make them subservient to ends which previously they appeared to obstruct. And as this process develops we find ourselves becoming more and more doubtful as to whether it will reach any conclusive end. The horizon is eternally receding from us, the spiral nebulae forever thrusting outwards into limitless space. The familiar and comfortable world of 'things' is meanwhile dissolving into abstract forces, a whirling dance of electrons, of atoms which are never the 'same' atoms from one moment to another of their restless existence. Does what we see bear any relation whatever to the external reality? Can we ever be certain that physics itself is 'true'?

Speculative thought has been dried up at its source by the realisation that science alone can never help to reveal ultimate truth, but can show us only expanding areas of what is relatively true. It was because of this that Wittgenstein was constrained to renounce all attempts to erect systems of philosophy, even negative systems, and was particularly averse to theories which take mathematics or natural science as the ideal. But while the scientist remains content to work within the areas of relative truth and to leave teleological questions alone, his self-denial does not forbid others from making use of his knowledge in the attempt to trace a coherent pattern in the diversity of human experience. We have evidence from other sources that it is possible to improve man's perceptual apparatus and extend it, and by that means we may break through the impasse. It is only necessary that the ideas we bring into play should not be of a kind that science has shown to be false on grounds within its own province.

The limits of scientific competence should be clearly understood. It is a common error to suppose that science has accounted for a phenomenon when it has given it a name, and that it has explained a cause when it has merely described a process. To take an example, 'natural selection' is accepted as one of the primary factors in evolution. But if we ask what causes natural selection—precisely why does a living organism choose one course of action rather than another, or whence comes the instinctive urge to mate in a certain way that 'happens' to be conformable to biological needs—science is silent. It does not know the answer. It has named a process, and shown how it works, but it has not discovered the reason for it. To say that there is no reason is to evade the issue. The purpose may be assumed to tie in the final result, but that is legislating after the event. A certain phenomenon may be produced by accident, but for a long and involved series of such accidents to bring forth in the end a highly-organised and equipped animal of the type of the higher vertebrates is stretching pure chance too far. All the evidence points towards some kind of drive behind the process, but this theory is vitiated by the fact that the drive does not go directly towards the fulfilment of its purpose. It blunders along by a painful process of trial and error—stopping, retracing its steps, coming to dead ends, and scattering the debris of its failures along the path of geological time, yet always ensuring that in some way its surviving stages are contributory to the ultimate result, whatever that may be. This drive, or demiurge, cannot be a creator-god, for if it were, it would achieve its purpose with greater economy and, presumably, with more regard for ethical principles. That these are completely lacking in nature is one of the strongest arguments against the emergent theory. All the indications in fact are opposed to the idea of a supreme deity, whether God be conceived as a complete being or as an evolving and progressively revealed spiritual principle. Yet when all this is granted we are still left with the vacuum created by the lack of a purposive directing force. The question still remains: Can biological processes be explained in purely physical terms, or do the problems of structure, function, and organisation necessitate some kind of teleology? The scientist may reject the "vitalism" which Hans Driesch postulated as a necessity, but something of the kind is needed to account for organic evolution.

Buddhism meets the challenge with the concept of the force of craving, an impersonal urge to fulfilment continually renewing itself in successive manifestations. The "*demiurge*" and the "*élan vital*" are both functionally represented in this concept. Here we have not a 'something' which has visualised the final result from the beginning and has been capable of creating from nothing and moving directly towards its consummation, but a blindly groping urge which shows itself in the instinctive behaviour of animals and on the deeper psychological levels of human beings. It is the one great creative impulse to which all the laws of the universe are subservient.

Far from precluding the possibility of other states of being besides our own, science makes them, by inference, a logical necessity. The facts suggest that, in the words of Sir Oliver Lodge, "an enlarged psychology, and possibly an enlarged physiology—possibly even an enlarged physics—will have to take into account and rationalize a number of phenomena which so far have been mainly disbelieved or ignored."

It is as well to bear in mind that the existence of extra-terrestrial modes of being had always been recognised until science, by confining the method on grounds of knowledge to the material level, caused an unprecedented antagonism to metaphysical ideas. The revolution in outlook justified itself in many ways, but a new rationalism is emerging which has its roots in the enigmatic territory that modern physics has revealed beyond the tangible world.

Understanding of how rebirth in the human states takes place is sometimes obscured by misconceptions regarding certain biological principles, especially those relating to the transmission of hereditary characteristics. Here it is necessary to realise that the various parts of an organism are not received intact from the parents but developed out of comparatively simple structures present in the egg. There is no real analogy between heredity and the legal notion of inheritance of property. One speaks loosely of a given hereditary character being 'transmitted' from parent to offspring, but obviously this is impossible since the only materials which can be thus transmitted are those contained in the uniting sex cells, the eggs and spermatozoa in higher animals. "An individual receives from his parents not a set of fully-formed characters but a set of determinants or genes, as a consequence of whose activities the hereditary characters are developed. This concept of hereditary determinants is fundamental for an understanding of heredity" (Prof. G.H. Beale, Lecturer in Genetics, Edinburgh University, 1957). The determinants are therefore only a contribution to the sum total of characters, or personality. The extent to which they are decisive must depend very largely on other factors, not all of which are to be accounted for by environment. Heredity and the predispositions from past *kamma* may be complimentary to one another, as when attachment leads to repeated rebirths in the same racial group, or even in the same family; or the kammic tendencies may modify or counteract the hereditary characteristics. It is only if rebirth is taken to mean the transmigration of a 'soul' that there is any conflict between it and the known facts of genetics.

The emphasis laid upon *anattā* is fundamental to the Buddhist point of view. There is no 'soul' in the sense of an enduring entity; in its place there is mental energy flowing out from living creatures which after their death continues its current of causality by assembling out of physical substances a new being. But this new being, which is the continuation of the kammic cause-effect current of the previous one, does not necessarily have to be a human being. It may be an animal or it may be a being existing in other realms, where it produces a body in accordance with the particular laws of generation obtaining in those realms. If it has brought about a birth in the *deva* or *peta-loka* (which are justifiably called 'spirit' realms, since 'spirit' has nothing to do with 'soul' but denotes a particular type of body, different from the bodies of the terrestrial plane) it continues with a more or less recognisable personality. It is similar enough in general characteristics to the person who died to be recognisable as belonging to the same current of causal identity, and so we call it the 'same' person, just as we say that John Smith at ninety is the 'same' person as John Smith the infant which he once was. Actually they are not the same, except in this conventional sense—they merely belong to the same continuum of cause and effect. The new being, *deva* or *peta*, also retains memories of the previous life, and if emotional links or other attachments are strong, it continues to share the interests of people living on this, our own plane. Furthermore, when personality is very strongly marked it is all the more likely to reproduce characteristics which make it identifiable as the 'same' person in a new manifestation.

In this way Buddhism accounts for the phenomena of the séance room. Rebirth in these other realms, or *loka,* does not necessitate a soul any more than does rebirth as a human being or animal. When the result of the *kamma* that has caused the rebirth in the *deva* or *peta* realms is exhausted, the mental energy once more flows out to operate through the conditions of the physical world and human rebirth takes place again. Or it may be that another *deva* or *peta* rebirth will come about, or a rebirth in any other of the thirty-one planes of existence according to the nature of the residual *kamma*.

There are several lines of enquiry on which investigation into rebirth may be carried out. It has been possible to indicate only a few of them here. The serial continuity of life, which so many people in all ages have felt instinctively to be a truth, however, carries with it the force of an intellectual conviction to all who seek for a purpose and a moral pattern in human experience. It is not too much to say that the whole of man's future development depends upon an acceptance of rebirth and a fuller understanding of the ethical principles it brings to light. Mankind is now ripe for a complete reassessment of values and a restatement of the universal principles on which our moral and spiritual convictions rest. Unless this is undertaken, we stand in danger of a catastrophic destruction of all those virtues by which man has risen to his present position in the hierarchy of living beings. It is only by the acceptance of rebirth as a fact that the sense of moral responsibility in an ordered universe can be restored.

Everyman's Ethics

Four Discourses of the Buddha

Adapted from the translations of

Nārada Thera

WHEEL PUBLICATION NO. 14

Adapted from the translations and notes in *The Light of the Dhamma* by the Venerable Nārada Thera.
The introductory notes to the last three texts have been supplied by the editor of this series.

Sigālovāda Sutta
The Layman's Code of Discipline

Sigāla was the son of a Buddhist family residing at Rājagaha. His parents were devout followers of the Buddha, but the son was indifferent to religion. The pious father and mother could not by any means persuade their son to accompany them to visit the Buddha or his disciples and hear the noble Doctrine. The son thought it practically useless to pay visits to the Sangha, as such visits may entail material loss. He was only concerned with material prosperity; to him spiritual progress was of no avail. Constantly he would say to his father: "I will have nothing to do with monks. Paying homage to them would make my back ache, and my knees stiff. I should have to sit on the ground and soil and wear out my clothes. And when, at the conversations with them, after so sitting, one gets to know them, one has to invite them and give them offerings, and so one only loses by it."

Finally as the father was about to die, he called his son to his deathbed, and enquired whether he would at least listen to his parting advice. "Most assuredly, dear father, I shall carry out any order you may be pleased to enjoin on me," he replied. "Well then, dear son, after your morning bath worship the six quarters." The father asked him to do so hoping that one day or other, while the son was so engaged, the Buddha or his disciples would see him, and make it an occasion to preach an appropriate discourse to him. And since deathbed wishes are to be remembered, Sigāla carried out his father's wish, not, however, knowing its true significance.

Now, it was the custom of the Buddha to rise from his sleep at four o'clock and after experiencing Nibbānic bliss for an hour to pervade the whole world with his boundless thoughts of loving-kindness. It is at this hour that he surveys the world with his great compassion to find out to what fellow being he could be of service on that day. One morning Sigāla was caught in the net of the Buddha's compassion; and with his vision the Buddha, seeing that Sigāla could be shown a better channel for his acts of worship, decided: "This day will I discourse to Sigāla on the layman's Vinaya (code of discipline). That discourse will be of benefit to many folk. There must I go." The Buddha thereon came up to him on his way for alms to Rājagaha; and seeing him engaged in his worship of the six quarters, delivered this great discourse which contains in brief, the whole domestic and social duty of the layman.

Commenting on this sutta, the Venerable Buddhaghosa says, "Nothing in the duties of a householder is left unmentioned. This sutta is called the Vinaya of the householder. Hence in one who practices what he has been taught in it, growth is to be looked for, not decay." And Mrs. Rhys Davids adds: "The Buddha's doctrine of love and goodwill between man and man is here set forth in a domestic and social ethics with more comprehensive detail than elsewhere. And truly we may say even now of this Vinaya or code of discipline, so fundamental are the human interests involved, so sane and wide is the wisdom that envisages them, that the utterances are as fresh and practically as binding today and here as they were then at Rājagaha. 'Happy would have been the village or the clan on the banks of the Ganges where the people were full of the kindly spirit of fellow-feeling, the noble spirit of justice which breathes through these naive and simple sayings.' Not less happy would be the village, or the family on the banks of the Thames today, of which this could be said."

Thus have I heard:

On one occasion the Exalted One was dwelling in the Bamboo Grove, the Squirrels' Sanctuary, near Rājagaha.

Now at the time, young Sigāla, a householder's son, rising early in the morning, departing from Rājagaha, with wet clothes and wet hair, worshipped with joined hands the various quarters—the East, the South, the West, the North, the Nadir, and the Zenith.

Then the Exalted One, having robed himself in the forenoon took bowl and robe, and entered Rājagaha for alms. Now he saw young Sigāla worshipping thus and spoke to him as follows:

"Wherefore do you, young householder, rising early in the morning, departing from Rājagaha, with wet clothes and wet hair, worship, with joined hands these various quarters—the East, the South, the West, the North, the Nadir, and the Zenith?"

"My father, Lord, while dying, said to me: The six quarters, dear son, you shall worship. And I, Lord, respecting, revering, reverencing and honouring my father's word, rise early in the morning, and leaving Rājagaha, with wet clothes and wet hair, worship with joined hands, these six quarters."

"It is not thus, young householder, the six quarters should be worshipped in the discipline of the noble."

"How then, Lord, should the six quarters be worshipped in the discipline of the noble? It is well, Lord, if the Exalted One would teach the doctrine to me showing how the six quarters should be worshipped in the discipline of the noble."

"Well, young householder, listen and bear it well in mind; I shall speak."—"Very good, Lord," responded young Sigāla.

And the Exalted One spoke as follows:

"Inasmuch, young householder, as the noble disciple (1) has eradicated the four vices in conduct,[1] (2) inasmuch as he commits no evil action in four ways, (3) inasmuch as he pursues not the six channels for dissipating wealth, he thus, avoiding these fourteen evil things, covers the six quarters, and enters the path leading to victory in both worlds: he is favoured in this world and in the world beyond. Upon the dissolution of the body, after death, he is born in a happy heavenly realm.

(1) "What are the four vices in conduct that he has eradicated? The destruction of life, householder, is a vice and so are stealing, sexual misconduct, and lying. These are the four vices that he has eradicated."

Thus spoke the Exalted One. And when the Master had thus spoken, he spoke yet again:

> Killing, stealing, lying and adultery,
> These four evils the wise never praise.

(2) "In which four ways does one commit no evil action? Led by desire does one commit evil. Led by anger does one commit evil. Led by ignorance does one commit evil. Led by fear does one commit evil.[2] "But inasmuch as the noble disciple is not led by desire, anger, ignorance, and fear, he commits no evil."

---

1. *Kamma-kilesa*, lit., "action-defilement." Commentary: "*Kammakileso ti kammañca taṃ kilesasampayuttattā kileso cāti kammakileso. Sakilesoyeva hi pāṇaṃ hanati, nikkileso na hanati, tasmā pāṇātipāto "kammakileso"ti vutto.*"

2. These are the four *agati*, "evil courses of action": *chanda, dosa, moha, bhaya.*

Thus spoke the Exalted One. And when the Master had thus spoken, he spoke yet again:

Whoever through desire, hate or fear,
Or ignorance should transgress the Dhamma,
All his glory fades away
Like the moon during the waning half.
Whoever through desire, hate or fear,
Or ignorance never transgresses the Dhamma,
All his glory ever increases
Like the moon during the waxing half.

(3) "What are the six channels for dissipating wealth which he does not pursue?

(a) indulgence in intoxicants which causes infatuation and heedlessness;
(b) sauntering in streets at unseemly hours;
(c) frequenting theatrical shows;
(d) indulgence in gambling which causes heedlessness;
(e) association with evil companions; and
(f) the habit of idleness.

(a) "There are, young householder, these six evil consequences in indulging in intoxicants which cause infatuation and heedlessness:

(i) loss of wealth,
(ii) increase of quarrels,
(iii) susceptibility to disease,
(iv) earning an evil reputation,
(v) shameless exposure of body,
(vi) weakening of intellect.

(b) "There are, young householder, these six evil consequences in sauntering in streets at unseemly hours:

(i) he himself is unprotected and unguarded,
(ii) his wife and children are unprotected and unguarded,
(iii) his property is unprotected and unguarded,
(iv) he is suspected of evil deeds,[3]

3. Crimes committed by others.

(v) he is subject to false rumours,
(vi) he meets with many troubles.

(c) "There are, young householder, these six evil consequences in frequenting theatrical shows. He is ever thinking:

(i) where is there dancing?
(ii) where is there singing?
(iii) where is there music?
(iv) where is there recitation?
(v) where is there playing with cymbals?
(vi) where is there pot-blowing?[4]

(d) "There are, young householder, these six evil consequences in indulging in gambling:

(i) the winner begets hate,
(ii) the loser grieves for lost wealth,
(iii) loss of wealth,
(iv) his word is not relied upon in a court of law,
(v) he is despised by his friends and associates,
(vi) he is not sought after for matrimony; for people would say that he is a gambler and is not fit to look after a wife.

(e) "There are, young householder, these six evil consequences in associating with evil companions, namely: any gambler, any libertine, any drunkard, any swindler, any cheat, any rowdy is his friend and companion.

(f) "There are, young householder, these six evil consequences in being addicted to idleness: He does no work, saying:

(i) that it is extremely cold,
(ii) that it is extremely hot,
(iii) that it is too late in the evening,
(iv) that it is too early in the morning,
(v) that he is extremely hungry,
(vi) that he is too full.

"Living in this way, he leaves many duties undone, new wealth he does not get, and wealth he has acquired dwindles away."

4. A kind of amusement.

Thus spoke the Exalted One. And when the Master had thus spoken, he spoke yet again:

"One is a bottle friend; one says, 'friend, friend' only to one's face; one is a friend and an associate only when it is advantageous.

Sleeping till sunrise, adultery, irascibility, malevolence, evil companions, avarice—these six causes ruin a man.

The man who has evil comrades and friends is given to evil ways, to ruin does he fall in both worlds—here and the next.

Dice, women, liquor, dancing, singing, sleeping by day, sauntering at unseemly hours, evil companions, avarice—these nine[5] causes ruin a man.

Who plays with dice and drinks intoxicants, goes to women who are dear unto others as their own lives, associates with the mean and not with elders—he declines just as the moon during the waning half.

Who is drunk, poor, destitute, still thirsty whilst drinking, frequents the bars, sinks in debt as a stone in water, swiftly brings disrepute to his family.

Who by habit sleeps by day, and keeps late hours, is ever intoxicated, and is licentious, is not fit to lead a household life.

Who says it is too hot, too cold, too late, and leaves things undone, the opportunities for good go past such men.

But he who does not regard cold or heat any more than a blade of grass and who does his duties manfully, does not fall away from happiness."

* * *

These four, young householder, should be understood as foes in the guise of friends:

(1) he who appropriates a friend's possessions,
(2) he who renders lip-service,
(3) he who flatters,
(4) he who brings ruin.

(1) "In four ways, young householder, should one who appropriates be understood as a foe in the guise of a friend:

5. The Pali original has here "six causes"—two compound words and one double-term phrase are counted as units.

(i) he appropriates his friend's wealth,
(ii) he gives little and asks much,
(iii) he does his duty out of fear,
(iv) he associates for his own advantage.

(2) "In four ways, young householder, should one who renders lip-service be understood as a foe in the guise of a friend:

(i) he makes friendly profession as regards the past,
(ii) he makes friendly profession as regards the future,
(iii) he tries to gain one's favour by empty words,
(iv) when opportunity for service has arisen, he expresses his inability.

(3) "In four ways, young householder, should one who flatters be understood as a foe in the guise of a friend:

(i) he approves of his friend's evil deeds,
(ii) he disapproves his friend's good deeds,
(iii) he praises him in his presence,
(iv) he speaks ill of him in his absence.

(4) "In four ways, young householder, should one who brings ruin be understood as a foe in the guise of a friend:

(i) he is a companion in indulging in intoxicants that cause infatuation and heedlessness,
(ii) he is a companion in sauntering the streets at unseemly hours,
(iii) he is a companion in frequenting theatrical shows,
(iv) he is a companion in indulging in gambling which causes heedlessness."

Thus spoke the Exalted One. And when the Master had thus spoken, he spoke yet again:

"The friend who appropriates,
the friend who renders lip-service,
the friend that flatters,
the friend who brings ruin—
these four as enemies the wise behold,
avoid them from afar as paths of peril.

"These four, young householder, should be understood as warm-hearted friends:

(1) he who is a helpmate,
(2) he who is the same in happiness and sorrow,
(3) he who gives good counsel,
(4) he who sympathises.

(1) "In four ways, young householder, should a helpmate be understood as a warm-hearted friend:

(i) he guards the heedless,
(ii) he protects the wealth of the heedless,
(iii) he becomes a refuge when one is in danger,
(iv) when there are commitments he provides one with double the supply needed.

(2) "In four ways, young householder, should one who is the same in happiness and sorrow be understood as a warm-hearted friend:

(i) he reveals his secrets,
(ii) he conceals one's own secrets,
(iii) in misfortune he does not forsake one,
(iv) his life even he sacrifices for one's sake.

(3) "In four ways, young householder, should one who gives good counsel be understood as a warm-hearted friend:

(i) he restrains one from doing evil,
(ii) he encourages one to do good,
(iii) he informs one of what is unknown to oneself,
(iv) he points out the path to heaven.

(4) "In four ways, young householder, should one who sympathises be understood as a warm-hearted friend:

(i) he does not rejoice in one's misfortune,
(ii) he rejoices in one's prosperity,
(iii) he restrains others speaking ill of oneself,
(iv) he praises those who speak well of oneself."

Thus spoke the Exalted One. And when the Master had thus spoken, he spoke yet again:

"The friend who is a helpmate,
the friend in happiness and woe,
the friend who gives good counsel,
the friend who sympathises too—
these four as friends the wise behold
and cherish them devotedly
as does a mother her own child.

The wise and virtuous shine like blazing fire.
He who acquires his wealth in harmless ways
like to a bee that honey gathers,[6]
riches mount up for him
like ant hill's rapid growth.

With wealth acquired this way,
a layman fit for household life,
in portions four divides his wealth:
thus will he friendship win.

One portion for his wants he uses,[7]
two portions on his business spends,
the fourth for times of need he keeps."

* * *

"And how, young householder, does a noble disciple cover the six quarters?

"The following should be looked upon as the six quarters. The parents should be looked upon as the East, teachers as the South, wife and children as the West, friends and associates as the North, servants and employees as the Nadir, ascetics and brahmins as the Zenith.[8]

6. Dhammapada v. 49: "As a bee, without harming the flower, its colour or scent, flies away, collecting only the honey..."

7. This portion includes what is spent on good works: gifts to monks, charity, etc.

8. "The symbolism is deliberately chosen: as the day in the East, so life

"In five ways, young householder, a child should minister to his parents as the *East* :

(i) Having supported me I shall support them,
(ii) I shall do their duties,
(iii) I shall keep the family tradition,
(iv) I shall make myself worthy of my inheritance,
(v) furthermore I shall offer alms in honour of my departed relatives.[9]

"In five ways, young householder, the parents thus ministered to as the *East* by their children, show their compassion:

(i) they restrain them from evil,
(ii) they encourage them to do good,
(iii) they train them for a profession,
(iv) they arrange a suitable marriage,
(v) at the proper time they hand over their inheritance to them.

"In these five ways do children minister to their parents as the East and the parents show their compassion to their children. Thus is the East covered by them and made safe and secure.

"In these five ways, young householder, a pupil should minister to a teacher as the *South*:

(i) by rising from the seat in salutation,[10]
(ii) by attending on him,

---

begins with parents' care; teacher's fees and the South are the same word: *dakkhiṇa*; domestic cares follow when the youth becomes man, as the West holds the later daylight; North is "beyond" (*uttara*), so by help of friends, etc., he gets beyond troubles."—(Rhys Davids)

9. This is a sacred custom of the Aryans who never forgot the dead. This tradition is still faithfully observed by the Buddhists of Sri Lanka who make ceremonial offerings of alms to the monks on the eighth day, in the third month, and on each anniversary of the demise of the parents. Merit of these good actions is offered to the departed after such ceremony. Moreover after every *puñña-kamma* (good action), a Buddhist never fails to think of his parents and offer merit. Such is the loyalty and the gratitude shown to parents as advised by the Buddha.

10. *The Path of Purification*, trans. by Ñāṇamoli, Kandy: BPS 1997, p.597

(iii) by eagerness to learn,
(iv) by personal service,
(v) by respectful attention while receiving instructions.

"In five ways, young householder, do teachers thus ministered to as the *South* by their pupils, show their compassion:

(i) they train them in the best discipline,
(ii) they see that they grasp their lessons well,
(iii) they instruct them in the arts and sciences,
(iv) they introduce them to their friends and associates,
(v) they provide for their safety in every quarter.

"The teachers thus ministered to as the South by their pupils, show their compassion towards them in these five ways. Thus is the South covered by them and made safe and secure.

"In five ways, young householder, should a wife as the *West* be ministered to by a husband:

(i) by being courteous to her,
(ii) by not despising her,
(iii) by being faithful to her,
(iv) by handing over authority to her,
(v) by providing her with adornments.

"The wife thus ministered to as the *West* by her husband shows her compassion to her husband in five ways:

(i) she performs her duties well,
(ii) she is hospitable to relations and attendants[11]
(iii) she is faithful,
(iv) she protects what he brings,
(v) she is skilled and industrious in discharging her duties.

"In these five ways does the wife show her compassion to her husband who ministers to her as the West. Thus is the West covered by him and made safe and secure.

"In five ways, young householder, should a clansman minister to his friends and associates as the *North*:

11. lit., "the folk around" (*parijana*).

(i) by liberality,
(ii) by courteous speech,
(iii) by being helpful,
(iv) by being impartial,
(v) by sincerity.

"The friends and associates thus ministered to as the *North* by a clansman show compassion to him in five ways:

(i) they protect him when he is heedless,
(ii) they protect his property when he is heedless,
(iii) they become a refuge when he is in danger,
(iv) they do not forsake him in his troubles,
(v) they show consideration for his family.

"The friends and associates thus ministered to as the North by a clansman show their compassion towards him in these five ways. Thus is the North covered by him and made safe and secure.

"In five ways should a master minister to his servants and employees as the *Nadir*:

(i) by assigning them work according to their ability,
(ii) by supplying them with food and wages,
(iii) by tending them in sickness,
(iv) by sharing with them any delicacies,
(v) by granting them leave at times.

"The servants and employees thus ministered to as the *Nadir* by their master show their compassion to him in five ways:

(i) they rise before him,
(ii) they go to sleep after him,
(iii) they take only what is given,
(iv) they perform their duties well,
(v) they uphold his good name and fame.

"The servants and employees thus ministered to as the Nadir show their compassion towards him in these five ways. Thus is the Nadir covered by him and made safe and secure.

"In five ways, young householder, should a householder minister to ascetics and brahmins as the *Zenith*:

(i) by lovable deeds,
(ii) by lovable words,
(iii) by lovable thoughts,
(iv) by keeping open house to them,
(v) by supplying their material needs.

"The ascetics and brahmins thus ministered to as the *Zenith* by a householder show their compassion towards him in six ways:

(i) they restrain him from evil,
(ii) they persuade him to do good,
(iii) they love him with a kind heart,
(iv) they make him hear what he has not heard,
(v) they clarify what he has already heard,
(vi) they point out the path to a heavenly state.

"In these six ways do ascetics and brahmins show their compassion towards a householder who ministers to them as the Zenith. Thus is the Zenith covered by him and made safe and secure."

Thus spoke the Exalted One. And when the Master had thus spoken, he spoke yet again:

"The mother and father are the East,
The Teachers are the South,
Wife and children are the West,
The friends and associates are the North.

Servants and employees are the Nadir,
The ascetics and brahmins are the Zenith;
Who is fit to lead the household life,
These six quarters he should salute.

Who is wise and virtuous,
Gentle and keen-witted,
Humble and amenable,
Such a one to honour may attain.

Who is energetic and not indolent,
In misfortune unshaken,
Flawless in manner and intelligent,

Such a one to honour may attain.

Who is hospitable, and friendly,
Liberal and unselfish,
A guide, an instructor, a leader,
Such a one to honour may attain.

Generosity, sweet speech,
Helpfulness to others,
Impartiality to all,
As the case demands.

These four winning ways make the world go round,
As the linchpin in a moving car.
If these in the world exist not,
Neither mother nor father will receive,
Respect and honour from their children.

Since these four winning ways
The wise appraise in every way,
To eminence they attain,
And praise they rightly gain."

When the Exalted One had spoken thus, Sigāla, the young householder, said as follows:

"Excellent, Lord, excellent! It is as if, Lord, a man were to set upright that which was overturned, or were to reveal that which was hidden, or were to point out the way to one who had gone astray, or were to hold a lamp amidst the darkness, so that those who have eyes may see. Even so, has the doctrine been explained in various ways by the Exalted One.

"I take refuge, Lord, in the Buddha, the Dhamma, and the Sangha. May the Exalted One receive me as a follower; as one who has taken refuge from this very day to life's end."

Mahā-maṅgala Sutta
Blessings

This famous text,[12] cherished highly in all buddhist lands, is a terse but comprehensive summary of Buddhist ethics, individual and social. The thirty-eight blessings enumerated in it are an unfailing guide on life's journey. Rightly starting with "avoidance of bad company," which is essential to all moral and spiritual progress, the Blessings culminate in the achievement of a passion-free mind, unshakeable in its serenity. To follow the ideals put forth in these verses is the sure way to harmony and progress for the individual as well as for society, country and mankind.

"The Mahā-maṅgala Sutta shows that Buddha's instructions do not always take negative forms, that they are not always a series of classifications and analysis, or concerned exclusively with monastic morality. In this sutta we find family morality expressed in most elegant verses. We can imagine the happy blissful state of household life attained as a result of following these injunctions." (From *The Ethics of Buddhism* by S. Tachibana, Colombo 1943, Bauddha Sahitya Sabha).

Thus have I heard. On one occasion the Exalted One was dwelling at Anāthapiṇḍika's monastery, in Jeta's Grove,[13] near

---

12. This Sutta appears in the Suttanipāta (v. 258 ff) and in the Khuddakapāṭha. See Mahāmaṅgala Jātaka (No. 453). For a detailed explanation see *Life's Highest Blessing* by Dr. R. L. Soni, Wheel No. 254/256.

13. Anāthapiṇḍika, lit., "He who gives alms to the helpless"; his former name was Sudatta. After his conversion to Buddhism, he bought the grove belonging to Prince Jeta, and established a monastery which was subsequently named Jetavana. It was in this monastery that the Buddha observed most of his *vassāna* periods (rainy seasons—the three months' retreat beginning with the full-moon of July). Many are the discourses delivered and many are the incidents connected with the Buddha's life that happened at Jetavana. It was here that the Buddha ministered to the sick monk neglected by his companions, advising them: "Whoever, monks, would wait upon me, let him wait upon the sick." It was here that the Buddha so poignantly taught the law of impermanence, by asking the bereaved young woman Kisā Gotamī who

Sāvatthī.[14] Now when the night was far spent, a certain deity, whose surpassing splendour illuminated the entire Jeta Grove, came to the presence of the Exalted One and, drawing near, respectfully saluted him and stood at one side. Standing thus, he addressed the Exalted One in verse:

The Deity:

Many deities and men, yearning after good, have pondered on blessings.[15] Pray, tell me the greatest blessing!

The Buddha:

Not to associate with the foolish,[16] but to associate with the wise; and to honour those who are worthy of honour—this is the greatest blessing.

To reside in a suitable locality,[17] to have done meritorious actions in the past and to set oneself in the right course[18]—this is the greatest blessing.

To have much learning, to be skilful in handicrafts,[19] well-trained in discipline,[20] and to be of good speech[21]—this is the greatest blessing.

---

brought her dead child, to fetch a grain of mustard seed from a home where there has been no bereavement.

14. Identified with modern Sahet-Mahet, near Balrampur.

15. According to the Commentary, *maṅgala* means that which is conducive to happiness and prosperity.

16. This refers not only to the stupid and uncultured, but also includes the wicked in thought, word and deed.

17. Any place where monks, nuns and lay devotees continually reside, where pious folk are bent on the performance of the ten meritorious deeds, and where the Dhamma exists as a living principle.

18. Making the right resolve for abandoning immorality for morality, faithlessness for faith, and selfishness for generosity.

19. The harmless crafts of the householder by which no living being is injured and nothing unrighteous done; and the crafts of the homeless monk, such as stitching the robes, etc.

20. *Vinaya* means discipline in thought, word and deed. The commentary speaks of two kinds of discipline—that of the householder, which is abstinence from the ten immoral actions (*akusala-kammapatha*), and that of the monk which is the non-transgression of the offences enumerated in the *Pātimokkha* (the code of the monk's rules) or the "fourfold moral purity" (*catu-parisuddhi-sīla*).

21. Good speech that is opportune, truthful, friendly, profitable and spoken

To support father and mother, to cherish wife and children, and to be engaged in peaceful occupation—this is the greatest blessing.

To be generous in giving, to be righteous in conduct,[22] to help one's relatives, and to be blameless in action—this is the greatest blessing.

To loathe more evil and abstain from it, to refrain from intoxicants,[23] and to be steadfast in virtue—this is the greatest blessing.

To be respectful,[24] humble, contented and grateful; and to listen to the Dhamma on due occasions[25]—this is the greatest blessing.

To be patient and obedient, to associate with monks and to have religious discussions on due occasions—this is the greatest blessing.

Self-restraint,[26] a holy and chaste life, the perception of the Noble Truths and the realisation of Nibbāna—this is the greatest blessing.

A mind unruffled by the vagaries of fortune,[27] from sorrow freed, from defilements cleansed, from fear liberated[28]—this is the greatest blessing.

Those who thus abide, ever remain invincible, in happiness established. These are the greatest blessings."[29]

---

with thoughts of loving-kindness.

22. Righteous conduct is the observance of the ten good actions (*kusala-kammapatha*) in thought, word and deed: freeing the mind of greed, ill-will and wrong views; avoiding speech that is untruthful, slanderous, abusive and frivolous; and the non-committal of acts of killing, stealing and sexual misconduct.

23. Total abstinence from alcohol and intoxicating drugs.

24. Towards monks (and of course also to the clergy of other religions), teachers, parents, elders, superiors, etc.

25. For instance, when one is harassed by evil thoughts.

26. Self-restraint (*tapo*): the suppression of lusts and hates by the control of the senses; and the suppression of indolence by the rousing of energy.

27. *Loka-dhamma*, i.e., conditions which are necessarily connected with life in this world; there are primarily eight of them: gain and loss, honour and dishonour, praise and blame, pain and joy.

28. Each of these three expressions refers to the mind of the arahant: *asoka*: sorrowless; *viraja*: stainless, i.e., free from lust, hatred and ignorance; *khema*: security from the bonds of sense desires (*kāma*), repeated existence (*bhava*), wrong views (*diṭṭhi*), and ignorance (*avijjā*).

29. The above-mentioned thirty-eight blessings.

Parābhava Sutta
Downfall

While the Maṅgala Sutta deals with the way of life conducive to progress and happiness, the Parābhava Sutta supplements it by pointing out the causes of downfall. He who allows himself to become tarnished by these blemishes of conduct blocks his own road to worldly, moral and spiritual progress, and lowers all that is truly noble and human in man. But he who is heedful of these dangers keeps open the road to all those thirty-eight blessings of which human nature is capable.

Thus have I heard. Once the Exalted One was dwelling at Anāthapiṇḍika's monastery, in the Jeta Grove, near Sāvatthī.

Now when the night was far spent, a certain deity, whose surpassing splendour illuminated the entire Jeta Grove, came to the presence of the Exalted One and, drawing near, respectfully saluted him and stood at one side. Standing thus, he addressed the Exalted One in verse:

The Deity:

Having come here with our questions to the Exalted One, we ask thee, O Gotama, about man's decline. Pray, tell us the cause of downfall!

The Buddha:

Easily known is the progressive one, easily known he who declines. He who loves Dhamma progresses; he who is averse to it declines.

The Deity:

Thus much do we see: this is the first cause of one's downfall. Pray, tell us the second cause.[30]

The Buddha:

The wicked are dear to him, with the virtuous he finds no delight, he prefers the creed of the wicked—this is a cause of one's downfall.

Being fond of sleep, fond of company, indolent, lazy and irritable—this is a cause of one's downfall.

Though being well-to-do, not to support father and mother who are old and past their youth—this is a cause of one's downfall.

To deceive by falsehood a Brahmin or ascetic or any other mendicant—this is a cause of one's downfall.

To have much wealth and ample gold and food, but to enjoy one's luxuries alone—this is a cause of one's downfall.

To be proud of birth, of wealth or clan, and to despise one's own kinsmen—this is a cause of one's downfall.

To be a rake, a drunkard, a gambler, and to squander all one earns—this is a cause of one's downfall.

Not to be contented with one's own wife, and to be seen with harlots and the wives of others—this is a cause of one's downfall.

Being past one's youth, to take a young wife and to be unable to sleep for jealousy of her—this is a cause of one's downfall.

To place in authority a woman given to drink and squandering, or a man of a like behaviour—this is a cause of one's downfall.

To be of noble birth, with vast ambition and of slender means, and to crave for rulership—this is a cause of one's downfall.

Knowing well these causes of downfall in the world, the noble sage endowed with insight shares a happy realm.

30. These lines are repeated after each stanza, with the due enumeration.

Vyagghapajja Sutta
Conditions of Welfare

In this sutta, the Buddha instructs rich householders how to preserve and increase their prosperity and how to avoid loss of wealth. Wealth alone, however, does not make a complete man nor a harmonious society. Possession of wealth all too often multiplies man's desires, and he is ever in the pursuit of amassing more wealth and power. This unrestrained craving, however, leaves him dissatisfied and stifles his inner growth. It creates conflict and disharmony in society through the resentment of the underprivileged who feel themselves exploited by the effects of unrestrained craving.

Therefore the Buddha follows up on his advice on material welfare with four essential conditions for spiritual welfare: confidence (in the Master's enlightenment), virtue, liberality and wisdom. These four will instil in man a sense of higher values. He will, then, not only pursue his own material concern, but also be aware of his duty towards society. To mention only one of the implications: a wisely and generously employed liberality will reduce tensions and conflicts in society. Thus the observing of these conditions of material and spiritual welfare will make for an ideal citizen in an ideal society.

Thus have I heard. Once the Exalted One was dwelling amongst the Koliyans,[31] in their market town named Kakkarapatta. Then Dīghajanu,[32] a Koliyan, approached the Exalted One, respectfully saluted him and sat on one side. Thus seated, he addressed the Exalted One as follows:

"We, Lord, are laymen who enjoy worldly pleasure. We lead a life encumbered by wife and children. We use sandalwood of Kāsi. We deck ourselves with garlands, perfume and unguents. We use gold and silver. To those like us, O Lord, let the Exalted One preach the Dhamma, teach those things that lead to weal and

---

31. The Koliyans were the rivals of the Sākyans. Queen Mahā Māyā belonged to the Koliyan clan and King Suddhodana to the Sākyan clan.

32. Literally, "long-kneed."

happiness in this life and to weal and happiness in future life."

Conditions of Worldly Progress

"Four conditions, Vyagghapajja,[33] conduce to a householder's weal and happiness in this very life. Which four?

"The accomplishment of persistent effort (*uṭṭhāna-sampadā*), the accomplishment of watchfulness (*ārakkha-sampadā*), good friendship (*kalyāṇamittatā*) and balanced livelihood (*sama-jīvitā*).

"What is the accomplishment of persistent effort?

"Herein, Vyagghapajja, by whatsoever activity a householder earns his living, whether by farming, by trading, by rearing cattle, by archery, by service under the king, or by any other kind of craft—at that he becomes skilful and is not lazy. He is endowed with the power of discernment as to the proper ways and means; he is able to carry out and allocate (duties). This is called the accomplishment of persistent effort.

"What is the accomplishment of watchfulness?

"Herein, Vyagghapajja, whatsoever wealth a householder is in possession of, obtained by dint of effort, collected by strength of arm, by the sweat of his brow, justly acquired by right means—such he husbands well by guarding and watching so that kings would not seize it, thieves would not steal it, fire would not burn it, water would not carry it away, nor ill-disposed heirs remove it. This is the accomplishment of watchfulness.

"What is good friendship?

"Herein, Vyagghapajja, in whatsoever village or market town a householder dwells, he associates, converses, engages in discussions with householders or householders' sons, whether young and highly cultured or old and highly cultured, full of faith (*saddhā*),[34] full of virtue (*sīla*), full of charity (*cāga*), full of wisdom (*paññā*). He acts in accordance with the faith of the faithful, with the virtue of the virtuous, with the charity of the charitable, with the wisdom of the wise. This is called good friendship.

"What is balanced livelihood?

---

33. "Tigers' Path"; he was so called because his ancestors were born on a forest path infested with tigers. Vyagghapajja was Dīghajānu's family name.

34. *Saddhā* is not blind faith. It is confidence based on knowledge.

"Herein, Vyagghapajja, a householder knowing his income and expenses leads a balanced life, neither extravagant nor miserly, knowing that thus his income will stand in excess of his expenses, but not his expenses in excess of his income.

"Just as the goldsmith,[35] or an apprentice of his, knows, on holding up a balance, that by so much it has dipped down, by so much it has tilted up; even so a householder, knowing his income and expenses leads a balanced life, neither extravagant nor miserly, knowing that thus his income will stand in excess of his expenses, but not his expenses in excess of his income.

"If, Vyagghapajja, a householder with little income were to lead an extravagant life, there would be those who say—'This person enjoys his property like one who eats udumbara figs.'[36] If, Vyagghapajja, a householder with a large income were to lead a wretched life, there would be those who say—'This person will die like a starveling.'

"The wealth thus amassed, Vyagghapajja, has four sources of destruction: debauchery, drunkenness, gambling, and friendship, companionship and intimacy with evil-doers.

"Just as in the case of a great tank with four inlets and outlets, if a man should close the inlets and open the outlets and there should be no adequate rainfall, decrease of water is to be expected in that tank, and not an increase; even so there are four sources for the destruction of amassed wealth—debauchery, drunkenness, gambling, and friendship, companionship and intimacy with evil-doers.

"There are four sources for the increase of amassed wealth: abstinence from debauchery, abstinence from drunkenness, non-indulgence in gambling, and friendship, companionship and intimacy with the good.

"Just as in the case of a great tank with four inlets and four outlets, if a person were to open the inlets and close the outlets, and there should also be adequate rainfall, an increase in water is certainly to be expected in that tank and not a

35. *Tulādharo,* lit., "carrier of the scales."

36. *Udambarakhādaka.* The Commentary explains that one who wishes to eat udumbara figs shakes the tree, with the result that many fruits fall but only a few are eaten, while a large number are wasted.

decrease, even so these four conditions are the sources of increase of amassed wealth.

"These four conditions, Vyagghapajja, are conducive to a householder's weal and happiness in this very life."

Conditions of Spiritual Progress

"Four conditions, Vyagghapajja, conduce to a householder's weal and happiness in his future life. Which four?

"The accomplishment of faith (*saddhā-sampadā*), the accomplishment of virtue (*sīla-sampadā*), the accomplishment of charity (*cāga-sampadā*) and the accomplishment of wisdom (*pañña-sampadā*).

"What is the accomplishment of faith?

"Herein a householder is possessed of faith, he believes in the Enlightenment of the Perfect One (*Tathāgata*): 'Thus, indeed, is that Blessed One: he is the pure one, fully enlightened, endowed with knowledge and conduct, well-gone, the knower of worlds, the incomparable leader of men to be tamed, the teacher of gods and men, all-knowing and blessed.' This is called the accomplishment of faith.

"What is the accomplishment of virtue?

"Herein a householder abstains from killing, stealing, sexual misconduct, lying, and from intoxicants that cause infatuation and heedlessness. This is called the accomplishment of virtue.

"What is the accomplishment of charity?

"Herein a householder dwells at home with heart free from the stain of avarice, devoted to charity, open-handed, delighting in generosity, attending to the needy, delighting in the distribution of alms. This is called the accomplishment of charity.

"What is the accomplishment of wisdom?

"Herein a householder is wise: he is endowed with wisdom that understands the arising and cessation (of the five aggregates of existence); he is possessed of the noble penetrating insight that leads to the destruction of suffering. This is called the accomplishment of wisdom.

"These four conditions, Vyagghapajja, conduce to a householder's weal and happiness in his future life.

Energetic and heedful in his tasks,
Wisely administering his wealth,
He lives a balanced life,
Protecting what he has amassed.

Endowed with faith and virtue too,
Generous he is and free from avarice;
He ever works to clear the path
That leads to weal in future life.

Thus to the layman full of faith,
By him, so truly named 'Enlightened,'
These eight conditions have been told
Which now and after lead to bliss."

Dependent Origination

(Paṭicca Samuppāda)

commentary by

Piyadassi Thera

WHEEL PUBLICATION NO. 15

Introduction

Dependent origination, *paṭicca-samuppāda*, is a basic teaching of Buddhism. The doctrine therein being so deep and profound it is not possible within the limited scope of this essay to make an extensive survey of the subject. Based solely on the teaching of the Buddha an attempt is made here to elucidate this doctrine, leaving aside the complex details.

Scholars and writers have rendered this term into English in various ways: "dependent origination," "dependent arising," "conditioned co-production," "causal conditioning," "causal genesis," "conditioned genesis," "causal dependencies." Throughout this essay the term dependent origination is used. Dependent origination is not a discourse for the unintelligent and superficial, nor is it a doctrine to be grasped by speculation and mere logic put forward by hair-splitting disputants. Hear these words of the Buddha:

"Deep, indeed, Ānanda, is this *paṭicca-samuppāda*, and deep does it appear. It is through not understanding, through not penetrating this doctrine, that these beings have become entangled like a matted ball of thread, become like *muñja* grass and rushes, unable to pass beyond the woeful states of existence and *saṃsāra*, the cycle of existence."[1]

Those who fail to understand the real significance of this all-important doctrine mistake it to be a mechanical law of causality, or even a simple simultaneous arising, nay a first beginning of all things, animate and inanimate. Be it remembered that there is no First Cause with a capital 'F' and capital 'C' in Buddhist thought, and dependent origination does not attempt to dig out or even investigate a first cause. The Buddha emphatically declared that the first beginning of existence is something inconceivable,[2] and that such notions and speculations of a beginning may lead to mental derangement.[3] If one posits a "First Cause" one is justified in asking for the cause of that "First Cause," for nothing can

1. Mahānidāna Sutta, DN 15.
2. Anamatagga Saṃyutta, S II 179.
3. A IV 77.

escape the law of condition and cause which is patent in the world to all but those who will not see.

According to Aldous Huxley:

> "Those who make the mistake of thinking in terms of a first cause are fated never to become men of science. But as they do not know what science is, they are not aware that they are losing anything. To refer phenomena back to a first cause has ceased to be fashionable, at any rate in the West...we shall never succeed in changing our age of iron into an age of gold until we give up our ambition to find a single cause for all our ills, and admit the existence of many causes acting simultaneously, of intricate correlations and reduplicated actions and reactions."[4]

A Creator God who rewards and punishes the good deeds and ill deeds of the creatures of his creation has no place in Buddhist thought. A theist, however, who attributes beings and events to an omnipotent Creator God would emphatically say, "It is God's will; it is sacrilege to question the authority." This God-idea, however, stifles the human liberty to investigate, to analyse, to scrutinize, to see what is beyond this naked eye, and retards insight.

Let us grant for argument's sake that 'x' is the "first cause." Now does this assumption of ours bring us one bit nearer to our goal, our deliverance? Does it not close the door to it? Buddhism, on the other hand, states that things are neither due to one cause (*eka-hetuka*), nor are they causeless (*ahetuka*). The twelve factors of *paṭicca-samuppāda* and the twenty-four conditioning relations (*paccaya*) shown in the Paṭṭhāna, the seventh and the last book of the Abhidhamma Piṭaka, clearly demonstrate how things are "multiple-caused" (*aneka-hetuka*); and in stating that things are neither causeless nor due to one single cause, Buddhism antedated modern science by twenty-five centuries.

We see a reign of natural law—beginningless causes and effects and naught else ruling the universe. Every effect becomes in turn a cause and it goes on forever (as long as ignorance and craving are allowed to continue). A coconut, for instance, is the principal cause or near cause of a coconut tree. 'X' has two parents,

4. Aldous Huxley, *Ends and Means* (London, 1945), pp. 14–15.

four grandparents, and thus the law of cause and effect extends unbrokenly like the waves of the sea—*ad infinitum*.

It is just impossible to conceive of a first beginning. None can trace the ultimate origin of anything, not even of a grain of sand, let alone of human beings. It is useless and meaningless to go in search of a beginning in a beginningless past. Life is not an identity, it is a becoming. It is a flux of psychological and physiological changes, a conflux of mind and body (*nāma-rūpa*).

> "There is no reason to suppose that the world had a beginning at all. The idea that things must have a beginning is really due to the poverty of our imagination. Therefore, perhaps, I need not waste any more time upon the argument about the first cause."[5]

Instead of a first cause, the Buddha speaks of conditionality. The whole world is subject to the law of cause and effect, in other words, action and reaction. We cannot think of anything in this cosmos that is causeless and unconditioned.

As Viscount Samuel says: "There is no such thing as chance. Every event is the consequence of previous events; everything that happens is the effect of a combination of a multitude of prior causes; and like causes always produce like effects. The laws of causality and of the uniformity of nature prevail everywhere and always."[6]

Buddhism teaches that all compounded things come into being, presently exist, and cease (*uppāda, ṭhiti, bhaṅga*) dependent on conditions and causes. Compare the truth of this saying with that oft-quoted verse of the Arahat Thera Assaji, one of the Buddha's first five disciples, who crystallized the entire teaching of the Buddha when answering the question of Upatissa who later became known as Arahat Thera Sāriputta.

Upatissa's question was: "What is your teacher's doctrine? What does he proclaim?"

And this was the answer:

"Ye dhammā hetuppabhavā—tesaṃ hetuṃ tathāgato āha,

---

5. Bertrand Russell, *Why I Am Not a Christian* (London, 1958), p. 4.

6. Viscount Samuel, *Belief and Action* (London: Penguin Books, 1939), p. 16.

tesaṃ ca yo nirodho—evaṃvādi mahāsamaṇo."

"Whatever from a cause proceeds, thereof
The Tathāgatha has explained the cause,
Its cessation too he has explained.
This is the teaching of the Supreme Sage."[7]

Though brief, this expresses in unequivocal words dependent origination or conditionality.

As the text says, during the whole of the first week, immediately after his enlightenment, the Buddha sat at the foot of the Bodhi Tree at Gayā experiencing the supreme bliss of emancipation. When the seven days had elapsed, he emerged from that *samādhi*, that state of concentrative thought, and during the first watch of the night thought over the dependent origination, as to how things arise (*anuloma*) thus: "When this is, that comes to be; with the arising of this, that arises, namely: dependent on ignorance, volitional formations; dependent on formations, consciousness...and so on. This is the arising of this whole mass of suffering."[8]

Then in the middle watch of the night, he pondered over the dependent origination as to how things cease (*paṭiloma*)[9] thus: "When this is not, that does not come to be; with the cessation of this, that ceases, namely: with the utter cessation of ignorance, the cessation of volitional formations...and so on. Thus is the cessation of this whole mass of suffering."

In the last watch of the night, he reflected over the dependent origination, both as to how things arise and cease thus: "When this exists, that comes to be; with the arising of this, that arises.

7. Vin I 40.

8. The entire formula consisting of the twelve factors is found at the end of this essay

9. Generally the two Pāli words *anuloma* and *paṭiloma* are translated as "direct order" and "reverse order." However, it is not quite correct to say "reverse order," for that means from the end towards the beginning or in the opposite order. Both the arising and the ceasing of the factors of dependent origination are from beginning to end. For instance, with the arising of ignorance arise volitional formations and so on. With the ceasing of ignorance cease volitional formations, and so on.

When this does not exist, that does not come to be; with the cessation of this, that ceases, namely: dependent on ignorance, arise volitional formations...and so on. Thus is the ending of this whole mass of suffering."[10]

One may justifiably be inclined to pose the question: Why did the Buddha not set forth the doctrine of dependent origination in his first discourse,[11] the sermon delivered to the five ascetics, his erstwhile companions, at Benares? The answer is this: the main points discussed in that all-important sermon are the Four Noble Truths: suffering, its cause, its cessation, and the way to the cessation of suffering, the Noble Eightfold Path. There is no statement in it about dependent origination; but one who understands the philosophical and doctrinal significance of dependent origination certainly understands that the twelvefold *paṭicca-samuppāda*, dependent origination, both in its order of arising and ceasing (*anuloma* and *paṭiloma*), is included in the Four Noble Truths.

The *paṭicca-samuppāda* in its order of arising manifests the process of becoming (*bhava*), in other words, the appearance of suffering (*dukkha*, the first truth); and how this process of becoming or suffering is conditioned (*dukkha-samudaya*, the second truth). In its order of ceasing the *paṭicca-samuppāda* makes plain the cessation of this becoming, this suffering (*dukkha-nirodha*, the third truth), and how it ceases (*dukkha-nirodha-gāmini paṭipadā*, the fourth truth). The Buddha-word with regard to this fact appears in the Aṅguttara Nikāya thus:

"And what, monks, is the noble truth of the origination of suffering? Dependent on ignorance arise volitional formations; dependent on volitional formations, consciousness; dependent on consciousness, mentality-materiality (mental and physical combination); dependent on mentality-materiality, the sixfold base (the five physical sense organs and consciousness as the sixth); dependent on the sixfold base, contact; dependent on contact, feeling; dependent on feeling, craving; dependent on craving, clinging; dependent on clinging, the process of becoming (rebirth); dependent on the process of becoming, ageing and death, sorrow, lamentation, pain, grief and despair come to pass. Thus does the

10. Ud 2.

11. Dhammacakkappavattana Sutta, Vin I 10–12; S V 420.

whole mass of suffering arise. This, monks, is called the noble truth of the origination of suffering.

"And what, monks, is the noble truth of the cessation of suffering? Through the entire cessation of ignorance cease volitional formations; through the cessation of volitional formations, consciousness...(and so on)...the cessation of the whole mass of suffering. This, monks, is called the cessation of suffering."[12]

It is now abundantly clear from the foregoing that the *paṭicca-samuppāda*, with its twelve factors, is the teaching of the Buddha and not, as some are inclined to think, the work of some writers on the Dhamma of later times. It is unreasonable, even dangerous, to rush to conclusions without fully understanding the significance of the *paṭicca-samuppāda*.

Dependent origination, or the doctrine of conditionality, is often explained in severely practical terms, but it is not a mere pragmatical teaching, though it may appear to be so, owing to such explanation resorted to for brevity's sake. Those conversant with the Tipiṭaka (the Buddhist Pali Canon) know that in the teachings of the *paṭicca-samuppāda* is found that which brings out the basic principles of knowledge (*ñāṇa*) and wisdom (*paññā*) in the *saddhamma*, the Good Law. In this teaching of the conditionality of everything in the world, that is the five aggregates, can be realized the essence of the Buddha's outlook on life. So if the Enlightened One's explanation of the world is to be rightly understood, it has to be through a full grasp of this central teaching summed up in the dictum: "*ye dhammā hetuppabhavā* ..." referred to above.

The doctrine of *paṭicca-samuppāda* is not the work of some divine power; it is not a creation. Whether a Buddha arises or not the fact is:

> "When this is, that comes to be;
> With the arising of this, that arises.
> When this is not, that does not come to be;
> With the cessation of this, that ceases."[13]

This conditionality goes on forever, uninterrupted and uncontrolled by any external agency or power of any sort.

12. A I 176.
13. MN 79/M II 32.

The Buddha discovered this eternal truth, solved the riddle of life, unravelled the mystery of being by comprehending, in all its fullness, the *paṭicca-samuppāda* with its twelve factors, and expounded it, without keeping back anything essential, to those who yet have sufficient intelligence to wish for light.

I. Ignorance (*Avijjā*)

Let us now deal with the twelve actors of the *paṭicca-samuppāda*, one by one, in due order. The first point for discussion is *avijjā* (Sanskrit, *avidyā*), ignorance. *Moha*, delusion and *aññāṇa*, non-knowledge, are synonyms for *avijjā*. What is *avijjā*? It is the non-knowledge of the Supreme Enlightenment. In other words, not knowing the Four Noble Truths. It is also not knowing dependent origination. Owing to this nescience, the uninstructed worldling entertains wrong views. He regards the impermanent as permanent, the painful as pleasant, the soulless as soul, the godless as god, the impure as pure, and the unreal as real. Further, *avijjā* is the non-perception of the conglomerate nature of the five aggregates (*pañcakkhandhā*), or mind and body.

Ignorance or delusion is one of the root causes of all unwholesome (*akusala*) actions, all moral defilements. All conceivable wrong notions are the result of ignorance. Independently of this crowning corruption no evil action, whether mental, verbal or physical, could be performed. That is why ignorance is enumerated as the first link of the chain of the twelvefold *paṭicca-samuppāda*. Nevertheless, ignorance should not be regarded as a *prima causa*, a first beginning, or an ultimate origin of things. It is certainly not the first cause; there is no conception of a first cause in Buddhist thought. The doctrine of *paṭicca-samuppāda* can be illustrated by a circle, for it is the cycle of existence, *bhavacakka*. In a circle any given point may be taken as the starting point. Each and every factor of the *paṭicca-samuppāda* can be joined together with another of the series, and therefore no single factor can stand by itself or function independently of the rest. All are interdependent and inseparable. Nothing is independent, or isolated. Dependent origination is an unbroken process. In this process nothing is stable or fixed, but all is in a whirl. It is the arising of ever changing conditions dependent on similar evanescent conditions. Here there is neither absolute non-existence nor absolute existence, only bare phenomena roll on (*suddhadhammā pavattanti*).

Ignorance, the first factor of the series, therefore, is not the sole condition for volitional formations, the second factor (*saṅkhāra*). A tripod, for instance, is supported by its three legs; it stands upright because of the interdependence of the legs. If one gives way, the other two fall to the ground unsupported. So, too, the factors of this *paṭicca-samuppāda* support one another in various ways.

II. Volitional Formations (*Saṅkhārā*)

Avijjāpaccayā saṅkhārā, "dependent on ignorance arise rebirth-producing volitional formations." The term *saṅkhāra* has also another meaning. In the statement, "*sabbe saṅkhārā aniccā*" or "*aniccā vata saṅkhārā*" (all compounded things are impermanent), the term "*saṅkhārā*" applies to all compounded and conditioned things, i.e. all things that come into being as the effect of causes and conditions and which themselves act as causes and conditions in turn to give rise to other effects. In the *paṭicca-samuppāda*, however, *saṅkhārā* is restricted to mean simply all good and evil actions (*kusala-akusala kamma*), all actions, physical, verbal and mental (*kāya-saṅkhāra, vacī-saṅkhāra*, and *citta-saṅkhāra*) which will bring about reactions. It is difficult to give a satisfactory English equivalent to the term *saṅkhāra*. Let us, therefore, understand it in this context as rebirth-producing volitional activities, or volitional formations, or simply as kamma.

Ignorance, *avijjā*, which has taken root in man is the blindness that prevents a man from seeing his actions as they really are, and so allows craving to drive him on to further actions. If there were no ignorance, there would be no such actions. In the absence of actions conditioned by ignorance, there will be no rebirth, and the whole mass of suffering will cease. In order to exemplify how the twelve factors of the *paṭicca-samuppāda* act upon a connected sequence of lives, the formula has been conceived as extending over three consecutive existences—past, present and future.

Ignorance and volitional formations belong to the previous birth. Wholesome *saṅkhāras* are capable of bringing about a good rebirth, i.e. birth in a good state of existence. Unwholesome *saṅkhāras* can cause a bad rebirth or birth in an evil state of existence. It must be mentioned that all *saṅkhāras*, all good and evil actions, have ignorance as condition. Here a question may be raised as to how actions conditioned by ignorance could bring about good rebirth.

All attainment of good (*kusala*), from the state of virtuous worldling (*kalyāṇaputhujjana*) and the "lesser stream-winner" (*cūḷasotāpanna*) to that of the consummate one (*arahat*), is due to the balance of insight over delusion and of detachment over craving. Good actions are the direct consequence of whatever clear understanding there may be in the doer. It is not because of delusion and craving that a man gives up killing, etc., but because he has the wisdom to see the evil consequences of such actions and also because he is moved by such qualities as compassion and virtue. It is not possible, except for the perfect ones, to act from complete insight or detachment. To the generality of men such knowledge is unthinkable. As Eddington says, "If 'to know' means 'to be quite certain of' the term is of little use to those who wish to be undogmatic."[14] And if to be detached means to be neutral always, such detachment is for the imperfect quite impossible and meaningless. But occasional detachment is possible, and a measure of knowledge adequate for understanding the good is available for an intelligent man of virtue, for producing actions that are wise and unsoiled by the yearning for rewards in this life. There is much that is done in the world today with no hope of reward, or recognition, out of compassion or for the furtherance of knowledge and peace. Such actions definitely are based on knowledge and detachment, not perhaps in the dogmatic, scholastic, or merely metaphysical sense, but in the light of sane, undogmatic thought. Good actions may well have ulterior motives, for instance, the yearning for the fruits of the good; but even in such instances, though tainted by greed and to that extent by delusion, there are in such good actions, for instance in liberality, the detachment to let go and the knowledge of seeing the evils of not giving at all, and the advantage of giving. The presence of craving and ignorance in a person does not mean that he can never act with insight and detachment.

14. Eddington, *The Philosophy of Physical Science* (Cambridge University Press, 1939).

Now it must also be understood that although man is capable of performing good actions unsoiled by strong desire for rewards in this life, there may be in him, unconsciously working, a tender longing for good rebirth, or a feeling of desire for rewards in the hereafter. Again, though he may be doing an action out of compassion and without any ulterior motives, he may still be lacking in full awareness of the real nature of life—its being impermanent, sorrow-stricken, and void of an abiding entity or soul. This non-knowledge of the real nature of life, though not so gross and strong as the delusion that induces a heinous act, can yet induce kammically wholesome action leading to a good rebirth. A good rebirth even in the heavens, is, however, temporary, and may be followed immediately by an unhappy rebirth.

Such non-knowledge motivates and colours the good act. If, for instance, the performance of good actions is motivated by the desire for the resultant happiness in a good rebirth in a heavenly realm, or on earth, then that is the ignorance of the impermanence and unsatisfactory nature of all existence, which becomes a condition of good rebirth, i.e. and inducement or support condition (*upanissaya paccaya*). In these, and other ways, ignorance may act as a condition of good rebirth by motivating or colouring good volitional activities (*saṅkhārā*) of a mundane (*lokiya*) nature. Such is the intrinsic nature of ignorance.

Ignorance of the real nature of life is primarily the ignorance of the Four Noble Truths. It is because of this non-knowledge of the truths that beings take birth again and again.

Says the Buddha:

> "Monks, it is through not understanding, not penetrating the Four Noble Truths that we have run so long, wandered on so long in this long long way, both you and I...But when these Four Noble Truths are understood and penetrated, rooted out is the craving for existence, destroyed is that which leads to renewed becoming, and there is no more coming to be."[15]

Only the actions of one who has entirely eradicated all the latent tendencies (*anusaya*), and all the varied ramifications of sorrow's cause, are incapable of producing rebirth; for such actions

15. D II 90; S V 430; Vin I 229.

are issueless. He is the *arahat*, Consummate One, whose clarity of vision, whose depth of insight penetrates into the deepest recesses of life, in whom craving has quite ceased through cognizing the true nature that underlies all appearance. He has transcended all appearance. He has transcended all capacity for error through the perfect immunity which penetrative insight, *vipassanā*, alone can give. He is, therefore, released from ignorance (*avijjā*) and his actions no more bring about rebirth.

III. Consciousness (*Viññāṇa*)

Saṅkhārapaccayā viññānaṃ, "dependent on rebirth-producing volitional formations (belonging to the previous birth), arises consciousness (re-linking or rebirth consciousness)." To express it in another way, dependent on the kamma, or good and evil actions of the past, is conditioned the conscious life in this present birth. Consciousness, therefore, is the first factor (*nidāna*), or first of the conditioning links belonging to the present existence. *Avijjā* and *saṅkhārā*, ignorance and volitional formations belonging to the past, together produce *viññāṇa*, consciousness in this birth. We read in the Mahānidāna Sutta of the Dīgha Nikāya, how "once ignorance and craving are destroyed, good and evil actions no more come into being, consequently no more rebirth consciousness will spring up again in a mother's womb." Hence it is clear that rebirth is caused by one's own good and evil actions, and is not work of a supreme being, a Creator God, nor is it due to mere chance.

As this consciousness or *viññāṇa* is the first in the stream of consciousness (*citta-santati*) belonging to one single existence (*bhava*), it is also known as *paṭisandhi-viññāṇa*, re-linking consciousness. The term *paṭisandhi* literally means re-linking, re-uniting, re-joining. It is re-birth, re-entry into the womb. Rebirth is the arising, the coming to be, the being born, in the future (*paṭisandhīti āyatiṃ uppatti*). It is called re-uniting because of its linking back the new existence to the old (*bhavantara paṭisandhānato paṭisandhīti vuccati*). The joining of the new to the old is the function of re-uniting or re-linking. Therefore, it is said, the function of re-uniting is the joining together of (one) existence with (another) existence (*bhavato bhavassa paṭisandhānaṃ paṭisandhi kiccaṃ*). *Paṭisandhi-viññāṇa* is the kamma resultant consciousness (*vipāka viññāṇa*) present at rebirth, connecting the new existence with the immediately preceding one, and through that with the entire past of the "being" reborn. This resultant consciousness is due to previous rebirth-producing volitional formations (*saṅkhārā* or *kamma*).

In the Aneñjasappāya Sutta,[16] the *vipāka viññaṇa* is referred to as *saṃvattanikaṃ viññāṇaṃ*, the consciousness that links on, that proceeds in one life as *vipāka* from the kamma in the former life.

When it is said, "the consciousness that links on," it does not mean that this consciousness abides unchanged, continues in the same state without perishing throughout this cycle of existence. Consciousness is also conditioned, and therefore is not permanent. Consciousness also comes into being and passes away yielding place to new consciousness. Thus this perpetual stream of consciousness goes on until existence ceases. Existence in a way is consciousness. In the absence of consciousness no "being" exists in this sentient world.

In the Buddhist doctrine of rebirth the third factor required for rebirth, the *gandhabba*, is called "the rebirth consciousness," which is another term for the *paṭisandhi-viññāṇa*, relinking consciousness.[17] There is the last moment of consciousness (*cuti citta*) belonging to the immediately previous life. Immediately following the cessation of that consciousness there arises the first moment of consciousness of the present birth, which as stated above, is termed relinking consciousness (*paṭisandhi-viññāṇa*). Between these two moments of consciousness, however, there is no interval, there is no *antarābhava* or *antarābhava-satta*, which means "either a being in the womb or a being in between the state of death and that of rebirth," as some of the Mahāyāna schools of thought maintain (*asti antar bhavah*).[18] It should be clearly understood that this relinking consciousness is not a "self" or a "soul" or an ego entity that experiences the fruits (*vipāka*) of good and evil deeds. The Mahātaṇhāsaṅkhaya Sutta records the following incident:

---

16. MN 106.
17. MN 38/M I 265–66.
18. Lankāvatāra Sūtra.

During the time of the Buddha there was a monk called Sāti who held the following view: "In so far as I understand the Dhamma taught by the Buddha, it is the same consciousness that transmigrates and wanders about (in rebirth)."

The monks who heard of this tried to dissuade Sāti, saying, "Do not, brother Sāti, speak thus, do not misrepresent the Lord; neither is misrepresentation of the Lord proper, nor would the Lord speak thus. For, brother Sāti, in many a figure is dependent origination spoken of in connection with consciousness by the Lord, saying: 'Apart from condition there is no origination of consciousness.'"

But Sāti would not change his view. Thereupon the monks reported the matter to the Buddha, who summoning him, spoke to him thus:

"Is it true, as is said, that a pernicious view like this has arisen in you, Sāti: 'In so far as I understand the Dhamma taught by the Lord, it is this consciousness itself that runs on, fares on, not another'?"

"Even so do I, Lord, understand the Dhamma taught by the Lord: 'It is this consciousness itself that runs on, fares on, not another.'"

"What is this consciousness, Sāti?"

"It is that which expresses, which feels (*vado vedeyyo*) and experiences the result of good and evil deeds now here, now there."

"But to whom, foolish man, have you heard me teaching the Dhamma in this way? Have I not in many ways explained consciousness as arising out of conditions, that apart from conditions there is no arising of consciousness? But now you, foolish man, misrepresent me because of your own wrong grasp."[19]

The Buddha then explained the different types of consciousness and made clear, by means of examples, how consciousness arises depending on conditions.

In the words of the Buddha, the *paṭicca-samuppāda* is a very deep and intricate doctrine, and in this difficult doctrine the most subtle and deep point, difficult to grasp, is this third link, consciousness, *viññāṇa* or *paṭisandhi-viññāṇa*; for it is this link that explains rebirth.

19. MN 38/MN I 258.

IV. Mentality-Materiality (*Nāma-Rūpa*)

Viññāṇapaccayā nāma-rūpaṃ, "dependent on consciousness arises mentality-materiality." The term *nāma* here stands for the mental states (*cetasika*), in other words, the three mental groups: namely, feeling (*vedanākkhandha*), perception (*saññākkhandha*), and volitional or mental formations (*saṅkhārakkhandha*).

The so called "being" (*satta*, Skt. *sattva*) is composed of five aggregates or groups (*pañcakkhandha*); namely, physical body, feeling, perception, volitional formations, and consciousness (*rūpa, vedanā, saññā, saṅkhārā* and *viññāṇa*). If consciousness is taken as the mind, then feeling, perceptions and volitional formations are the concomitants or factors of that mind. Now when we say dependent on consciousness arises *nāma-rūpa*, mentality-materiality, materiality means the physical body, its organs, faculties, and functions. Mentality means the factors of the mind mentioned above. In other words, *viññāṇa-paccayā nāma-rūpaṃ* means dependent on consciousness arise the three mental concomitants (feeling, perception, and volitional formations) that compose mentality, along with the conascent material body in its first embryonic stage.

Consciousness and its factors (*citta-cetasika*) are always interrelated and interdependent. Consciousness cannot arise and function independently of its factors, nor can the factors arise and function without consciousness. They arise simultaneously (*sahajāta-paccaya*) and have no independent existence.

V. The Sixfold Base (*Saḷāyatana*)

Nāma-rūpapaccayā saḷāyatanaṃ, "dependent on mentality-materiality arises the sixfold base," the five physical sense organs—eye, ear, nose, tongue, and body—and the mind base (*manāyatana*). *Manāyatana* is a collective term for the many different classes of consciousness, i.e. for the five kinds of sense-consciousness and the many kinds of mind-consciousness. Hence, five bases are physical phenomena, namely eye, ear, nose, tongue, and body; and the sixth, mind base, is identical with consciousness.[20]

20. Nyanātiloka Thera, *Fundamentals of Buddhism* (Colombo, 1949), p.67.

The function of *viññāṇa*, consciousness, is varied. The third factor of the chain is made known to us as *viññāṇa*; now here again we hear of a sixth base, *manāyatana*, which is identical with consciousness. But here by *manāyatana* different types of consciousness are meant. It should be borne in mind that consciousness is not something that is permanent and everlasting. It undergoes change, not remaining the same for two consecutive moments; it comes into being and immediately passes away yielding place to a new consciousness. "These mental phenomena are, as it were, only the different aspects of those units of consciousness which like lightning every moment flash up and immediately thereafter disappear forever."[21]

If there were no *nāma-rūpa* (mentality-materiality), no *saḷāyatana* (sixfold base) could arise. Because of *rūpa*, the physical sense organs, eye, ear, etc. appear, and because of *manāyatana* (different types of consciousness) the physical sense organs function. Thus *nāma-rūpa* and *saḷāyatana* are inescapably interrelated and interdependent.

VI. Contact (*Phassa*)

Saḷāyatanapaccayā phasso, "dependent on the sixfold base arises contact." In the preceding proposition we saw the sixfold base or *āyatanas*, eye, ear, etc.; they are internal bases (*ajjhattika-āyatana*). External to one's material body, there are the corresponding five sense objects—form, sound, smell, taste, and tactile objects—and further, the mental objects. These are known as the six external bases (*bāhira-āyatana*). These external bases are food for our internal bases. Hence they are interrelated. Although there is this functional relationship between these six sense organs and their objects, awareness comes with *viññāṇa* or consciousness. Hence it is said, "If consciousness arises because of eye and forms it is termed visual consciousness."

Now, when eye and forms are both present, visual consciousness arises dependent on them. Similarly with ear and sounds, and so on, down to mind and mental objects (ideas). Again, when the three, namely, eye, forms, and eye-consciousness

21. Ibid., p. 65.

come together, it is their coincidence that is called "contact" (or impression). From contact there arises feeling, and so on.[22]

Thus it is clear that contact (*phassa*) is conditioned by both the internal sixfold base (*ajjhattika-āyatana*) and the external sixfold base (*bāhira-āyatana*).

In brief, "dependent on the sixfold base arises contact or impressions," means: The visual contact conditioned by the eye; the sound contact conditioned by the ear; the smell contact conditioned by the nose; the taste contact conditioned by the tongue; the bodily contact conditioned by the body; the mental contact conditioned by the mind.

VII. Feeling (*Vedanā*)

Phassa paccayā vedanā, "dependent on contact arises feeling." Feeling is sixfold: feeling born of visual contact; feeling born of sound contact; feeling born of smell contact; feeling born of taste contact; feeling born of body contact, and feeling born of mental contact.

Feeling may be pleasurable (*sukha*), painful (*dukkha*), or neutral, i.e. neither pleasurable nor painful (*adukkhamasukha* = *upekkhā*).

As stated in the preceding clause, sense objects can never be cognized by the particular sensitivity without the appropriate kind of consciousness, but when these three factors come together, there arises contact. With the arising of contact, simultaneously there arises feeling (*vedanā*) and it can never be stopped by any power or force. Such is the nature of contact and feeling. The experiencing of desirable or undesirable kamma-results of good and evil actions performed here or in a previous birth, is one of the prior conditions due to which feeling can arise.

Seeing a form, hearing a sound, smelling an odour, tasting a flavour, touching some tangible thing, cognizing a mental object (idea), we experience feeling; but it cannot be said that all beings experience the same feeling with the same object. An object, for instance, which may be felt agreeable by one, may be felt unpleasant by another, and neutral by still another. Feeling also may differ

22. Madhupiṇḍika Sutta, MN 18, and Mahātaṇhāsaṅkhaya Sutta, MN 38.

in accordance with circumstances. A sense object which once evoked unpleasant feelings in us may possibly produce pleasant feelings in us under different circumstances, in a totally different background—geographical condition, climatic conditions, etc. Thus we learn how feeling is conditioned by contact.

VIII. Craving (*Taṇhā*)

Vedanāpaccayā taṇhā, "dependent on feeling arises craving." Craving has its source, its genesis, its rise in feeling. All forms of appetite are included in *taṇhā*. Greed, thirst, desire, lust, burning, yearning, longing, inclination affection, household love—these are some of the many terms that denote *taṇhā*, which in the words of the Buddha is the leader to becoming (*bhavanetti*). Becoming, which manifests as *dukkha*, as suffering, frustration, painful excitement, is our own experience. The enemy of the whole world is lust or craving through which all evils come to living beings. Through clear understanding of craving, the origin of craving, the cessation of craving, the true way of practice leading to the cessation of craving, one disentangles this tangle.

What then is craving? It is this craving which causes re-becoming, rebirth, accompanied by passionate pleasure, and finding fresh delight now here, now there, namely, craving for sense pleasures (*kāma-taṇhā*), craving for continued existence, for becoming (*bhava-taṇhā*), and craving for non-existence, for self-annihilation (*vibhava-taṇhā*).[23] "Where does craving arise and take root? Where there is the delightful and the pleasurable, there craving arises and takes root. Forms, sounds, smells, tastes, bodily contacts, and ideas are delightful and pleasurable, there craving arises and takes root."[24]

Craving, when obstructed by some cause, is transformed into wrath and frustration. "From craving arises grief, from craving arises fear. To one free from craving there is no grief. Whence fear?"[25]

23. S V 421.
24. DN 22/D II 308–309.
25. Dhp 216.

Man is always attracted by the pleasant and the delightful, and in his search for pleasure he ceaselessly runs after the six kinds of sense objects and clings to them. He little realizes that no amount of forms, sounds, smells, tastes, tangibles, and mental objects will ever satisfy the eye, ear, nose, tongue, body, and mind. In this intense thirst for either possessions or the gratification of desires, he gets bound to the wheel of saṃsāra, is twisted and torn between the spokes of agony, and securely closes the door to final deliverance. The Buddha was most emphatic against this mad rush, and warned:

> "Pleasure is a bond, a joy that's brief,
> Of little taste, leading to drawn-out pain.
> The wise know that the hook is baited."[26]

All mundane pleasures are fleeting; like sugar-coated pills of poison they deceive us, insidiously working harm. As stated above, whenever craving for these objects is connected with sensual pleasures, it is called "sensuous craving." When it is associated with the belief in eternal personal existence, then it is called "craving for continued existence." This is what is known as *sassata-diṭṭhi* or eternalism. When craving is associated with the belief in self-annihilation at death, then it is called "craving for self-annihilation" (*vibhava-taṇhā*); this is what is known as *uccheda-diṭṭhi* or nihilism.

Craving is conditioned not only by pleasurable and agreeable feelings, but by unhappy and unpleasant feelings, too. A man in distress craves and thirsts to get rid of it, and longs for happiness and release. To express it in another way, the poor and the needy, the sick and the disabled, in brief, all sufferers, crave for happiness, security, and solace. On the other hand, the rich, the healthy, who have not glimpsed the sufferings of the distressed, and who are already experiencing pleasure, also crave. They crave and long for more and more pleasures. Thus craving is insatiable. As cattle go in search of fresh pasture so do people go in quest of fleeting pleasures, constantly seeking fuel for this life-flame. Their greed is inordinate.

"All is burning, all is in flames." And what is the "all" that is in flames, that is burning? The five sense organs and the five sense objects are burning. Mind and thoughts are burning. The

26. Sn 61.

five aggregates of grasping (*pañca upādānakkhandha*) are burning. With what are they burning? With the fire of craving, with the fire of hate, with the fire of delusion."[27]

A fire keeps burning so long as there is fuel. The more fuel we add, the more it burns. It is the same with the fire of life.

Craving is an insatiable fire and no fire is ever contented. Such is the nature of this corruption that spreads right up to the highest plane of existence (*bhavagga*) with respect to spheres, and right up to the *gottabhū citta*, the threshold of sainthood, with respect to mind-flux. Where there is no self-desire, there indeed is no sense desire either; and where there is no self-desire, there all ill dies out like a flame whose fuel is spent.

It is only when suffering comes as its consequence, and not before, that one realizes the viciousness of this poisonous creeper of craving which winds itself round all who are not arahats or perfectly pure ones who have uprooted its tap-root, ignorance. The more we crave, the more we suffer; sorrow is the tribute we have to pay for having craved. Wherefore, know this craving as our foe here, in saṃsāra, that guides us to continued and repeated sentient existence, and so builds the "House of Being."

The Buddha on attaining full enlightenment spoke these joyful words:

> "Repeated births are each a torment,
> Seeking but not finding the 'House Builder,'
> I wandered through many a saṃsāric birth.
> O House Builder, thou art seen,
> Thou wilt not rebuild the house.
> All thy rafters have been shattered,
> Demolished has thy ridge pole been.
> My mind has now attained the unformed Nibbāna,
> The extinction of craving is achieved."[28]

---

27. Vin I 34–35. For details see Thera Piyadassi, *The Buddha's Ancient Path* (BPS, 5th ed., 1987), p. 163.
28. Dhp 153, 154.

IX. Clinging (*Upādāna*)

Taṇhāpaccayā upādānaṃ "dependent on craving arises clinging." This is the mental state that clings to, or grasps, the object even as a piece of raw meat that sticks to a saucepan. Because of this clinging, which is described as craving in a high degree, man becomes a slave to passion, and falls into the net he himself has made of his passion for pleasure, like the caterpillar that spins itself a tangle in which it lives.

Upādāna, clinging or attachment, is fourfold: (i) attachment to sensuous pleasures or sense desires (*kāma-upādāna*); (ii) attachment to wrong and evil views (*diṭṭhi-upādāna*); (iii) attachment to mere external observances, rites and rituals (*sīlabbata-upādāna*); and (iv) attachment to self or a lasting soul-entity (*attavāda-upādāna*).

Kāma here means both the craving and the craved object (*kilesa-kāma* and *vatthu-kāma*), and when that craving for such desired objects becomes intensified, it is known as *kāma-upādāna* or clinging. Man entertains thoughts of craving, and in proportion as he fails to ignore them, they grow till they get intensified to the degree of tenacious clinging.

All the various wrong views (*diṭṭhi*) that were in existence during the time of the Buddha can be included in annihilationism (*uccheda-diṭṭhi*) and eternalism (*sassata-diṭṭhi*). To some, especially to the intellectuals, at times the giving up of a view that they have cherished is more difficult than giving up objects of sense. Of all wrong views the clinging to a belief in a soul or self or an abiding ego-entity (*attavāda-upādāna*) is the strongest, foremost and most pernicious.

It is not without good reason that the Buddha rejected the notion of a self or soul (*attā*). In this conflux of mind and body which undergoes change without remaining the same for two consecutive moments, the Buddha could not see a lasting, indestructible soul. In other words, he could locate no abiding soul in this ever-changing "being." The Master, therefore, emphatically denied an *attā* either in the five aggregates (material form, feeling, perception, volitional formations, consciousness) or elsewhere. "All this," he said, "is void of an *attā* or anything of the nature of an *attā* (*suññaṃ idaṃ attena vā attaniyena vā*)."[29] If this wrong notion is got rid of, all the existing wrong and pernicious views automatically cease.

The Master's clear injunction to Mogharāja is:

Suññato lokaṃ avekkhassu—mogharāja sadā sato
attānudiṭṭhiṃ ūhacca—evaṃ maccu taro siyā

"O Mogharāja, ever mindful,
See the world as void.
Having eradicated the view of a self
One may overcome death." (Sn 1119)

The doctrine of *anattā* (*anātmā*) is exclusively Buddhistic and is distinguishable from every other religion and philosophy. It is the heart and core of the Buddha's teaching. It was the recognition that this self (*attā*) is an illusion, a mirage, that made the Buddha's doctrine so singular and so revolutionary.

All the existing religions do believe in a soul or self and they claim it to be all-powerful, all-pervading, indestructible and permanent. To the believers in a soul, soul is a permanent entity that has taken root in all beings.

Some say that this *ātmā* spreads throughout the length and breadth of the body like oil in a sesame seed; others say that it surrounds the body in the form of an imperceptible light, which light one perceives when cleansed of all impurities. Still others profess that it is within us, like a gem twinkling in a casket. Still others say it is consciousness, or perception, or sensation, or volition and some conclude that this *ātmā* consists of both mind and body—*nāma* and *rūpa*.

Buddhism advocates no such unchanging entity or soul or ātmā. In conventional usage we speak of a "being," "I," etc., but in the highest sense there exists no "being"; there is no "I" personality. Each one of us is the manifestation of his or her kammic-force, and a composition of nothing but an ever-changing conflux of mind and body. This mind and body separated from each other lose something of their potency and cannot function alone indefinitely. But as a boat and a boatman together cross the

29. MN 22/M I 138.

stream, and as a lame man mounted on the shoulders of a blind man reach their destination, so mind and body when wedded together function best.

Unceasingly does the mind and its factors change; and just as unceasingly, though at a slower rate, the body alters from moment to moment. The conflux of mind and body goes on as incessantly as the waves of the sea, or as the Buddhist say *nadī soto viya*, like a flowing stream. Thus the "being" or mind and body, *saṃsāra* or the procession of events, is utterly free from the notion of a *jīvatma* or *paramātma*, microcosmic soul or macrocosmic soul.

X. Becoming (*Bhava*)

Upādānapaccayā bhavo, "dependent on clinging arises becoming." Becoming is twofold, and should be understood as two processes: kamma-process (*kamma-bhava*) and kamma-resultant process (*upapatti-bhava*). *Kamma-bhava* is the accumulated good and evil actions, the "kammically active side of life." *Upapatti-bhava* is "the kammically passive and morally neutral side of life," and signifies the kamma-resultant rebirth-process in the next life. The next life may be in any sphere or plane—that of sensuous existence (*kāma-bhava*), that of form (*rūpa-bhava*), or that of formless existence (*arūpa-bhava*).

In the first clause (*avijjāpaccayā saṅkhārā*), *saṅkhārā* is explained as good and evil actions (*kamma*); if that is so, is it not repetitive to say that *kamma-bhava*, mentioned here, also means good and evil actions? The *paṭicca-samuppāda*, we must know, is concerned not only with the present life but with all the three lives—past, present, and future. Kamma, or the good and evil actions mentioned in the first clause, belong to the past—and on those past actions the present life depends. The kamma that is referred to here in this clause, *upādānapaccayā bhavo*, belongs to the present life and that in turn causes future life. *Upādānapaccayā bhavo* meaning clinging (*upādāna*) is the condition of the kamma-process, or actions, and of the kamma-resultant rebirth process.

XI. Birth (*Jāti*)

Bhavapaccayā jāti, "dependent on becoming arises birth." Here birth means not the actual childbirth, but the appearance of the five aggregates (material form, feeling, perception, formations, and consciousness) in the mother's womb. This process is conditioned by *kamma-bhava.*

The present birth is brought about by the craving and clinging kamma-volitions (*taṇhā-upādāna*) of the past birth, and the craving and clinging acts of will of the present birth bring about future rebirth. According to the teaching of the Buddha, it is this kamma-volition that divides beings into high and low.

"Beings are heirs of their deeds; bearers of their deeds, and their deeds are the womb out of which they spring,"[30] and through their deeds alone they must change for the better, remake themselves, and win liberation from ill.

We are reaping what we have sown in the past; some of our reapings, we know, we have even sown in this life. In the same way, our actions here mould the hereafter, and thus we begin to understand our position in this mysterious universe. If we, through our ignorance, craving, and clinging in the long night of saṃsāric wandering, have not shaped ourselves as we are, how could there be such difference and dissimilarity between living beings as we see in the world today? Can we conceive of a mind, a single mind, vast and confused enough to plan out such a motley sentient world as surrounds us?

Thus kamma is the corollary of rebirth, and rebirth, on the one hand, is the corollary of kamma. Here it may be asked: If kamma is the cause of rebirth and if Buddhism emphatically denies a soul or a transcendental ego, how does this kammic process bring about rebirth?

Well, "No force is ever lost, and there is no reason to think that the force manifest in each being as mind and body is ever lost. It ever undergoes transformations. It is changing now, every moment of our lives. Nor is it lost at death. The vitalizing mind flux is merely reset. It resets in conditions harmonizing with itself, even as broadcast sounds reset in a receiver tuned to the particular

30. MN 135/M III 203.

wavelength. It is the resetting of this vital flux, in fresh conditions, that is called rebirth. Each reborn being starts with a unique set of latent possibilities, the accumulated experiences of the past. That is why character differs, why each endows himself with what theists call 'gifts,' and infinite possibilities."[31]

There is nothing that passes or transmigrates from one life to another. Is it not possible to light one lamp from another and in this process does any flame pass from one to the other? Do you not see the continuity of the flame? It is neither the same flame nor a totally different one.

The kammic process (*kamma-bhava*), therefore, is the force in virtue of which reaction follows actions; it is the energy that, out of a present life, conditions a future life in unending sequence.

"Desire gives rise to deed; deed gives rise to result; result exhibits itself as new corporeality endowed with new desire. Deed is as inevitably followed by result as the body by its shadow. This is merely the universal natural law of conservation of energy extended to the moral domain. As in the universe no energy can ever be lost, so also in the individual nothing can be lost of the resilient force accumulated by desire. This resilient energy is always transmuted into fresh life and we live eternally through our lust to live. The medium, however, that makes all existence possible is kamma."[32]

XII. Ageing and Death (*Jarāmaraṇa*)

Jātipaccayā jarāmaraṇaṃ, "dependent on birth arise ageing and death," and with them naturally come sorrow, lamentation, pain, grief, and despair. Birth is inevitably followed by ageing and death; in the absence of birth there will be no ageing and death. Thus this whole mass of suffering arises dependent on the twelvefold dependent origination. Ageing and death are followed by birth, and birth, on the other hand, is followed by ageing and death. The pair thus accompany each other in bewildering succession. Nothing mundane is still; it is all in flux. People build up wishful

---

31. Dr. Cassius A. Pereira (later Kassapa Thera), "What I Believe?" *Ceylon Observer*, October 1937.

32. Paul Dahlke, *Buddhist Essays* (London, 1908), p. 115.

hopes and plans for the morrow, but one day, sudden perhaps and unexpected, there comes the inevitable hour when death puts an end to this brief span of life, and brings our hopes to naught. So long as man is attached to existence through his ignorance, craving, and clinging, for him death is not the final end. He will continue his career of whirling along with the wheel of existence, and will be twisted and torn between the spokes of agony. Thus, looking around us in the world at the different types of men and women, and at the differences in their varying fortunes, we know that these cannot be due to mere chance.

An external power or agency that punishes the ill deeds and rewards the good deeds of beings has no place in Buddhist thought. Buddhists do not resort to any especially graced person or pray to any imperceptible individual to grant them deliverance. Not even the supreme Buddha could redeem them from saṃsāra's bond. In ourselves lies the power to mould our lives. Buddhists are *kammavādins*, believers in the efficacy of actions, good and evil.

According to the teachings of the Buddha, the direct cause of the distinctions and inequalities of birth in this life is the good and evil actions of each individual in past lives. In other words, each person is reaping what he has sowed in the past. In the same way, his actions here mould his hereafter.

In all actions, good and evil, mind is the most important factor. "All mental states have mind as their forerunner; mind dominates, everything is mind-made. If one speaks or acts with a polluted mind, pain follows him in consequence as the cartwheel follows the foot of the beast of burden." In like manner, "in consequence of mentations made, words spoken and deeds done with a pure and placid mind, happiness follows him even like the inseparable shadow."[33]

Man is always changing either for good or for evil. This changing is unavoidable and depends entirely on our own actions and environment.

The world seems to be imperfect and ill-balanced. We are too often confronted with many a difficulty and shortcoming. People differ from one another in many ways and aspects. Among us human beings, let alone the animal kingdom, we see some

33. Dhp 1, 2.

born as miserable wretches, sunk in deep distress and supremely unhappy; others born into a state of abundance and happiness enjoying a life of luxury and knowing nothing of the world's woe. Again, a chosen few are gifted with keen intellect and great mental capacity while many are wrapped in ignorance. How is it that some of us are blessed with health, beauty, sincere friends, and amiable relatives while others are despicable weaklings, destitute and lonely? How is it that some are born to enjoy long life while others pass away in the full bloom of youth? Why are some blessed with affluence, fame, and recognition? Why are some chosen few given in full measure all the things which human beings deserve while others are utterly neglected? These are intricate problems that demand a solution.

If we but pause for a moment and impartially investigate and intelligently inquire into things, we will find that these wide differences are not the work of an external agency or a superhuman being. We will find that we ourselves are responsible for our deeds whether good or ill and that we ourselves are the makers of our own kamma.

Says the Buddha:

"According to the seed that is sown,
So is the fruit ye reap therefrom.
The doer of good (will gather) good,
The doer of evil, evil (reaps).
Sown is the seed and planted well;
Thou shalt enjoy the fruit thereof."[34]

It is impossible to conceive of an external agency or some all-powerful being who distributes his gifts to different persons in diverse measures, and who at times showers all his gifts on the same individual. Is it not more rational to say that:

"Who toiled a slave may come anew a prince,
For gentle worthiness and merit won.
Who ruled a king may wander earth in rags
For things done and undone."

Light of Asia

34. S I 227; *The Kindred Sayings*, I. p. 293.

Buddhists do not blame the Buddha or a superhuman being or a deva or an especially graced person for the ills of humanity or praise them for the happiness people experience.

It is knowledge of kamma and kamma-vipāka, the law of cause and effect, or moral causation, that urges a true Buddhist to refrain from evil and do good. He who understands cause and effect knows well that it is his own actions and nothing else that make his life miserable or otherwise. He knows that the direct cause of the distinctions and inequalities of birth in this life is the good and evil actions of each individual in past lives and in this life.

Man today is the result of millions of repetitions of thought and action. He is not ready-made; he becomes, and is still becoming. His character is predetermined by his own choice. The thought, the act which he chooses, that by habit he becomes.

It should, however, be remembered that according to Buddhism not everything that occurs is due to past actions. During the time of the Buddha, sectarians like Nigaṇṭha Nātaputta, Makkhali Gosala, and others, held the view that whatever the individual experiences, be it pleasant or unpleasant or neither, all come from former actions or past kamma.[35] The Buddha, however, rejected this theory of an exclusive determination by the past (*pubbekatahetu*) as unreasonable. Many things are the result of our own deeds done in this present life, and of external causes. Hence it is not true to say that all things that occur are due to past kamma or actions.

Is it not absurd for a student who fails in his examination due to sheer laxity on his part, to attribute the failure to his past kamma? Is it not equally ridiculous for a person to rush about carelessly, bang himself against a stone or some similar thing, and ascribe the mishap to his past kamma? One can multiply such instances to show that not everything is due to actions performed in the past.

But when the causes and conditions of things are destroyed, automatically the effects also cease to be. Sorrow will disappear if the varied rootlets of sorrow's cause are eliminated. A man, for instance, who burns to ashes a mango seed, puts an end to

35. MN 101; DN 2. This view is examined at A I 137.

its germinating power and that seed will never produce a mango plant. It is the same with all compounded things (*saṅkhārā*), animate or inanimate. As kamma is our own manufacture we have the power to break this endless chain, this Wheel of Existence (*bhavacakka*). Referring to those enlightened ones who have conquered themselves through the uprooting of the defilements, the Buddha says in the Ratana Sutta:

> "Their past (kamma) is spent, their new (kamma) no more arises, their mind to future becoming is unattached. The germ (of rebirth-consciousness) has died, they have no more desire for re-living. Those wise ones fade out (of existence) like the flame of this lamp."[36]

It is said that as the Buddha spoke these words he saw the flame of a lamp go out.

The *paṭicca-samuppāda*, with its twelve links starting with ignorance and ending in ageing and death, shows how man, being fettered, wanders in saṃsāra birth after birth. But by getting rid of these twelve factors man can liberate himself from suffering and rebirth. The Buddha has taught us the way to put an end to this repeated wandering. It is by endeavouring to halt this Wheel of Existence that we may find the way out of this tangle. The Buddha-word which speaks of this cessation of suffering is stated thus:

> "Through the entire cessation of ignorance cease volitional formations;
> Through the cessation of volitional formations, consciousness ceases;
> Through the cessation of consciousness, mentality-materiality ceases;
> Through the cessation of mentality-materiality, the sixfold base ceases;
> Through the cessation of the sixfold base, contact ceases;
> Through the cessation of contact, feeling ceases;
> Through the cessation of feeling, craving ceases;
> Through the cessation of craving, clinging ceases;

36. Sn 235.

Through the cessation of clinging, becoming ceases;
Through the cessation of becoming, birth ceases;
Through the cessation of birth, cease ageing and death, sorrow, lamentation, pain, grief, and despair. Thus does this whole mass of suffering cease."[37]

Though in Buddhism time is considered as a mere concept (*paññatti*), in the language of the apparent truth (*sammuti-sacca*) we speak of three periods of time, namely, the past, the present and the future, and the *paṭicca-samuppāda* formula can be taken as representing them. The two factors ignorance and volitional formations (*avijjā* and *saṅkhārā*) belong to the past; the next eight, beginning with consciousness (*viññāṇa*) belong to the present; and the last pair, birth and ageing and death, belong to the future.

In this Wheel of Existence there are then three connecting links (*sandhi*). Between volitional formations (*saṅkhārā*), the last factor of the past, and consciousness (*viññāṇa*), the first factor of the present, there is one link consisting of past cause and present fruit (*hetu-phala*). Consciousness, mentality-materiality, the sixfold base, contact, and feeling are effects in the present life caused by ignorance and volitional formations of the past. Because of these five factors there come into being three other factors, namely, craving, clinging, and becoming, which will cause birth in the future. Therefore, between feeling and craving there is another link consisting of present fruit and present cause (*phala-hetu*). Because of craving, clinging, and becoming of the present, there come into being birth, ageing, and death in the future. Therefore, between becoming and birth there is another link. These three links consist of four sections: (i) ignorance, volitional formations; (ii) consciousness, mentality-materiality, the sixfold base, contact, feeling; (iii) craving, clinging, becoming; (iv) birth and ageing and death.

"There were five causes in the past,
And now there is a fivefold fruit,
There are five causes now as well,
And in the future fivefold fruit."[38]

37. A I 176.

38. *The Path of Purification*, trans. by Ñāṇamoli (Kandy: BPS, 1997), p.597.

The text mentions ignorance and volitional formations as past causes. "But one who is ignorant, hankers, and hankering, clings, and with his clinging as condition there is becoming; therefore craving, clinging, and becoming are included as well. Hence it is said: 'In the previous kamma-process becoming, there is delusion, which is ignorance; there is accumulation, which is formations; there is attachment, which is craving; there is embracing, which is clinging; there is volition, which is becoming; thus these five things in the previous kamma-process becoming are conditions for rebirth-linking here (in the present becoming).'"[39]

Now the fivefold fruit in the present life as given in the text is represented by five factors: consciousness, mentality-materiality, the sixfold base, contact, feeling.

There are five causes we now produce, of which the text gives only craving, clinging, and becoming. "But when becoming is included, the formations that precede it or that are associated with it are included too. And by including craving and clinging, the ignorance associated with them, deluded by which a man performs kamma, is included too. So they are five."

The fivefold fruit we reap in the future. This is represented by consciousness, mentality-materiality, the sixfold base, contact, feeling. The text gives also birth and ageing and death as the future fivefold fruit. Birth really is represented by these five beginning with consciousness and ending in feeling. Ageing and death is the ageing and death of these five.

On close analysis, it becomes clear that in this dependent origination, *paṭicca-samuppāda*, in this repeated process of rebirth, in this cycle of existence, there is nothing permanent, no enduring soul-entity that passes from one birth to the next. All *dhammas* are causally dependent, they are conditioned (*sabbe dhammā paṭiccasamuppannā*), and this process of events is utterly free from the notion of a permanent soul or self.

The Buddha declares: "To believe the doer of the deed will be the same as the one who experiences its results (in the next life), this is the one extreme. To believe that the doer of the deed and the one who experiences its results are two different persons, this is the other extreme. Both these extremes the Tathāgata, the

39. Ibid.

Perfect One, has avoided and taught the truth that lies in the middle of both, namely: "Through ignorance conditioned are the kamma formations and so on (see formula). Thus arises this whole mass of suffering."

Hence the ancients said:

"There is no doer of a deed
Or one who reaps the deed's result;
Phenomena alone flow on—
No other view than this is right.

For here there is no Brahmā God,
Creator of the round of births;
Phenomena alone flow on—
Cause and component their condition."[40]

In concluding this essay on dependent origination, a confusion that may arise in the reader's mind should be forestalled. If according to dependent origination things are determined by conditions, one may be inclined to think that the Buddha encouraged fatalism or determinism, and that human freedom and free will are put aside.

But what is fatalism? According to the *Dictionary of Philosophy*, "Fatalism is determinism, especially in its theological form which asserts that all human activities are predetermined by God." Determinism, according to the *Oxford English Dictionary*, is "the philosophical doctrine that human action is not free but necessarily determined by motives, which are regarded as external forces acting upon the will." The doctrine of kamma refutes that. A clear understanding of Buddhism shows that the Buddha never subscribed to the theory that all things are unalterably fixed, that all things happen by inevitable necessity—that is strict determinism (*niyativāda*), nor did he uphold the theory of complete indeterminism (*adhicca-samuppanna*). Everywhere we see certain laws and conditions functioning, and one of these is *cetanā* or volition, which is kamma. There is no law giver, no external agency to interfere with the mental and material happenings. Through causes and conditions things come to be.

40. Ibid. pp. 622–23

Thus is this endless play of action and reaction kept in perpetual motion by kamma, concealed by ignorance, and propelled by craving. In no way does this affect the freedom of the will and the responsibility of man for his acts (his kamma).

Lastly a word about "free will": will is not something static. It is not a positive entity, or a self-existent thing. Will is quite momentary like any other mental state; there is, therefore, no "will" as a "thing" to be either free or not free. The truth is that "will" is conditioned and a passing phenomenon.

To the genuine Buddhist the primary concern of life is not mere speculation, or vain voyages into the imaginary regions of high fantasy, but the gaining of true happiness and freedom from all suffering. *Paṭicca-samuppāda*, which speaks of suffering (*dukkha*), and the cessation of suffering, is the central concept of Buddhism, and represents the finest flower of Indian thought.

Paṭicca-Samuppāda (*anuloma*)

Dependent Origination (in direct order; the arising)

i-ii. *Avijjāpaccayā saṅkhārā*
ii-iii. *Saṅkhārāpaccayā viññāṇaṃ*
iii-iv. *Viññāṇapaccayā nāma-rūpaṃ*
iv-v. *Nāma-rūpapaccayā saḷāyatanaṃ*
v-vi. *Saḷāyatanapaccayā phasso*
vi-vii. *Phassapaccayā vedanā*
vii-viii. *Vedanāpaccayā taṇhā*
viii-ix. *Taṇhāpaccayā upādānaṃ*
ix-x. *Upādānapaccayā bhavo*
x-xi. *Bhavapaccayā jāti*
xi-xii. *Jātipaccayā jarā-maraṇaṃ soka-parideva-dukkha-domanassupāyasā sambhavanti. Evam etassa kevalassa dukkhakkhandhassa samudayo hoti.*

Paṭicca-Samuppāda (*paṭiloma*)

Dependent Origination (the ceasing)

i-ii. *Avijjāya tveva asesavirāganirodhā saṅkhāranirodho*
ii-iii. *Saṅkhāranirodhā viññāṇanirodho*
iii-iv. *Viññāṇanirodhā nāma-rūpanirodho*
iv-v. *Nāma-rūpanirodhā saḷāyatananirodho*
v-vi. *Saḷāyatananirodhā phassanirodho*
vi-vii. *Phassanirodhā vedanānirodho*
vii-viii. *Vedanānirodhā taṇhānirodho*
viii-ix. *Taṇhānirodhā upādānanirodho*
ix-x. *Upādānanirodhā bhavanirodho*
x-xi. *Bhavanirodhā jātinirodho*
xi-xii. *Jātinirodhā jarā-maraṇaṃ soka-parideva-dukkha-domanassupāyāsā nirujjhanti. Evam etassa kevalassa dukkhakkhandhassa nirodho hoti.*

(S II 1/SN 12:1)

Translation

The Arising of the Wheel of Existence

i-ii. Dependent on ignorance arise volitional or mental formations.
ii-iii. Dependent on volitional formations arises relinking or rebirth consciousness.
iii-iv. Dependent on consciousness arise mentality-materiality.
iv-v. Dependent on mentality-materiality arises the sixfold base.
v-vi. Dependent on the sixfold base arises contact.
vi-vii. Dependent on contact arises feeling.
vii-viii. Dependent on feeling arises craving.
viii-ix. Dependent on craving arises clinging.
ix-x. Dependent on clinging arises becoming.
x-xi. Dependent on becoming arises birth.
xi-xii. Dependent on birth arises ageing and death, and sorrow, lamentation, pain, grief, and despair. Thus there is the origination of this whole mass of suffering.

The Cessation of the Wheel of Existence

i-ii. Through the entire cessation of this ignorance, volitional formations cease.
ii-iii. Through the cessation of volitional formations, rebirth consciousness ceases.
iii-iv. Through the cessation of rebirth consciousness, mentality-materiality ceases.
iv-v. Through the cessation of mentality-materiality, the sixfold base ceases.
v-vi. Through the cessation of the sixfold base, contact ceases.
vi-vii. Through the cessation of contact, feeling ceases.
vii-viii. Through the cessation of feeling, craving ceases.
viii-ix. Through the cessation of craving, clinging ceases.
ix-x. Through the cessation of clinging, becoming, ceases.
x-xi. Through the cessation of becoming, birth ceases.
ix-xii. Through the cessation of birth, ageing and death cease, and sorrow, lamentation, pain, grief, and despair. Thus there is the cessation of this whole mass of suffering.

ABOUT PARIYATTI

Pariyatti is dedicated to providing affordable access to authentic teachings of the Buddha about the Dhamma theory (*pariyatti*) and practice (*paṭipatti*) of Vipassana meditation. A 501(c)(3) nonprofit charitable organization since 2002, Pariyatti is sustained by contributions from individuals who appreciate and want to share the incalculable value of the Dhamma teachings. We invite you to visit www.pariyatti.org to learn about our programs, services, and ways to support publishing and other undertakings.

Pariyatti Publishing Imprints

Vipassana Research Publications (focus on Vipassana as taught by S.N. Goenka in the tradition of Sayagyi U Ba Khin)

BPS Pariyatti Editions (selected titles from the Buddhist Publication Society, copublished by Pariyatti)

MPA Pariyatti Editions (selected titles from the Myanmar Pitaka Association, copublished by Pariyatti)

Pariyatti Digital Editions (audio and video titles, including discourses)

Pariyatti Press (classic titles returned to print and inspirational writing by contemporary authors)

Pariyatti enriches the world by

- disseminating the words of the Buddha,
- providing sustenance for the seeker's journey,
- illuminating the meditator's path.

www.ingramcontent.com/pod-product-compliance
Lightning Source LLC
Chambersburg PA
CBHW020347170426
43200CB00005B/78